# SOCIAL WORK I<br>DIVERSE SOCIE

## Transformatory practice with<br>black and minority ethnic individuals<br>and communities

Edited by Charlotte Williams<br>and Mekada J. Graham

First published in Great Britain in 2016 by

Policy Press
University of Bristol
1-9 Old Park Hill
Bristol BS2 8BB
UK
t: +44 (0)117 954 5940
e: pp-info@bristol.ac.uk
www.policypress.co.uk

North American office:
Policy Press
c/o The University of Chicago Press
1427 East 60th Street
Chicago, IL 60637, USA
t: +1 773 702 7700
f: +1 773-702-9756
e:sales@press.uchicago.edu
www.press.uchicago.edu

© Policy Press 2016

British Library Cataloguing in Publication Data
A catalogue record for this book is available from the British Library.

Library of Congress Cataloging-in-Publication Data
A catalog record for this book has been requested.

ISBN 978-1-4473-2262-7 paperback
ISBN 978-1-4473-2261-0 hardcover
ISBN 978-1-4473-2264-1 ePub
ISBN 978-1-4473-2265-8 Mobi

Cover design by Andrew Corbett
Printed and bound in Great Britain by CPI Group (UK) Ltd, Croydon, CR0 4YY
Policy Press uses environmentally responsible print partners

Dedicated to
Mekada's mum, Norah Mary Graham
and
Charlotte's mum, Catherine Alice Hughes

# Contents

# Notes on the editors
# and contributors

## The editors

**Mekada J. Graham** is Professor and Director/Chair in Social Work at California State University Dominguez Hills, California, USA. She has published extensively in social work-related fields over the past 15 years. Her research interests include childhood studies and issues of social justice, social inequality and postmodern approaches in social work education and practice. She is co-editor of the Special Issue of the *British Journal of Social Work* (2014) entitled: 'A World on the Move: Migration, Mobilities and Social Work'. She is currently working on a new book, *Reflective thinking in social work: lessons from student narratives* to be published by Routledge.

**Charlotte Williams**, OBE, is Professor and Deputy Dean of Social Work at RMIT University, Melbourne, Australia. She is a qualified social worker and has over 25 years of experience in social work education. Her ongoing research interest focuses on issues of race and cultural diversity in social policy, social work education and practice. Her most recent publications include: *Race and ethnicity in a welfare society* (co-authored with M. Johnson) (Open University Press, 2010), and guest editorship with Mekada J. Graham of the Special Issue of the *British Journal of Social Work* (2014) entitled: 'A World on the Move: Migration, Mobilities and Social Work'.

## Contributing authors

**Dan Allen** of Salford University has a background in social work research and practice with Roma, Gypsy and Traveller children, families and communities. By attempting to link the fundamental concerns of social work practice with theory development and wider contextual challenges, Dan continually seeks to improve service provision and advance the knowledge, values and skills that inform social work practices and traditions with Gypsy, Roma and Traveller people on a more general basis.

**Claudia Bernard** is Professor of Social Work in the Department of Social Therapeutic and Community Studies, Goldsmiths, University of London. Her research interests lie in investigating the intersection of race, gender, social class and child and family welfare. She is principally interested in developing research methodologies that open up new ways for understanding violence and abuse in the lives of vulnerable children from stigmatised and marginalised communities. She has written widely on child abuse and gender-based violence, including a book entitled *Constructing lived experiences: representations of black mothers in child sexual abuse discourses* (Ashgate, 2001). She is presently co-editing a book on *Safeguarding black children* (Jessica Kingsley, 2016).

**Kish Bhatti-Sinclair**'s research interests include 'race' and racism, ethics, values, and empowering practice, both with children and adults. Projects in 2015 include a project evaluation of the Think Family Programme, West Sussex Children's Services and a report on the data analysis of black and minority ethnic children in looked after care for Wandsworth Borough Council. Recent publications include 'Race, racism and culturally appropriate interventions', in *International Encyclopedia of Social and Behavioural Sciences* (Elsevier, 2015).

**Stefan Brown** is a social work lecturer at Royal Holloway University. He teaches on the MSc Social Work programme. His areas of interest are mental health policy and practice, mental capacity and multidisciplinary working. He is a registered social worker and has worked in mental health services.

**Beverley Burke** is a senior lecturer in social work at Liverpool John Moores University, UK. She has practised as a social worker with children and families and has published widely in the areas of anti-oppressive practice, values and ethics. Beverley is co-editor of the practice section of the international peer-reviewed academic *Journal Ethics and Social Welfare*.

**Janet Carter Anand** is Professor of International Social Work at the University of Eastern Finland, Kuopio, Finland. She was a social worker for over 25 years before taking up an academic career. She has lectured in Social Work at the University of Tasmania, Australia; Trinity College Dublin, Republic of Ireland; and Queen's University Belfast, United Kingdom. Professor Anand's teaching and research interests are in the areas of adult services, social gerontology and the internationalisation of the social work curriculum. The concepts of critical reflection and critical cultural competence are central to her approach to teaching and global mindedness in social work practice.

**Sarah Cemlyn** is a research fellow and former social work lecturer at Bristol University, with a background in community development, social work and advocacy, and undertook the first English national study of social work's responses to Gypsies and Travellers. Her research with Gypsies, Travellers and Roma has focused on promoting rights, equality and anti-discrimination in social work, education, health and accommodation services, and engaging with activists in reflecting on community development and campaigning.

**Chaitali Das** completed her Master's in Social Work at the University of Mumbai and then worked on child-related issues, such as children in sex work and street children. Subsequently, she moved to London to do her PhD on British–Indian families of divorce. She later moved to Belfast and was a lecturer in social work at Queen's University Belfast. Her interests include international social work, community social work, cultural competence and minority ethnic groups. She currently lives and works in Germany doing research, training and consultancy on these topics.

**M. Rafik Gardee**, MBE LRCP&S (Eire), DPH (Glas), FFPHM (UK), MFPHM (Ire), was the Director of the National Resource Centre for Ethnic Minority Health in Scotland. He was awarded an MBE for his work in equality and diversity within health-care services in Scotland. He has interfaced with developed and developing populations internationally, in academic and rapid appraisal research, especially within Muslim and minority ethnic communities.

**Philomena Harrison** trained as a psychiatric social worker and has worked as a lecturer in social work at Liverpool John Moores University, UK, and now at Liverpool Hope University, UK. Philomena was the Director of Mental Health at the University of Salford, UK. Besides designing and delivering anti-oppressive practice and cultural competence to a range of health and social care professionals, she has undertaken therapeutic work with children and young people on issues of 'race' and identity, and has presented and written in the area of race, anti-oppressive practice and cultural competence at national and international events.

**Tue Hong Baker** is the Chief Executive Officer of the North Wales Regional Equality Network (NWREN). NWREN is a grassroots-led organisation whose primary function is to challenge discrimination and promote equality of access and opportunity for all citizens across North Wales. To date, NWREN has undertaken a number of major research projects, operates a drop-in centre, delivers education and training, works in partnership with statutory and voluntary sector agencies, and offers support to individuals faced with discrimination and inequality.

**Frank Keating** is a senior lecturer in health and social care in the Department of Social Work at Royal Holloway University of London, where he is Director of Research and Graduate studies. Frank's teaching focuses on mental health, social work theory, research methods and 'race' and ethnic studies. His main research interests are ethnicity, gender and mental health, particularly focusing on African and Caribbean communities. He is a strong advocate for racial equality in mental health services through his writing, teaching and public speaking.

**Michael Lavalette** is Professor of Social Work and Social Policy at Liverpool Hope University and national coordinator of the Social Work Action Network (UK). He has just completed a book (with Stephen Cunningham) on the history of school student strikes in Britain, *The School's Out* (Bookmarks, 2016) and is working on a book (with Iain Ferguson and Vassilios Ioakimidis) on radical social work in international context.

**Siân E. Lucas** is a lecturer in social work at the University of Stirling. She has carried out research with young people and social workers about their experiences of offering and receiving interpreting. Siân is interested in ways that academic inquiry can benefit social work policy and practice. Her research interests centre around the spoken language, namely, child language brokering and social work with minority-language speakers, with a focus on discourse analysis.

**Rhetta Moran** has worked within and across the statutory community and voluntary sectors for 30 years in local, national and international arenas. She is most interested in applying her communication skills through the development of praxis that releases human potential for constructive learning and change. She co-edited *Doing research with refugees* (Policy Press, 2006).

**Donna Price** is currently a senior lecturer in social work at the University of Chichester following a career of over 25 years in social work practice and significant professional development in child protection and children's safeguarding issues. Donna's professional and research interests lie in the area of child protection, and, more specifically, the management of identified sexual risk in family settings, and she continues to provide independent consultation and assessment in this regard.

**Raghu Raghavan** is Professor of Mental Health at De Montfort University Leicester. He is the Acting Head of Research in the School of Nursing and Midwifery and Nursing and Midwifery Research Centre (NMRC). Raghu leads the Mental Health and Disability Research Group. His clinical background is in health psychology and learning disability nursing, with expertise in participatory research with service users and family carers for service development. His current research consists of exploring: the conceptualisation of dementia in minority ethnic communities; faith, mental health service access and recovery; the perception of eating disorders in the South Asian community; and the resilience of disabled young people and their carers.

**Lena Robinson**, PhD, is Professor of Social Work at CQ University, Australia. She has published and researched widely in the field of race, ethnicity, culture and social work practice. She has recently completed an international study on the adaptation of Muslim youth in the West.

**Roma Thomas** is Research Fellow, International Social Development, at the Institute for Applied Social Research at the University of Bedfordshire. She is course co-ordinator for an MA in International Social Work and Social

Development. Her research interests include young masculinities and the practice and theories of professionals.

**Shantel Thomas** is a senior practitioner in children's social services. She completed a Master's in Social Work at Goldsmith's University of London in 2008 and specialised in front-line child protection work in local authority children and families social work since qualifying. Her Master's dissertation was concerned with exploring the influence of childhood experiences of domestic violence on black teenage mothers, and their understanding of positive intimate relationships. Her main practice and research interests are in understanding violence and abuse in the lives of vulnerable children from marginalised communities. She previously worked as a family court adviser with the Children and Families Court Advisory Support Service (Cafcass), and this role involved being the 'voice of children', particularly during protracted private law cases.

# Part One
# Theory and practice

# ONE

# Building transformative practice

*Charlotte Williams and Mekada J. Graham*

## Introduction

Across the decades, high-profile cases, such as the death of Tyra Henry (1984), Rocky Bennett (1998), Victoria Climbié (2000) and Hylene Essilifie (2007), among others, are often cited as evidence of the practice gap in appropriately meeting the needs of black and minority ethnic (BME) service users or in developing acceptable and effective interventions. While these sad and tragic cases have provided a spur to major changes in policy and practice, whether in the field of child welfare, mental health or youth justice, they are but the tip of the iceberg and can only hint at some of the complexities that characterise this terrain. Difficulties in the encounter between state social work and ethnically and racially diverse publics are not new. In the UK, the mismatch at this interface has been recognised, politicised, theorised and extensively documented most significantly since the mass migrations following the Second World War (Williams and Johnson, 2010). By all accounts, service delivery for BME groups has been flawed, leading to poor outcomes in health, housing, education, employment and social care. In this encounter, a number of lessons have been learned and internalised on both sides of the social services counter; some for the good, some for the bad. Perhaps one of the most significant learnings is that this interface is not static. It is, in essence, not so much an encounter as a dynamic, in which far-reaching change has occurred and continues to occur in the nature of service delivery, within the social work profession itself and in terms of the nature and extent of ethnic and racial diversity. This book is about practice. It is about what is going on in the field and what we can learn from it.

In this opening chapter, we want to explore some of the contemporary challenges and opportunities of the practice context and look towards what we tentatively call *embedded transformatory practice* in setting the scene for the chapters to come. Our critical starting point is the need to reframe what is increasingly named '*the problem of diversity*', that is, to reframe ethnic diversity not as a problematic encounter for social work, but as something fundamental to social work itself – its knowledge, value base and social identity.

Our arguments are simple. We seek to reset professional thinking about what the problematic is at the heart of the contemporary impasse in what is generally called anti-racist or race equality practice. We argue for the need to acknowledge the contexts in which these debates about practice and practices occur as highly contested territories: that is to say, territories that reflect particular localised political contexts, are highly relational and dynamic, and, at the same time, refract the grand narratives of social work practice.

Accordingly, we suggest the need for theories of change that are built in situ and engage with a critical interrogation of local and national contexts as significant to making a difference. In this chapter, we develop on our understanding of the implementation gap, arguing that the analysis of theoretical models has evolved without sufficient grounding in the practice context and with the neglect of the contributions of minority groups so crucial to the development of appropriate service delivery. We bemoan the failure to confront the tensions within the liberal value base of social work but look ahead to the project that is this text: *building embedded transformative practice*.

## Minority ethnic disadvantage and social work

Within social work, we must be concerned about the sustained and deepening nature of ethnic and racial inequalities (EHRC, 2015; IRR, 2015). Ethnicity is a factor known to be linked to social disadvantage. The so-called 'ethnic penalty' has long been recognised and some considerable evidence supports the notion that this is pervasive and sustained across the countries of the UK (EHRC, 2015; Davies et al, 2011). Amid growing immiseration among vulnerable groups in this age of austerity, BME groups fare very badly (Lavalette and Penketh, 2014; *The Guardian*, 2014). Their discontent as consumers of services is ever apparent.

While the sources of ethnic and racial disadvantage are complex and varied between groups, discriminations in service delivery are known to play a key role. Accordingly, there must be concern about evidence of institutional ineptitude and lethargy in meeting race equality requirements (SCIE, 2006). Access to welfare for minority ethnic groups has been problematic throughout the 20th century, and despite shifts and changes in service delivery models and approaches to diversity and despite the strengthening of equalities legislation, we are far from getting it right (Craig, 2007; Williams and Johnson, 2010). In addition, a long history of self-provisioning and self-help is being gradually undercut as the buoyancy of BME service organisations has been severely curtailed. Organisations close to communities and vital to well-being increasingly find themselves overstretched and under-resourced (Bowes and Sim, 2006).

As a profession, we are being confronted more and more with the need to acknowledge and respond to this shortfall by activists, academics and polemicists, but most significantly by service users themselves, their kin and carers. Despite a significant body of theory in relation to working with ethnic and cultural diversity, there remains an identifiable gap between professional aspirations and the reality of making a difference on the ground. A burgeoning literature exists on the related topics of cross-cultural social work, cultural competency, anti-racist practice and anti-oppressive practice (Okitikpi and Aymer, 2010; Bhatti-Sinclair, 2011). In addition, social work education and training in the UK, as in most Western developed countries, seeks to embed relevant and transferable skills for working with the complexities of increased diversity and prescribes mandatory requirements for newly qualifying practitioners and for continuous professional development (SWTF, 2009). Yet, practitioners struggle to give a clear account of how they implement anti-discriminatory and anti-racist practice (see, eg, Williams and Parrott, 2013). Operational concerns for pragmatic and reactive responses too often outweigh the moral mandate to secure changes in the ways things are done, and overall an accommodative orientation that endorses the status quo wins the day (Reisch and Jani, 2012).

More recently, commentators have pointed to an impasse in the development and pursuit of the social justice ambitions of social work (Olson, 2008; Solas, 2008; Kam, 2014) and to a retreat from multicultural and anti-racist theorising and practice (Lavalette and Penketh, 2014). It is almost as if there is nothing more to say: that the theorising has been done and recognition of the issue has been institutionally mainstreamed by legislative and policy developments following the Race Relations Act 2000. McLaughlin (2005), for example, has argued that the legislative developments put in place for regulating and monitoring organisational responses have resulted in the institutionalisation of anti-racist and anti-oppressive practice and consequently led to an attrition or depoliticisation of these concerns. Others point to the eroding effects of neoliberal policies on public sector delivery and the impact of associated managerialist approaches on social workers' capacity to fulfil their social justice mission (Ferguson, 2007).

In the endeavour to straddle the mismatch between professional rhetoric and the realities of action on the practice floor, an examination of practice wisdoms is suggested. How are these issues being accommodated in practice? What strategies are available to those on the front line in shaping service responses? How can we capture these practice wisdoms? Practice theories in social work are important points of analysis in making sense of interactions, the interpretations of policy agendas, the opportunities and constraints in context for purposeful action and interventions, and how these are negotiated vis-a-vis the service user and other stakeholders. The focus of this text is on a selection of bedrock contemporary practice themes and how they are interpreted in relation to specific fields of practice with BME populations. These are not exhaustive, but insightful in building an inductive theory of transformative practice. However, we first turn our attention to a consideration of the issues that produce what has been called the *implementation gap* and ask: what are the contemporary challenges for social work?

## Traversing the implementation gap

Practitioners may have little trouble in identifying some of the key barriers to effective anti-racist and confident race equality practice. They will talk about a lack of political will and leadership, organisational resource restraint, and restrictive short-sighted policy measures that categorise and restrict eligibilities. They will name the stringencies of a neoliberal managerialism that stifles creativity and innovation. They may cite organisational racisms and discriminations that infiltrate their work or the force of other priorities that displace these concerns, particularly in areas of low minority presence. They may point to the lack of BME service user/organisational infrastructure, input and involvement, and they may even argue there is a lack of know-how. These factors present a constant challenge to practice and they are central to the grind of anti-racist work. Despite the fact that they are operating within a strong legal framework for equalities practice post-2000, in which organisational learning and competency has developed apace, Bhatti-Sinclair (2011) argues that these legislative instruments provide merely a framework for practice and require moral force as a motivating factor, skill in interpretation and continuous professional development on the part of practitioners to operationalise them with craft and care. She demonstrates the limitations of legal measures and calls for social work organisations to lift their game in complying with anti-racist policies and to build service strategies on better empirical research evidence and more significant engagement and participation of minority groups. Practitioners, she says, have a moral duty to inform themselves, develop their knowledge and skills, and 'confidently defend anti-racist practice in the 21st century' (Bhatti-Sinclair, 2011: xvi).

It is worth making a few broader points here by way of acknowledging the complexities and tensions apparent in working within liberal-democratic welfare organisations. A public service culture based on the liberal values of one-size-fits-all universalism, individualism and resource residualisation will always be found wanting in terms of responding to contemporary diversity (Williams and Johnson, 2010). The modernising project in welfare arrangements has aimed to insert difference and diversity into the heart of welfare delivery but, at the same time, this has brought new challenges for social work. Social work publics have changed, as have the nature of their relationships with user groups. Social workers are operating in a policy climate hostile to diversity in which considerations must extend outward from what Bhavani et al (2005) call 'situated' or localised racism to a consideration of discourses on a national and cross-national level that demonise and stigmatise minority groups (Williams and Graham, 2014). At the same time, thinking and theorising about the nature of interventions and responses to diversity are shifting within the profession and a measure of introspection has led to some deep questioning of the social work role, professionalism and identity vis-a-vis racialised minorities. We want to pause here and consider these points in more detail in as much as they present new challenges to traversing the implementation gap.

## The changing nature of ethnic diversity in the UK

We live in a new era of ethnic diversity in Britain, one in which the discourses and terminology of post-war race relations has been surpassed by the complexities and array of contemporary multiculturalism. At the beginning of the 1990s, the BME population of the UK accounted for about 6–7% of all residents; now, the figure is double, some 14%, according to the 2011 Census. However, it is not just growth that characterises the contemporary scene; Britain's cities are superdiverse, to use Vertovec's (2008) term, best depicted as characterised by diversity within diversity. The post-war waves of immigration from the former colonies have now been surpassed by smaller waves of migration from a wider range of countries, including from within Europe. Migrants from all over the world present for services, including refugees and asylum seekers, irregular migrants, foreign nationals, migrant workers, Gypsies and Travellers, and Roma. The range of ethnicities, language and cultures is but one intersection of difference, others are gender and age profiles, different immigration status, rights and entitlements, skill levels, and geographic distribution. Neither are they necessarily settlers, but transient peoples, toing and froing in the push and pull of migration flows (Williams and Graham, 2014). The needs of new arrivals and transients are considerably different from those settled minorities who form some of the oldest black communities in Europe, such as in major cities across the UK – Liverpool, Cardiff, Edinburgh, Birmingham and London. In some of the UK's cities, those of minority ethnic background are no longer in the minority numerically. Leicester, Luton and Slough now join London in having a white British population that falls below 50%.

Among the settled communities, generational transitions, intermarriage and the growth of the mixed-race population have produced new and emerging ethnicities, hybridity and interesting intersections of culture (Fanshawe and Sriskandarajah, 2010). These new and changing needs imply significant challenges for service delivery (Phillimore, 2010), not simply to cope with the sheer complexity of superdiverse publics, but challenges in terms of consultation, participation and representation. The 'community' model underpinning the multicultural model of welfare provision has lost currency, as has the notion of collective mobilisation and agency, which implies much for the development of practice (Boccagni, 2015). As Boccagni (2015: 617) argues: 'A gap exists between the pedagogical merit of a multidimensional and flexible approach to clients' identities, needs and circumstances, as a compendium of the diversity notion; and the cognitive and organizational costs that this raises in practice'. Far-reaching change to the liberal value base of welfare institutions is implied by this demographic shift and to service delivery predicated on 'one-size-fits-all' universalism (Williams and Johnson, 2010).

An important intersection in this dynamic is place. Different parts of the UK are now governed by a divergent politics under devolution. The spatial distribution of minority ethnic groups shapes factors of service delivery (Williams and De Lima, 2006) and reflects historic patterns of settlement, ethnic mobilisation and provisioning. In some parts of the UK, the settlement of new arrivals following European expansion in 2004 placed significant pressure on specialist welfare services, information and appropriate language support, and left many without appropriate care. Multicultural provision struggles in areas where migrant populations are small, diverse or scattered, and public service agencies fail to cater, leaving practitioners on the front line to innovate and personalise services. What is implied are new terminologies and frames of reference, new skills and the openness and willingness to innovate and experiment in adapting to the new realities.

## A hostile policy and practice context

Against the backdrop of this vibrant picture of demographic change, profound and far-reaching changes have occurred within social work practice. In recent years, social work's activities and values have been circumscribed by the prevailing neoliberal models of welfare driving the contours of practice. Since the inception of the welfare state, neoliberal critiques of the state have gradually taken hold, embracing the idea that free markets best achieve human well-being (Rogowski, 2010). With a preference for market-driven reforms and new approaches to management, these changes transformed day-to-day social work practice through procedural activities, paperwork and budgets (Ferguson, 2007). Rogowski (2010), among others, notes the ways in which social workers are often too busy getting on with the day job such that they are in danger of losing sight of their professional uniqueness. These modernising developments, it is argued, lead to social workers having to work their way through a maze of new rules and procedures while simultaneously adhering to deadlines and targets to achieve organisational performance indicators. Social work itself is under pressure and this has not only constrained its potential for creativity and innovation, but also significantly undermined its social justice values (Lavalette and Penketh, 2014). This is keenly felt in terms of attention to anti-racist and race equality practice, which some would argue always had a tenuous foothold in the bureaucracy (Harrison and Turner, 2011).

The reconfiguring of multiculturalism under neoliberalism moves apace and has been marked by a number of notable trends evident in UK policy, as well as across Europe and other Western countries. The neoliberal tendency has resurrected an assimilationist discourse that amplifies demands for national unity, shared values, conformity and cohesion. This trend exaggerates difference as deviance and demands adherence to an ill-defined notion of a British way of life. Social workers on the front line are engaged in policing lifestyles, dress and other conspicuous aspects of cultural difference in an easy compliance with the neoliberal mandate (Lavalette and Penketh, 2014). There has been an evident distancing from the language of race and difference during the 2000s and a resurgent emphasis on Britishness, with discourses suggesting the *death of multiculturalism* and proposing that diversity has undermined the cohesive values of institutions such as the welfare state. At the same time, increasingly restrictive and hostile immigration policies have opened up space for the vilification and demonisation of *outsiders*, readily framed as a threat to national unity. These trends have been compounded by the overriding retrenchment and marketisation of services, including the co-option of the black voluntary sector amid a clear shift towards self-help and mutual aid. These institutional transformations forged through the dismantling of the welfare state reflect what Phillimore (2010) refers to as 'restrictivisation', compounding the disadvantage of vulnerable groups.

The climate for speaking out about race, minority ethnic service provision, migrant needs and issues of multiculturalism has significantly changed to the extent that most commentators suggest a depoliticisation of the politics of race equality and an attrition of effort. While some authors have argued that current reforms of the welfare state and social work have reduced the possibilities for social justice practice, others view these changes as opportunities to explore the potential of evolving developments in practice (Healy, 2000; McDonald and Jones, 2000).

These contemporary shifts within social work reflect far-reaching debates about the nature and role of social work's response to ethnic diversity. They are not simply questions of competing theoretical positions, but speak to the remit and identity of the social work profession. Reisch and Jani (2012), in their trenchant critique, assert the evolution of a social work practice that has accommodated itself to dominant cultural values that valorise the individual over community, equality of opportunity over equity, and expertise over mutual aid. The profession, they argue, endorses a change-oriented narrative while, at the same time, is preoccupied with *adaptation* rather than conflict. Reisch and Jani go on to suggest that the wrong model underpins the contemporary construction of social work practice. In proposing a repoliticisation of practice, Reisch and Jani (2012) argue for an engagement with conflict and change situated in the profession's history of radical practice, as well as local context-driven practice.

Undoubtedly, action on the ground refracts with these wider political discourses that constrain, contain and 'manage' minority ethnic lifestyles and well-being. These discourses act to frame minority ethnic individuals and communities as a problem for service delivery rather than as integral to it. The effectiveness of social work's response to diversity relies on a recognition of social work's ambivalent positioning vis-à-vis these discourses and the work of exposing and countering this framing.

## The trouble with theory

We are not short of models, or repertoires, of diversity filled with their own terminologies and discourses. These narratives of responses to racial and ethnic diversity reflect the social policy and practice contexts in which they emerge and come to prominence. Successive eras have produced their predominant orientation as the search for the holy grail goes on. This is the search for an approach that is going to produce that 'fit for purpose' worker – the one with the right amount of cultural knowledge, who is sufficiently but not overly politicised, who has interrogated herself on questions of power and duty, and, most recently, who has looked into the invisible knapsack of her own whiteness (McIntosh, 2004). At the same time, less attention has been given to the 'how to do', to understanding the relevance of ethnicity in particular situations and to the puzzles at the heart of the implementation of theory in practice.

Responding to ethnic and cultural diversity has and does reflect contestation for a number of reasons, not least the incorporation of a range of interpretations based on differing political and philosophical mainsprings. Distinct models of practice have surfaced, most notably, the anti-racist social work and anti-discriminatory/oppressive practice models that rose to prominence in the 1980s and 1990s (Thompson, 1993; Dominelli, 1998). These models transpired in response to concerns about ongoing discrimination, injustice and inequalities in service provision and practice and reflected the analysis of structural and institutional racism. The fact that this is an evolving field, full of critique and counter-critique, both helps and hinders practice applications. It suggests that there are no absolutes, no universal formulas, but rather a strong body of theory available to craft practice. Working with the principles that have been established demands considerable skill on the part of the practitioner. Okitikpi and Aymer (2010), for example, argue for a reclaiming of the anti-discriminatory practice project, which acknowledges the interstice of human interaction and exchange and engages with notions of meaning, identity, representation and agency as they are negotiated in practice.

Although there is no definitive model of anti-oppressive practice, it includes elements of radical, feminist and emancipatory approaches and seeks to capture a diversity of oppressions. In this framework, social problems are no longer to be explained solely by reference to long-standing class divisions, and as considerations of gender, race, disability, sexuality and age entered the social sciences lexicon, so they spilled over into human services and social work. Neither could these social disparities be explained or addressed simply by a focus on cultural differences as the multicultural approaches appeared to suggest. Such overly culturalised models of practice have been subject to considerable critique (see Das and Carter-Anand in Chapter Two), although they still retain considerable currency (Laird, 2008). In embracing cultural diversity and cross-cultural practice, multicultural social work prompted disagreements between the anti-oppressive practice approaches and that of cultural competence as the prescription for effective practice (Sundar et al, 2012).

Couched as a new practice model for social work, anti-oppressive practice was presented as the key approach that held promise for engaging with transformative practice given its focus on social justice and equality (Dominelli, 1998, 2002). In practice, this model embraces a person-centred philosophy, bringing together individual assistance with working to challenge issues on a structural level (see, eg, Baines, 2011). In turn, it recognises that social workers hold positions of power and influence through institutional structures, and therefore the potential for discrimination and oppression. Thus, practice requires ongoing critical examination and self-reflection and a practitioner more appreciative of the influence of their own identity and social status.

Both multicultural and anti-oppressive practice models for practice have been subject to intense critique and modification as the 'implementation gap' between theory and practice has proved almost impermeable. The critique of the anti-oppressive practice approach has been particularly trenchant from within and outside of the profession. Power, oppression and inequality on a structural level may be easy to analyse but translating them into an anti-oppressive practice on the micro-level has proved trickier (Harrison and Turner, 2011). Further, while social work positions itself as the champion against the wrongs of oppression and anti-oppressive practice is seen as the 'correct' way to make good these disparities, these assumptions are far from accepted. Beresford and Wilson (2000) took up this point by examining the claims of anti-discrimination practice from the service user's point of view. They challenge such assertions, arguing that this approach has failed to engage critically with social work's own position and practices and to ask: who determines what is defined as anti-oppressive practice in the first place? Aspirations embedded in social work do not necessarily resonate with service users and can appear to be lofty ideals rather than engaging their experiences and narratives to frame practice activities. For Beresford and Wilson, the service user becomes lost in the pursuit of theory (Beresford, 2012). Accordingly, it is possible that anti-oppressive practice can reproduce the very oppression that it claims to diminish by being tied to ideology and scholarship rather than knowledge from the ground up (Sakamoto and Pitner, 2005). These propositions imply a healthy scepticism in the development of theory and a commitment to what Das and Carter Anand call *pushing* theory (see Chapter Two, this volume). They imply greater consultation and more genuine engagement with the diversity of BME service users (see Hong Baker and Williams, Chapter Eight).

Anti-oppressive practice's overarching modernist view has increasingly been seen as lacking an understanding of the unique and specific expressions of oppression. This generic approach tends to avoid the way in which the multiplicity of oppressions varies in frequency, intensity and pervasiveness, and promotes 'a little of something for everyone approach', often driven by political considerations rather than systematic approaches (Graham and Schiele, 2010). This gap has been readily filled by postmodern perspectives that force a re-examination of social work's assumptions, most notably, attention to how professional knowledge is created and maintained, as well as the connections between theory and practice.

Postmodern thinking has filtered into social work practice, proposing different ways of conceiving identities and social divisions in society and extending practice beyond social change ambitions. The central themes of postmodernism have provided a critique of the modernist assumptions of universalism, scientific rationality, absolute truth and reliance on 'grand narratives' to explain social divisions. These approaches privilege the uniqueness of individuals, as well as embracing a more fragmented view of the collective dimensions of society and its institutions. These theories have contributed greatly to our body of knowledge through offering a more nuanced understanding of the complexities of race, ethnicity, power and privilege. In understanding race/ethnicity, gender and class, a postmodern perspective moves beyond simplistic binary categories, leading to an appreciation of the complexities of power relations in different contexts and situations. In this vein, notions of a single identity are replaced as the individual is conceived as complex web of intersectional identities. The term *intersectionality* emerged through attempts to understand how individual experiences reflect the interaction of multiple oppressions rather than just seeing them as one or more add-ons sitting alongside each other (Yuval-Davis, 2006).

For over a decade now, intersectionality has been used across disciplines as a tool of analysis for studying the ways in which the intersections of social categories contribute to the unique experiences of both oppression and privilege. This framework helps us to appreciate that people have multidimensional aspects to their identity and their lived experiences. By using this model, different types of discrimination that occur within these intersections can be revealed in order to assess their impact on these converging identities (Ortiz and Jani, 2013). However, this concept is as yet limited in terms of understanding a wider spectrum of axes of difference experienced by minority ethnic groups, including legal status and citizenship rights, migration history, length of stay, and so on, as they reflect the superdiversity of minority experience (Boccagni, 2015).

Postmodern analysis does, however, employ a greater scrutiny of practice methods through the recognition of different social locations/positions, revealing an even wider gap between theory and practice. At the same time, postmodern insights have opened up opportunities for the subjective experience and voice of the service user to be expressed in the construction of knowledge situated in and through the context of practice. For example, critical race studies has moved beyond a black–white paradigm and essentialist constructs of ethnicity to consider multiple intersections of race, ethnicity, gender and various identities as a critical form of expression. The voice of minority peoples in the form of narrative or storytelling has been foregrounded, not only as a way of conveying gendered and racialised experiences, but also to counter metanarratives, images, preconceptions and myths used as a way to maintain racial inequality (see Robinson and Gardee, Chapter Five; Thomas, Chapter Twelve). This centrality of experiential knowledge is critical to lines of inquiry about links to larger systems of power, dominance and inequity (Baines, 2002). This narrative and storytelling approach serves to illuminate the social and relational content of practice, bringing service users'/clients' experience to contribute to theorising. Ortiz and Jani (2013) articulate what this approach might look like in practice. First, they ask: what are the presuppositions embedded in the services, and how do these fit with people for whom these are designed to serve? This requires viewing the service user in the social context through connecting the client's problem with the social conditions in which it is located, as well as considering their accessibility to services (Ortiz and Jani, 2013).

In these and other ways, postmodern perspectives have unsettled the world of social work practice by undermining hierarchical arrangements of social workers as experts towards knowledge from the ground up in the daily experience of clients and practitioners as listeners and learners (Fook, 2002). Within the frame of postmodern thinking, social work practices are reconfigured and understood in different ways.

Despite its appeal in opening up perspectives of difference, however, Noble (2004: 292) considers that 'these 'post' theories, more specifically the postmodern critique, are quietly destabilizing and undermining social work's intellectual heritage'. The shift away from the analysis of social structures towards a focus on social meanings and individual identities is seen as having deradicalised social work.

What can we make, therefore, of this trouble with theory? How can we negotiate the competing concerns of attention to structure and to individual agency? Much relies on the craft of the practitioner to mobilise concerns with the big issues of power and oppression, with historical and localised context, with meaning and agency. All too often, social workers are pressed for time, without any space to reflect upon what they are doing, but this type of critical reflection is fundamental to 'pushing theory' into service. Relationship-based approaches have a long-standing place in social work. Over time, these approaches have evolved into what is broadly termed reflexive practice, which involves critical thinking, analysis and self-awareness. While the skill of reflection invites us to consider in-depth situations outside of ourselves, as in our daily professional life, reflexivity calls for strategies to question our own attitudes, thought processes, values and thinking from within that experience. Thinking critically, as Baines (2002) suggests, strengthens capacity, social analysis and critique. We make use of theory reflexively. In this way, the relationship between theory and practice is no longer a one-way-street process that moves from theory to practice, but rather a dialogical relationship in which knowledges (professional and user-led) and practice are integrated (see, eg, Lucas, Chapter Six). Within these relationships, reflexivity sharpens insights into the ways in which discourses influence and shape practice environments (see Thomas, Chapter Twelve). We reiterate here Okitikpi and Aymer's observation that work with and on behalf of minority ethnic service users demands considerable skill and continuous professional development on the part of the practitioner.

## Towards embedded transformatory practice

This breadth of approaches – sometimes complimentary, sometimes in contradiction – offers a useful starting point in building a framework for thinking about practice. The contribution of these theories has been to bring issues of individual, institutional and professional power and social-structural processes that compound disadvantage into view, to highlight the importance of agency and voice, and to signal the significance of context, both historical and present. The tendency, however, has been to focus on prescriptive formulas and 'dos and don'ts' rather than on emergent theory or what might be called dialogic or negotiated action and intervention. As Boccagni (2015: 609) observes: 'there is a rich and widespread repertoire of professional experiences but far less reflexivity and theoretical elaboration about the influence of diversity'. More attention is needed in understanding how ethnic diversity is named, categorised and mobilised in social work and social welfare interactions by professionals, their organisations and service users.

Here, we propose a loose framework for thinking about practice that will contextualise the work covered within this volume. This framework does not propose formulas, but is underpinned by value principles (see Burke and Harrison, Chapter Three), and offers lines of inquiry for action built on negotiation and dialogue. It calls for the profession to recognise its ambivalent positioning vis-à-vis the state's 'management' of minority groups and to consider how this is played out in specific cultural and political contexts.

**Figure 1.1: Towards embedded transformatory practice**

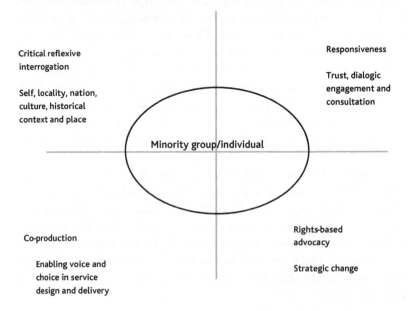

The model proposed here (see Figure 1.1) is a broad framework with four relevant trajectories for capturing the work that will unfold in this text. It is a model that acknowledges the voice of the minority group user(s) as the starting point and considers the 'affective' and relational aspects of encounters within service delivery. Its bedrock assumption is that BME participants in welfare are a resource to the processes of welfare delivery, receipt and reciprocity. In recognising this, the minority group/individual is placed at the heart of analysis and action from which practice intervention is built. In terms of critical reflexive interrogation, the framework prompts questions such as: what are the '*narratives of race*' at work here and how do they frame understandings of the issues presented? How am

I positioned in relation to this historicity and contemporary manifestation of discourses of ethnic difference and diversity?

As a profession, we are coming to understand more clearly the affective nature of such practice engagement and the creativity and innovation required to produce meaningful responses (see Cemlyn and Allen, Chapter Ten). Loss of trust in public services on the part of many BME groups means that considerable skill is required to bridge the paucity of their experience and to demonstrate responsiveness. The model proposes trust, dialogic engagement and consultation as essential to this. This direct micro-level work relies on the range of skills familiar to anti-oppressive practice, accommodating attention to power and power relationships and the ways in which social needs are constructed, framed and communicated, as discussed in several of the chapters. The effectiveness of the response builds on a critical and reflective interrogation of self and society, on aspects of locality, nation and culture, and organisational context that are core contextualising factors in any encounter. These need to be understood in as much as they shape practice and give historicity to the assessment process. Here, knowledge of local nuances or the situated nature of community demographics, histories, politics and place speak to practice. Examples of work from Wales, Northern Ireland and Scotland in this volume highlight the relevance of this contextual knowledge to the practice nexus (see Das and Carter-Anand, Chapter Two; Robinson and Gardee, Chapter Five; Hong Baker and Williams, Chapter Eight).

We then look to two further trajectories of responsibility, namely: co-production, working alongside users/user groups, drawing positively on their contributions and engaging in dialogue to produce relevant outcomes; and rights-based advocacy, speaking out for and alongside minority groups/individuals for more strategic change (see Moran and Lavalette, Chapter Seven; Cemlyn and Allen, Chapter Ten; Raghavan, Chapter Eleven).

Much good and innovative practice with BME groups, communities and individuals goes into attrition in the absence of robust evaluation and research. There is an evident need to distil messages from practice and to conduct more empirical research to explore how issues of difference and diversity are socially constructed, approached and negotiated in practice (see Bhatti-Sinclair and Price, Chapter Thirteen). How service users themselves define, present and negotiate diversity in seeking assistance is little understood (see Raghavan, Chapter Eleven) and how this diversity is situated in context-dependent ways (see Lucas, Chapter Six) requires elucidation and elaboration. Few studies empirically capture how the principles of anti-oppressive practice play out in public services (Strier and Binyamin, 2014) or how social workers actually engage with these issues in practice (Harrison and Turner, 2011).

This edited collection brings together academics and practitioners working at the forefront of issues of responding appropriately to ethnic and cultural difference. Many of the authors in this book have been major contributors in progressing writing on anti-racist and anti-oppressive practice in the UK, and have produced between them a wealth of literature that we want to recognise here (Bernard,

2001; Dalrymple and Burke, 2006; Clifford and Burke, 2008; Fernando and Keating, 2008; Bhatti-Sinclair, 2011; Lavalette and Penketh, 2014). This book complements this literature in drawing on practice scenarios to add insights to the knowledge base.

The book adopts the concept of 'embedded transformative practice' to explore, in Part One, the available theoretical ground, issues, tensions and debates, and argues for 'pushing theory' from experience in the field by engaging in dialogue with practitioners working on the front line. As such, it is a book about 'emergent theory', not a theory-driven book, and a book that draws on practice wisdom. The second half of the book takes forward key practice themes and draws on the contributor pairings to illustrate principles for practice. We have sought where possible to link an academic writer with a practitioner in producing each chapter, in line with our philosophy of *dialogic engagement* towards integrating theory and practice. We are hoping that this enterprise will in itself produce a novel methodology for the production of lessons for practice and a unique and eminently readable collection.

Each of the contributors seeks to develop understanding around their chosen theme, based on research evidence and knowledge in practice, and proceeds to demonstrate how this theme applies to practice utilising illustrative case scenarios. Part Two of the book is devoted to short case studies, projects and research that are illustrative of the ways in which it has been possible to traverse key constraints on practice through innovative, creative and participatory strategies. These studies demonstrate the ways in which the barriers to more reflective approaches are negotiated in the field, and each chapter offers findings from the front line that contribute to our understanding of practice development in the field of ethnic and cultural diversity. In the spirit of this endeavour and the notion of emergent theory, we reserve our thematic review of the chapters to the Conclusion, where we offer our reading of the text.

**References**

Baines, D. (2002) 'Race, class and gender in the everyday talk of social workers: the ways we limit the possibilities for radical practice', *Race Gender and Class Journal*, 9(1): 145–67.

Baines, D. (ed) (2011) *Doing anti-oppressive practice: building transformative politicized social work*, Halifax, NS: Fernwood Publishing.

Beresford, P. (2012) 'Service-user involvement', in M. Gray, J. Midgley and S. Webb (eds) *The Sage handbook of social work*, London: Sage.

Beresford, P. and Wilson, A. (2000) 'Anti-oppressive practice, emancipation or appropriation', *British Journal of Social Work*, 30(5): 553–73.

Bernard, C. (2001) *Constructing lived experiences: representations of black mothers in child sexual abuse discourses*, Aldershot: Ashgate Publishing.

Bhatti-Sinclair, K. (2011) *Anti-racist practice in social work*, Basingstoke: Palgrave/Macmillan.

Bhavani, R., Mirza, H. and Meetoo, V. (2005) *Tackling the roots of racism*, Bristol: The Policy Press.

Boccagni, P. (2015) '(Super)Diversity and the migration–social work nexus: a new lens on the field of access and inclusion?', *Ethnic and Racial Studies*, 38(4): 608–20.

Bowes, A. and Sim, D. (2006) 'Advocacy for black and minority ethnic communities: understandings and expectations', *British Journal of Social Work*, 36(7): 1209–25.

Clifford, D. and Burke, B. (2008) *Anti-oppressive ethics and values in social work*, Basingstoke: Palgrave Macmillan.

Craig, G. (2007) '"Cunning, unprincipled, loathsome": the racist tail wags the welfare dog', *Journal of Social Policy*, 36(4): 605–23.

Dalrymple, J. and Burke, B. (2006) *Anti-oppressive practice social care and the law* (2nd edn), Maidenhead: Open University Press.

Davies, R., Drinkwater, S., Joll, S., Jones, M., Lloyd-Williams, H., Makepeace, G., Parhi, M., Parken, A., Robinson, C., Taylor, C. and Wass, V. (2011) *An anatomy of economic inequality in Wales*, Cardiff: Equality and Human Rights Commission.

Dominelli, L. (1998) 'Anti-oppressive practice in context', in R. Adams, L. Dominelli and M. Payne (eds) *Social work: themes, issues and critical debates*, Basingstoke: Palgrave.

Dominelli, L. (2002) *Anti-oppressive social work theory and practice*, London: Palgrave Macmillan.

EHRC (Equality and Human Rights Commission) (2010) Equality Act, EHRC, http://www.legislation.gov.uk/ukpga/2010/15/contents

EHRC (2015) *How fair is Britain?*, http://www.equalityhumanrights.com/about-us/our-work/key-projects/how-fair-britain/full-report-and-evidence-downloads

Fanshawe, S. and Sriskandarajah, D. (2010) *"You can't put me in a box": superdiversity and the end of identity politics in Britain*, London: IPPR.

Ferguson, I. (2007) *Reclaiming social work*, London: Sage.

Fernando, S. and Keating, F. (ed) (2008) *Mental health in a multi-ethnic society* (2nd edn), London: Routledge.

Fook, J. (2002) *Social work: critical theory and practice*, London: Sage.

Graham, M. and Schiele, J. (2010) 'Anti-discriminatory and equality of oppressions models in social work: reflections from the UK and USA', *European Journal of Social Work*, 13(2): 231–44.

Harrison, G. and Turner, R. (2011) 'Being a "culturally competent" social worker', *British Journal of Social Work*, 41(2): 333–50.

Healey, K. (2000) *Social work practices: contemporary perspectives on change*, London: Sage.

IRR(Institute of Race Relations (2015) Inequality, housing and employment statistics, http://www.irr.org.uk/research/statistics/poverty/

Kam, P.K. (2014) 'Back to the "social" of social work: reviving the social work profession's contribution to the promotion of social justice', *International Social Work*, 57(6): 723–40.

Laird, S. (2008) *Anti-oppressive social work: a guide for developing cultural competence*, London: Sage.

Lavalette, M. and Penketh, L. (2014) *Race, racism and social work: contemporary issues and debates*, Bristol: The Policy Press.

McDonald, C. and Jones, A. (2000) 'Reconstructing and re-conceptualizing social work in the emerging milieu', *Australian Social Work*, 53(3): 3–11.

McIntosh, P. (2004) 'White privilege: unpacking the invisible knapsack', in M. Anderson and P. Hill-Collins (eds) *Race, class and gender: an anthology*, Belmont, CA: Wadsworth Publishing Co.

McLaughlin, K. (2005) 'From ridicule to institutionalization: anti-oppression, the state and social work', *Critical Social Policy*, 25(3): 283–305.

Noble, C. (2004) 'Postmodern thinking: where is it taking social work?', *Journal of Social Work*, 4(3): 289–304.

Okitikpi, T. and Aymer, C. (2010) *Key concepts in anti-discriminatory social work*, London: Sage.

Olson, J.J. (2008) 'Social work's professional and social justice projects', *Journal of Progressive Human Services*, 18(1): 45–69.

Ortiz, L. and Jani, J. (2013) 'Critical race theory: a transformational model for teaching diversity', *Journal of Social Work Education*, 46(2): 175–93.

Phillimore, J. (2010) 'Approaches to health provision in the age of superdiversity: accessing the NHS in Britain's most diverse city', *Critical Social Policy*, 31(1): 5–29.

Reisch, M. and Jani, J. (2012) 'The new politics of social work practice: understanding context to promote change', *British Journal of Social Work*, 42(6): 1132–50.

Rogowski, S. (2010) *Social work: the rise and fall of a profession?*, Bristol: The Policy Press.

Sakamoto, I. and Pitner, R.O. (2005) 'Use of critical consciousness in anti-oppressive social work practice: disentangling power dynamics at personal and structural levels', *British Journal of Social Work*, 35(4): 435–52.

SCIE (Social Care Institute for Excellence) (2006) *Are we there yet? Identifying the characteristics of social care organisations that successfully promote diversity*, London: SCIE, http://www.scie.org.uk/publications/raceequalitydiscussionpapers/redp03.asp

Solas, J. (2008) 'What kind of social justice does social work seek?', *International Social Work*, 51(6): 813–22.

Strier, R. and Binyamin, S. (2014) 'Introducing anti-oppressive social work practices in public services: rhetoric to practice', *British Journal of Social Work*, 44(8): 2095–112.

Sundar, P., Syvestre, J. and Bassi, A. (2012) 'Diversity and social work practice', in M. Gray, J. Midgley and S. Webb (eds) *The Sage handbook of social work*, London: Sage, pp 355–71.

SWTF (Social Work Task Force) (2009) *Building a safe, confident future*, London: General Social Care Council.

*The Guardian* (2014) 'Austerity has hit women, ethnic minorities and the disabled most', 31 July.

Thompson, N. (1993) *Anti discriminatory practice*, Basingstoke: Macmillan.

Vertovec, S. (2008) 'Superdiversity and its implications', *Ethnic and Racial Studies*, 30(6): 1024–54.

Williams, C. and De Lima, P. (2006) 'Devolution, multicultural citizenship and race equality: from laissez-faire to nationally responsible policies', *Critical Social Policy*, 26(3): 498–522.

Williams, C. and Graham, M. (2014) '"A world on the move": migration, mobilities and social work', *British Journal of Social Work*, 44(Supplement 1): i1–i17.

Williams, C. and Johnson, M. (2010) *Race and ethnicity in the welfare state*, Maidenhead: Open University Press.

Williams, C. and Parrot, L. (2013) 'From specialism to genericism: rising and falling to the challenges of responding to racial and ethnic diversity in social work education in Wales', *British Journal of Social Work*, 43(6): 1206–24.

Yuval-Davis, N. (2006) 'Intersectionality and feminist politics', *European Journal of Women's Studies*, 13(3): 193–209.

# TWO

# 'Pushing theory': applying cultural competence in practice – a case study of community conflict in Northern Ireland

*Chaitali Das and Janet Carter Anand*

## Introduction

This chapter provides a critical analysis of cultural competence with the intention of reconstructing a culturally transformative model of critical cultural competence relevant to the needs of globally minded social work practice. Postmodernism and post-colonial theory have helped challenge the universalism of British and European social work methods and interventions based on Eurocentric assumptions (Coates et al, 2006). However, a historical analysis of the development of cultural competence in the UK traces the adoption and eventual abandonment of radical anti-racist practice and education for a more limited model of cultural competence focusing on work with minority groups and 'other' cultures (Macey and Moxon, 1996; Dominelli, 1998; Chau et al, 2011). Neoliberalism has contributed to an obscuring of social inequalities in the UK and other Western countries by promoting assumptions that civil and political rights have been achieved for all. As a consequence, social workers' ability to 'speak out' against social injustice and for social, cultural and economic rights has been thwarted, resulting in the profession's retreat from political and social activism and a focus on technical rationality, equality and justification for the current system of service provision (Harrison and Melville, 2010). We, however, argue that a critical examination of power (critical), privilege (reflexivity), self-awareness (reflection) and rights-based practice (social change) are essential tools for anti-oppressive social work to address social, cultural, political and religious inequality.

The first section of this chapter outlines the concept of cultural competence and the historical derailing of the radical objectives of cultural competence within social work. We argue that the positioning or occupational space occupied by the profession may either open up or close down opportunities for cultural transformative practice and working for social justice and change. We further push the concept of cultural competence and suggest a critical reading of the concept, where knowledge, skills and values can enable an analytical process of considering different social, political and historical positions and create spaces for transformative practice (Fook, 2002; Furlong and Wight, 2011). We use the context of Northern Ireland (NI), as a society that has experienced colonisation, violent conflict and sectarianism racism, to illustrate how critical cultural competence offers renewed opportunities for transformative practice within complex cultural contexts.

## Cultural competency in social work education and practice

Cultural competence is a fundamental principle of anti-oppressive social work practice (Abrams and Moio, 2009) when working with individual service users, diverse groups and cultures (Chau et al, 2011), and yet it continues to be a contested concept (Laird, 2008). Current approaches to cultural competence focus on practitioners' awareness of different cultural beliefs and behaviours. Greater awareness of the global context of social work practice has resulted in the demand for more culturally competent social workers to work with minority and disability groups (Poxton et al, 2012). In contemporary social work contexts, the term 'diverse groups', in its broadest conceptualisation, has come to encompass all groups at risk of social exclusion and marginalisation (Sheppard, 2006; Abrams and Moio, 2009; Harrison and Turner, 2011). Social work education programmes are thus increasingly addressing issues of diversity through the theoretical underpinning of anti-oppressive practice (and cultural competence).

Cultural competence is broadly an ability to apply knowledge, values and skills that can actively promote understanding of individuals and groups, particularly oppressed groups whose cultures are often marginalised in the mainstream context. Weaver (1999) suggests that cultural competence must incorporate three basic attributes: knowledge, skills and values. 'Knowledge' refers to an understanding of the nuances and complexity of a group of people and how they have developed their history and belief systems, as well as any changes in belief systems through key events and contemporary issues presenting within communities. 'Skills' refers to a willingness to listen, reflect and be patient with individuals, groups and communities. Finally, 'values' refers to a belief in the issues of humanity and social justice for the group and an open and non-judgemental attitude.

Yet, the conceptualisation of cultural competence is fraught with ambiguity, confusion and inherent paradoxes. For example, cultural competence is frequently used interchangeably with concepts such as multicultural practice, cultural pluralism, cross-cultural training, diversity awareness, cultural awareness, cultural sensitivity and anti-racist practice. Sometimes, these terms reflect contradictory assumptions and agendas, such as the dilution of cultures into one culture (cultural assimilation), the creation of cultural melting pots (multiculturalism) or different cultures existing in parallel with one another (bi-culturalism and cultural pluralism). Cultural theories such as multiculturalism and cultural assimilation have been criticised for failing to address the cultural identity, needs and rights of minority groups at the expense of serving the interests of dominant cultural groups.

For social work educators and practitioners, the plethora of approaches, training models and standards of cultural competence (Laird, 2008) add to this ambiguity. Social work education tends to teach students the culture of diverse people as a 'commodity'. Rather than cultural competency as a practice-oriented activity requiring constant reflection, and reworking at every encounter, in practice, it is reduced to a series of 'do's and don'ts' for practitioners based on stereotypical pieces of information (Betancourt et al, 2005; Kumagai and Lypson, 2009). This results in an oversimplification of the concept of culture and encourages the use of broad generalisations and stereotyping (Ben-Ari and Strier, 2010; Chau et al, 2011; Furlong and Wight, 2011; Harrison and Turner, 2011).

Ben-Ari and Strier (2010) criticise cultural competency as it continues to recognise diverse groups as the 'other', which maintains a particular privileged discourse and promotes 'othering'. 'Minority' or 'diverse' groups are considered targets for culturally competent practice against the majority 'norm'. The focus on difference, particularly within cultural competency training, remains on minority race and culture. Programmes focus on racial and/or cultural issues and practices but not their development (Carter, 2001). Thus, minority cultures are always assessed or explained in contrast with the majority culture, which remains unquestioned, further perpetuating a Eurocentric perspective.

While cultural competence uses anti-oppressive practice perspectives and aims to address oppression, much of the focus remains on individual attitudes, with little focus on structural or institutional change. Applications of cultural competence are often used towards the provision of remedial, therapy-based services, which are systematically sustained through economic and political arrangements that reinforce the status quo, justify the system and perpetuate further social injustice (Vera and Speight, 2003). Often, the concept of culture is placed in isolation from the multiple layers of discrimination, for example, gender and responsibilities for caring, and emphasises risk issues rather than fostering an understanding of risk and support factors within cultural contexts. Such a conceptualisation of culture leads to the further minoritisation[1] of diverse groups and the entrenchment of their identities, limiting the capacities of minority groups for change or transformation (Nash, 2005).

While most programmes offer theoretical knowledge, the reality of integrating this knowledge into practice remains patchy and superficial with little focus on skills of reflection and critical self-awareness (Ledoux and Montalvo, 1999). Although most social work schools in the Western context increasingly offer a curriculum aimed at equipping students with knowledge and skills for culturally competent practice, they often lack a radical critical framework to understand diverse marginalised groups and peoples (Weaver, 1999; Haug, 2005; Kumagai and Lypson, 2009; Wehbi, 2009). Furthermore, the term 'competency' is also controversial as it may indicate proficiency in skills rather than a praxis-oriented process that requires constant engagement and reworking at every encounter. Acquisition of cultural competency is developmental (Bennett, 1993), requiring reflexivity and honest reflection to achieve the full integration of cultural awareness into everyday interactions.

## Historical development of cultural competency

The way in which social workers have conceptualised cultural competence has been influenced by contradictory social and political influences over time. Feminism and the civil rights movements in the 1960s played a significant role in the profession's engagement with cultural competence, encouraging social workers to challenge dominant white assumptions and questioning racist and discriminatory assumptions that problematise diversity and vulnerable and minority communities (Coates et al, 2006; Abrams and Moio, 2009). During the 1980s and 1990s, postmodernism and post-colonial influences have revised our awareness of cultural 'norms', together with the process of 'othering' and diversity. Postmodernism afforded an understanding of the ways in which people from diverse backgrounds are labelled as at risk, marginal or vulnerable and that the role of social work has the potential to not only challenge inequality, but also reproduce oppression, power and privilege (Sheppard, 2006; Abrams and Moio, 2009; Chau et al, 2011; Harrison and Turner, 2011). An awareness of how the complex relationship between the colonial and the colonised shapes what is diverse as a clear distinction between who has power and who is powerless was heralded as a commitment of anti-oppressive social work (Dominelli, 2002). The impact of post-colonial theory on professional social work practice was sharply experienced in former colonies such as South Africa, Australia and New Zealand, where practitioners actively sought to address historical injustices by acknowledging and privileging indigenous ways of knowing, being and doing (Weaver, 1999; Martin, 2003). However by the late 1990s and 2000s, the anti-racist and anti-oppressive agenda was largely depoliticised, alongside more global conservative political and economic trends. Anti-racist practice and education saw a backlash in the UK in favour of a less emotive and more common-sense approach to social work practice, reflecting the contemporary neoliberal agenda (Macey and Moxon, 1996; Dominelli, 1998). Likewise, the radicalism of South African social work during the apartheid years waned and shifted to more pragmatic day-to-day practice concerns (Harrison and Melville, 2010).

One explanation for professionals' lack of success in bringing about social change relates to the profession's knowledge, skills and value base, which remain embedded in modernist, Eurocentric ideas, resulting in the reproduction of the same power inequalities. In addition, practitioners increasingly find themselves working within contexts where they themselves feel powerless to address the tensions between the structural and the collective, and the local and the global (Jordan, 2004; Wehbi, 2009). While the postmodernist influence has resulted in an emphasis on critical understanding of and reflection on (Fook, 2002) different social, historical and political positions and how they interact (Furlong and Wight, 2011), social work interventions that remain embedded in a modernist framework are difficult to implement in the contemporary unstable, complex and disorderly postmodern realities of most disenfranchised and marginalised groups (Coates et al, 2006). Harrison and Turner (2011) argue that postmodern challenges have, in some ways, led to frustration and a re-emergence of conservatism, with a call for homogeneity in political contexts.

## Social work, critical cultural competence and the Northern Irish context

The context of NI offers the opportunity to explore the contradictions and challenges of culturally competent social work practice in a society that, along with a history of deep divisions and segregation, is undergoing transformative political, economic and demographical changes. Historically, social work practice in NI has been influenced by two interrelated experiences: colonialism and sectarianism. The unique nature the sectarian conflict experienced can be simplistically but briefly explained as a struggle between those (largely considered to be Catholic Republicans) who wish to see NI as a part of the Republic of Ireland and those (largely considered to be Protestant Unionists) who wish to see NI continue as a part of the UK (Cairns and Darby, 1998). However, this understanding of conflict suppresses the deep historical, cultural, religious, political, economic and psychological elements that can be traced back more than 300 years. The Troubles, spanning 30 years of active conflict between these two 'cultural' groups, was a more recent manifestation of the conflict that ended in 1998 with the Belfast Agreement, which instituted a power-sharing government between the two conflict groups (Cairns and Darby, 1998). While the Agreement has been successful in largely overcoming violent activities between the two groups, the unique interplay of cultural, religious and political conflicts persists in different forms in almost every fabric of NI society. This complex nature of cultural identity in Northern Ireland presents immense challenges for social workers trying to understand not only their personal cultural identity, but also how this may impact on working with individuals and communities with different profiles.

The legacy of the historical colonisation of the island of Ireland continues to have a significant impact on the development of social work in NI. Walton and Abo-El-Nasr (1988) suggests that a parallel process of interaction occurs between colonial and local forms of professional knowledge, values and practices. The first is that of the indigenisation of non-local practice by adopting imported ideas to make them relevant to local conditions, and the second involves the authentication of local practice to form a new locally relevant structure of ideas. In NI, this has meant that, on the one hand, the development of the social work profession has been based on English models and frameworks (Heenan and Birrell, 2011); however, on the other, issues of sectarianism have also influenced social work practice. Social work in NI tends towards a bureaucratic, legalistic and individual-centred model of practice, and during the height of sectarian conflict, it played a minimal role in addressing issues of the injustice and inequality of the Troubles. It is argued that during the 30 years preceding the Belfast Agreement, social workers worked in an environment where culture and identity were highly political and social workers operated from a perspective where culture and identity were not addressed in order to protect themselves and their clients (Pinkerton and Campbell, 2002; Houston, 2008). The social work profession's limited engagement with the Troubles as an issue of social justice may also be rationalised by the profession's ultimate reliance on the political regime of the time for the provision of roles, status and, most importantly, career opportunities. An agenda of anti-sectarian practice was later developed (and is still under way) to acknowledge the presence, manifestations and effects of sectarianism (Duffy et al, 2013). The question as to why the social work professional continues to take a relatively 'neutral' political position in response to sectarianism in NI stimulated our interest in the possibilities of a critical approach to cultural competence to address issues of power, oppression and conflict, both with the local context and internationally. The building blocks of our notion of critical cultural competence involve a nuanced *knowledge* and understanding of historical and contemporary issues, *skills* that can prepare social workers to find alternative possibilities and realities for transformative practice, and, finally, *values* that are committed to anti-oppression practice (Weaver, 1999). We consider each of these components in the following.

### Knowledge of history, culture, identities and contemporary issues

Social work practitioners caught up with the pressures of task-focused agency practice often neglect the importance of understanding how historical and cultural knowledge inform day-to-day professional practice. A historical perspective enables practitioners to chart the impact and basis of the NI conflict in religious, national, economic and political inequalities and oppression (Muldoon, 2002) and to avoid the often simplistic construction of the Troubles as a battle between Catholics and Protestants (Muldoon, 2002; Trew, 2004). Social work education seeks to provide students with a recognition that both Catholics and Protestants experience minoritisation within the larger context of the UK. While Catholics experience minoritisation in NI, Protestants experience minoritisation within the island of Ireland, as well as in Britain (Muldoon, 2002). While the Belfast or the Good Friday Agreement is an important recent development, which sought to establish shared political institutions in NI that include both Catholic and Protestant political groups in order to encourage cooperation and trust (Gallagher, 2004), the complexity of the NI situation, the successes and failures and the reasons thereof, and the possibilities for the future only become clear when one understands these historical precedents.

The importance of the cultural and ethnographic identities and lived experience of individuals and communities in NI has, at times, been neglected by the profession. Due to the conflict, in NI, culture remains highly charged and cultural artefacts and symbols (flags and other representations) are used to continue division and unresolved political conflict (Nash, 2005), making it particularly challenging for practitioners to navigate across different communities. Cultural relativism has tended to maintain the 'conflict' in post-conflict NI; segregation continues through symbols, demarcated territories, housing, schools and recreational activities (Trew, 2004). An understanding of how culture and identity can be used to create boundaries between two groups that are rigid and homogeneous, and that have mutually exclusive political aspirations (Brian and Shirlow, 1998; Bryne, 2001; Trew, 2004; Nash, 2005; Sluka, 2009), is therefore fundamental to social work practice in the NI context. For example, the essentialisation of identity – by focusing on selective aspects and reaffirming stereotyped images by ethnic and nationalist movements – has served to create divisive politics. Furthermore, these cultural identities are communicated trans-generationally and enable new sets of grievances to energise and re-energise the conflict, contributing to the enduring nature of the conflict (Ginty et al, 2007).

The rigid identity politics in NI limit the possibilities for alternative or different versions of identity, allegiance or political position (Trew, 2004; Nash, 2005), which are necessary to address conflict (Porter, 2000). The essentialisation of culture has also led to an ignorance of the diversity within NI, which is far more complex than the two supposedly monolithic groups (Cassidy and Trew, 1998). The complex interactions between lifestyle, class, welfare, place and identity are sidelined. Furthermore, NI is a society comprised not of two contesting ethnic groups, but also of other minority ethnic communities (Nash, 2005). NI is increasingly becoming a multicultural society, with immigration exceeding emigration through increasing flows of people from the European Union (EU) and around the world (NISRA, 2009). Issues of culture and identity are entangled in complex ways with equity and justice in NI and necessarily require a complex reading of identity, tradition and culture more widely.

Finally, knowledge of the linkages between history and the development of contemporary and future social issues are critical for practice. These include the changing nature of the sectarian context, issues of equality and justice, and issues of immigration and minority communities, as well as the broader European political context. Many researchers contend that since the Belfast Agreement, sectarian issues have become further exacerbated, with continued social, residential and educational segregation and an over-privileging of difference (Ginty et al, 2007; Bekerman et al, 2009; Sluka, 2009). In spite of the peace agreement, activities of paramilitaries and violence at residential interfaces continues (but with reduced overall intensity), though in different forms. Various peace efforts, including those by civil and community organisations, have not managed to push beyond single identity work towards building bridges across communities, and structural issues of injustice, inequality and conflict have remained unaddressed (Gallagher, 2004; Jarman, 2004; McDowell, 2008). Many social problems common across societies, such as drug use, have become underscored by the conflict, and subsequent peace processes have created more instability. The peace process has seen a decline in community bonds, with decreasing informal social networks accompanied by a growth of alienation and community fragmentation (Gallagher, 2004; Nash,

2005; Gilligan, 2006). Finally, NI is also dealing with an increasingly complex and global society, with changing immigration and emigration patterns, where issues of racism, sectarianism, gender and class issues interact in complex ways, challenging traditional notions of culture and tradition (Kinnval, 2004).

## Skills

Historical knowledge has to be combined with applied skills for culturally competent practice. Within NI, this involves the ability to work with people from different positions and create spaces for dialogue and creative problem solving. The development of appropriate language and framing when working in NI is essential for nuanced practice, particularly in a culturally and conflict charged situation. Critical skills also include the ability to seek appropriate knowledge and link them to practice settings across different levels of practice (individual, group, policy, institutional, professional). Engagement in NI requires an understanding of the complexity of sectarianism and the skills to recognise its various forms, as well as to address them in different ways. Finally, irrespective of work in a single identity context, cross-community, institutional, individual or group level, the skills to work with clients at their level with a goal of critical conscientisation is crucial.

Without personal skills, such as the ability to self-reflect, be self-aware and address personal bias, critical cultural competence cannot be implemented in practice. Engagement in cultural competence means not only working sensitively with others, but also recognising processes of praxis, ourselves and our own engagement. This is particularly difficult as we are constantly surrounded by dominant and oppressive ideologies. Critical self-awareness requires space and a willingness to deal with discomfort and to challenge our own inherent assumptions.

## Values

NI social work has a strong historical commitment to anti–oppressive practice; however, this has particular implications for practice within a post-conflict context. Weaver (1999) outlines humility and a non–judgemental attitude as key values that should shape cultural competence. For culturally competent practice in NI, this requires a willingness to respect the experiences of the people in NI, their historical process, culture and contemporary realities. Humility requires acknowledging people's contexts and practices and not trivialising and making simplistic or unfair comparisons with other methods, contexts or modes of practice. Cultural competence also requires a judicious use of skills and knowledge to challenge and address issues of social justice. This can often present risks and requires commitment and courage. However, risks should only be taken with serious engagement in reflexive practice and consideration of one's own position as an insider or outsider, an awareness of issues of privilege and power. A commitment to values of human rights is also essential to practice and should include praxis-oriented reflection that enables one to reflect on the underlying assumptions that workers may themselves hold for or against particular groups in NI.

## Working towards transformative practice within social work practice

NI social work faces significant challenges when engaging with the cultural in a sectarian context. However, in this section, we discuss what critical cultural competence in NI could possibly look like. In a post- conflict society, the role of social work involves addressing issues of segregation, conflict and oppression, and enabling processes for society to function along non-violent anti-discriminatory and social justice principles. However, the profession's engagement with contemporary issues still requires a major shift from the historical default position of cultural neutrality to active social engagement. The concept of transformation is therefore central to this discussion. Transformation is a process that fosters changes in the personal, structural, relational and cultural aspects of conflict, brought about over different time periods (the short, mid- and long term) and affecting different system levels at different times. According to Miall (2004), such a process requires engagement and change in asymmetrical relationships (interests and discourses) to balanced relationships through conscientisation, confrontation, negotiation and development. The professions require a re-engagement with community to consciously resist historical social injustice and inequality (Das et al, 2015). However, social work engagement in NI within community development approaches has been limited due to their failure to gain trust across communities. As explained, social work's relationship with communities in NI has been problematic due to their close alliance with state-based services and the high degree of mistrust towards state institutions in NI. Furthermore, within the bureaucratic, individualised, rationalised, neoliberal and service-driven environment, social workers have struggled to incorporate a social justice agenda in their work (Das et al, 2015).

## No justice without healing

Previously, we alluded to the nature of the relationship between the profession and civil society in NI, and perhaps the first stage in a transformative process involves the building of trust between the profession and the different communities across NI. This needs to parallel a broader resolution and transformation process in NI that links issues of justice to healing, and a vision that takes into account the kind of society people in NI want to inhabit (Gilligan, 2006; Sluka, 2009). Part of this process involves an honest analysis of the profession's historical involvement with power structures and processes that helped reproduce exclusionary cultural identities. Social work needs not only to focus on the traumatic impact of sectarianism and colonialism for individuals and communities, but also to recognise and address the contemporary structural issues for lasting conflict resolution (Bryne, 2001; Kinnval, 2004). The various processes of essentialisation and stigmatisation that plague NI are, in essence, products of social organisations where inequality is pervasive. Effective, fair and just institutions and legal frameworks are necessary first steps to address issues of social justice and conflict, and NI social work has a potential role is promoting the next stage of economic, social and cultural rights. Social workers in NI need to develop a visible agenda and vision for social justice in NI, and engage in these political and structural issues. While overarching generalised understandings of social justice and power are essential, it is equally important to consider the local and global interconnections and the particular ways in which structural inequalities are institutionally reproduced within NI.

## Cultural and identity work

Culture is central to all meaning-making processes. However, as discussed, the context of NI limits the free agency of people to actively and dynamically engage with cultural issues (McGlynn, 2011). In NI, the multicultural project must protect minority groups, but also adapt to tackle the legacy of conflict by challenging stereotypes, engaging with the 'other' perspective and reducing prejudice (McGlynn, 2011). Furthermore, cultural systems in NI limit and exclude many groups, including women, from participating in the conflict resolution process (McDowell, 2008). The implication for social work practice is to allow recognition and emergence of complex patterns of identity that cut across age, gender, sexuality, class, disability, ethnicity, temporality and geography. Professional practice that recognises cross-cutting identities can potentially enable alternative discourses of social struggles and pave the way for conscientisation and the raising of social justice issues beyond rigid ethnic categories. The challenge for the profession is to problematise the essentialisation of identity in NI, and while it may be still too difficult to question whether an individual or community is Catholic or Protestant, there are more subtle approaches to exploring under what circumstances, how and if one is Catholic or Protestant (Bekerman et al, 2009). Addressing the uneasy tension between cultural work and risk will require finding spaces for dialogue across differences without the assurance of consensus (Porter, 2000). Critical cultural competence involves opening up opportunities for discussion, or what Smith (1992) refers to as critical conscientisation, although practitioners will need to be prepared for the likely contradictions and challenges that will emerge from such political engagement.

Anti-sectarian approaches that challenge these divisions across groups in NI are increasingly acknowledged in social work practice and training (Duffy et al, 2013), but there are many more opportunities and possibilities to incorporate cultural competence that recognise the complexity of identity and culture. Within social work education, students are encouraged to become aware of the cultural dynamics in NI and engage with the complexities of their own cultures and identities. Given the segregation in housing and education in NI, university studies offer the first opportunity for many students to interact with other groups. As outlined, a cultural competence framework can not only support the recognition of diversity and minority groups, but also provide opportunities for working with majority groups. Some innovative approaches of bi-cultural work in New Zealand and multicultural practices in Australia provide interesting insights in terms of dealing with historical conflict, difference and self-identity (Aotearoa New Zealand Association of Social Workers, 2012; Sonn, 2012).

## Importance of working with partners across issues and different levels

Transformation is not a time-bound, objective-based outcome, but a process (McCully, 2006). In NI, the process of transformation is uneven and the peace accord is institutionally engineered by national and international elites, often without the integration and experience of peace at the group or individual level (Ginty and Du Toit, 2007). The integration of institutional and grass-roots approaches to conflict management and conflict resolution is lacking (Bryne, 2001; O'Brien, 2007). Although civil society and community approaches in NI are becoming increasingly significant, they have not totally succeeded in breaking down the sectarian divisions, and much more work is needed to transform the 'conflict-habituated' system into a 'peace-system' (Ginty et al, 2007; O'Brien, 2007). While civil society and community-based approaches can, indeed, play a key role in facilitating a culture of peace and democracy, they can also be used to control, to colonise, to maintain the status quo or to support particular political aims (O'Brien, 2007).

Nevertheless, non-governmental organisation (NGO) practitioners in NI have developed an in-depth understanding of the roots of conflict and have used pragmatic realism, critical anti-sectarianism and constructive optimism to create spaces for dialogue, conscientisation and alternative ways of understanding difference and identity (Miall, 2004; Nash, 2005; McCully, 2006). There is increasing optimism that the non-government sector in NI potentially provides opportunities for social work practitioners to engage in peace-building, relationship-building and institution-building over the longer term.

For transformative work, it remains vital for social workers to build partnerships with others, across societal, institutional, professional and community levels. Cultural competence that is not supported across levels cannot address justice issues and risks becoming a tokenistic exchange between social workers and clients and can, in fact, be more damaging by reiterating problematic power structures. Das et al (2015) suggest that social workers might, in fact, be in a very good position to serve as strategic partners across levels for such work.

## *Self*

Critical self-awareness is 'personal work' (Miller et al, 2004) but requires support from peers, educators and the profession as this is an uncomfortable process and one that can raise significant anxiety, confusion and unease about one's self (Sakomoto and Pitner, 2005). One of the key educational outcomes requires social work students to understand that critical self-reflection involves an awareness of the tensions that exist in every aspect of our lives and the constant resistance to practices of oppression and challenging. Practitioners need to be encouraged to be at ease with and adopt a position of 'not knowing' when working with individuals and communities and be prepared to rework their frames of reference for every case and context. For social workers practising in more procedural and statutory contexts, this may present as uncertainty and may be a challenge. In the social work literature, this repositioning is also referred to as 'Informed not knowing' (Furlong and Wight, 2011), 'secure unknowingness' (Clare, 2007) and 'Being aware of what you don't know' (Harrison and Turner, 2011). While cultural competence is associated with knowing the other, the processes of cultural competence also need to incorporate a process of knowing 'ourselves' and what we mean by our 'culture', and opening ourselves to other ways of knowing. We believe that this enables a critical cultural competence that can unpack power assumptions and lead to reciprocal partnership working with clients, enable working in partnership, and challenge persistent power frameworks.

Appropriate supervision and support for social work practitioners, education and training are all important and fundamental components of developing a culturally competent workforce within social work. This presents significant challenges and requires creative and innovative ways of teaching and learning. Some such approaches are well under way in NI, such as the service user input in teaching and service user and NGO partnerships in projects that enable more diverse voices to participate in dialogue across different levels.

## Conclusion

Cultural competence and anti-oppressive practice are extremely important concepts in social work. While we have problematised the current conceptualisation of cultural competence and its application in current social work, we nevertheless argue that it presents a useful framework to work with diversity, conflict and social injustice.

Critical cultural competence demands that social worker engagement with their clients is accompanied with deep and complex knowledge of the various historical, cultural and contemporary issues that shape the lives of their clients. Critical cultural competence also requires that social workers have the skills of being able to listen, retrieve information, sensitively probe, patience and empathy. Social workers need skills not only to work with clients, but also to be able to be self-reflective and reflexive at the same time. Finally, these knowledge and skills have to support a value base that recognises the humanity of people and their development, and is committed to social justice and openness/non-judgemental attitudes. Culturally competent professionals should be able to incorporate an acceptance of the complex political realities, contradictions and diversities (intersections of identities, class, sexuality, race) across different individuals and groups, and across different situations (Weaver, 1999; Chau et al, 2011). Ultimately, cultural competence offers the opportunity to deconstruct power issues and analyse them, and to reconstruct possible alternatives for critical practice. Finally, critical cultural competence requires creativity and flexibility to respond to particular contexts, partnership with others (particularly clients and communities) and the acceptance of uncertainty and the acceptability of what communities or clients may want.

In NI, we believe that critical cultural competence can lead to transformative social practice as it demands a commitment to issues of social justice, across different levels of practice, from the structural and institutional to the personal. In this context, critical cultural competence also involves understanding the nuances and complexity of the NI context not only within a historical perspective, but also in terms of contemporary issues. Cultural competence requires the analytical ability to view discrimination, social injustice and conflict from both indigenous and global perspectives. Skills necessary for such practice include a willingness to listen, resisting the simplification of issues, respecting and working in partnership with others, an ability to draw connections, developing an agenda for change, translating knowledge into action through creative means, and taking measured risks, but also critically reflecting on one's own self and position in order to be able to resist oppressive ideologies and processes.

We have attempted to outline the various knowledge, skills and values that may be relevant to contribute to transformative practice in NI and, indeed, what transformative practice may involve. Ultimately, however, the agenda for transformation must remain with local actors themselves, who have the greatest stake in transforming and determining the futures of their own societies.

## Note
[1] Minoritisation refers to processes by which certain groups are rendered as minority groups, and challenges the status of 'minority' as an inherent characteristic of the group (Burman and Chantler, 2005).

## References

Abrams, L.S. and Moio, J.A. (2009) 'Critical race theory and the cultural competence dilemma in social work education', *Journal of Social Work Education*, 45(2): 245–61.

Aotearoa New Zealand Association of Social Workers (2012) 'Bicultural partnership'. Available at: http://anzasw.org.nz/about/topics/show/58-bi-cultural-partnership (accessed 7 December 2014).

Bekerman, Z., Zembylas, M. and McGlynn, C. (2009) 'Working toward the de-essentialization of identity categories in conflict and postconflict societies: Israel, Cyprus, and Northern Ireland', *Comparative Education Review*, 53(2): 213–34.

Ben-Ari, A. and Strier, R. (2010) 'Rethinking cultural competence: what can we learn from Levinas', *British Journal of Social Work*, 40(7): 2155–67.

Bennett, M.J. (1993) 'Towards ethnorelativism: a developmental model of intercultural sensitivity', in R.M. Paige (ed) *Education for the intercultural experience*, Yarmouth, ME: Intercultural Press.

Betancourt, J.R., Green, A.R., Carrillo, J.E. and Park, E.R. (2005) 'Cultural competence and health care disparities: key perspectives and trends', *Health Affairs* 24(2): 499–505.

Brian, G. and Shirlow, P. (1998) 'An elusive agenda: the development of a middle ground in Northern Ireland', *Area*, 30(3): 245–54.

Bryne, S. (2001) 'Consociational and civic society approaches to peace building in Northern Ireland', *Journal of Peace Research*, 38(3): 327–52.

Burman, E. and Chantler, K. (2005) 'Domestic violence and minoritisation: legal and policy barriers facing minoritized women leaving violent relationships', *International Journal of Law and Psychiatry*, 28(1): 59–74.

Cairns, E. and Darby, J. (1998) 'The conflict in Northern Ireland: causes, consequences and controls', *American Psychologist*, 53(7): 754–60.

Carter, R.T. (2001) 'Back to the future in cultural competence training', *The Counseling Psychologist*, 29(6): 787–89.

Cassidy, C. and Trew, K. (1998) 'Identities in Northern Ireland: a multidimensional approach', *Journal of Social Issues*, 54(4): 725–40.

Chau, R.C.M., Yu, S.W.K. and Tran, C.T.L. (2011) 'The diversity based approach to culturally sensitive practices', *International Social Work*, 54(1): 21–33.

Clare, B. (2007) 'Promoting deep learning: a teaching, learning and assessment endeavour', *Social Work Education*, 26(5): 433–46.

Coates, J., Gray, M. and Hetherington, T. (2006) 'An "ecospiritual" perspective: finally, a place for indigenous approaches', *British Journal of Social Work*, 36(3): 381–99.

Das, C., O'Niell, M. and Pinkerton, J. (2015) 'Re-engaging with community work as a method of practice in social work: A view from Northern Ireland (NI)', *Journal of Social Work*. Available at: http://jsw.sagepub.com/cgi/reprint/1468017315569644v1.pdf?ijkey=nqGjb846NBHyB8o&keytype=finite

Dominelli, L. (1998) 'Anti-oppressive practice in context', in R. Adams, L. Dominelli and M. Payne (eds) *Social work: themes, issues and critical debates*, Houndmills: MacMillan Press.

Dominelli, L. (2002) *Anti-oppressive social work theory and practice*, Basingstoke: Palgrave.

Duffy, J., Das, C. and Davidson, G. (2013) 'Service user and carer involvement in role plays to assess readiness for practice', *Social Work Education: The International Journal*, 32(1): 39–54.

Fook, J. (2002) *Critical social work*, London: Sage Publications.

Furlong, M. and Wight, J. (2011) 'Promoting "critical awareness" and "critiquing cultural": towards disrupting received professional knowledges', *Australian Social Work*, 64(1): 38–54.

Gallagher, T. (2004) 'After the war comes peace? An examination of the impact of the Northern Ireland conflict on young people', *Journal of Social Issues*, 60(3): 629–42.

Gilligan, C. (2006) 'Traumatised by peace? A critique of five assumptions in the theory and practice of conflict- related trauma policy in Northern Ireland', *Policy & Politics*, 34(2): 325–45.

Ginty, R.M. and Du Toit, P. (2007) 'A disparity of esteem: relative group status in Northern Ireland after the Belfast Agreement', *Political Psychology*, 28(1): 13–31.

Ginty, R., Muldoon, O. and Ferguson, N. (2007) 'No war, no peace: Northern Ireland after the Agreement', *Political Psychology*, 28(1): 1–11.

Harrison, G. and Melville, R. (2010) *Rethinking social work in a global world*, Basingstoke: Palgrave McMillian.

Harrison, G. and Turner, R. (2011) 'Being a "culturally competent" social worker: making sense of a murky concept in practice', *British Journal of Social Work*, 41(2): 333–50.

Haug, E. (2005) 'Critical reflections on the emerging discourse of international social work', *International Social Work*, 48(2): 126–35.

Heenan, D. and Birrell, D. (2011) *Social work in Northern Ireland: conflict and change*, Bristol: The Policy Press.

Houston, S. (2008) 'Transcending ethno-religious identities: social work's role in the struggle for recognition in Northern Ireland', *Australian Social Work*, 61(1): 25–41.

Jarman N. (2004) 'From war to peace? Changing patterns of violence in Northern Ireland, 1990–2003', *Terrorism and Political Violence*, 16(3): 420–38.

Jordan, B. (2004) 'Emancipatory social work? Opportunity or oxymoron', *British Journal of Social Work*, 34(1): 5–19.

Kinnval, C. (2004) 'Globalization and religious nationalism: self, identity, and the search for ontological security', *Political Psychology*, 25(5): 741–67.

Kumagai, A.K. and Lypson, M.L. (2009) 'Beyond cultural competence: critical consciousness, social justice, and multicultural education', *Academic Medicine*, 84(6): 782–7.

Laird, S. (2008) *Anti-oppressive social work: a guide for developing cultural competence*, London: Sage.

Ledoux, C. and Montalvo, F.F. (1999) 'Multicultural content in social work graduate programs', *Journal of Multicultural Social Work*, 7(1): 37–55.

Macey, M. and Moxon, E. (1996) 'An examination of anti-racist and anti-oppressive theory and practice in social work education', *British Journal of Social Work*, 26(3): 297–314.

Martin, K.L. (2003) 'Ways of knowing, ways of being and ways of doing: a theoretical framework and methods for indigenous re-search and indigenous research. Voicing dissent, new talents 21c: next generation Australian studies', *Journal of Australian Studies*, 76: 203–14.

McCully, A. (2006) 'Practitioner perceptions of their role in facilitating the handling of controversial issues in contested societies: a Northern Irish experience', *Educational Review*, 58(1): 51–65.

McDowell, S. (2008) 'Commemorating dead "men": gendering the past and present in post-conflict Northern Ireland', *Gender, Place & Culture*, 15(4): 335–54.

McGlynn, C. (2011) 'Negotiating difference in post-conflict Northern Ireland: an analysis of approaches to integrated education', *Multicultural Perspectives*, 13(1): 16–22.

Miall, H. (2004) 'Conflict transformation: a multi-dimensional task', in A. Austin, M. Fischer and N. Ropers (eds) *Transforming Ethnopolitical Conflict: The Berghof Handbook*, Berlin: VS Verlag für Sozialwissenschaften, pp 67–90.

Miller, J., Hyde, C.A. and Ruth, B.J. (2004) 'Teaching about race and racism in social work: challenges for white educators', *Smith College Studies in Social Work*, 74(2): 409–26.

Muldoon, O.T. (2002) 'Children of the Troubles: the impact of political violence in Northern Ireland', *Journal of Social Issues*, 60(3): 453–68.

Nash, C. (2005) 'Equity, diversity and interdependence: cultural policy in Northern Ireland', *Antipode*, 37(2): 272–300.

NISRA (Northern Ireland Statistics and Research Agency) (2009) 'Long-term international migration estimates for Northern Ireland (2007–8)', NISRA. Available at: http://www.nisra.gov.uk/archive/demography/population/migration/NI_Migration_Report(2008).pdf (accessed 15 May 2010).

O'Brien, C. (2007) 'Integrated community development/conflict resolution strategies as "peace building potential" in South Africa and Northern Ireland', *Community Development Journal*, 42(1): 114–30.

Pinkerton, J. and Campbell, J. (2002) 'Social work and social justice in Northern Ireland: towards a new occupational space', *British Journal of Social Work*, 32(6): 723–37.

Porter, E. (2000) 'Risks and responsibilities creating dialogical spaces in Northern Ireland', *International Feminist Journal of Politics*, 2(2): 163–84.

Poxton, R., Taylor, J., Brenner, D., Cole, A. and Burke, C. (2012) *Reaching out to people with learning disabilities and their families from black and minority ethnic communities*, London: Foundation of People with Learning Disabilities.

Sakamoto, I. and Pitner, R.O. (2005) 'Use of critical consciousness in anti-oppressive social work practice: disentangling power dynamics at personal and structural levels', *British Journal of Social Work*, 35(4): 435–52.

Sheppard, M. (2006) *Social work and social exclusion: the idea of practice*, Aldershot: Ashgate.

Sluka, J. (2009) 'In the shadow of the gun. 'Not-war-not-peace' and the future of conflict in Northern Ireland', *Critique of Anthropology*, 29(3): 279–99.

Smith, M. (1992) 'Postmodernism, urban ethnography, and the new social space of ethnic identity', *Theory and Society*, 21: 493–531.

Sonn, C. (2012) 'Research and practice in the contact zone: crafting resources for challenging racialized exclusion', *Global Journal of Community Psychology Practice*, 3(1): 113–23.

Trew, K. (2004) 'Children and socio-cultural divisions in Northern Ireland', *Journal of Social Issues*, 60(3): 507–22.

Vera, E.M. and Speight, S.L. (2003) 'Multicultural competence, social justice, and counseling psychology: expanding our roles', *The Counseling Psychologist*, 31(3): 253–72.

Walton, R.G. and Abo-El-Nasr, M.M. (1988) 'Indigenization and authentization in terms of social work in Egypt', *International Social Work*, 31(2): 135–44.

Weaver, H.N. (1999) 'Indigenous people and the social work profession: defining culturally competent services', *Social Work*, 44(3): 217–25.

Wehbi, S. (2009) 'Deconstructing motivations: challenging international social work placement', *International Social Work*, 52: 48.

THREE

# Exploring the political and ethical dimensions of social work practice with the 'other'

*Beverley Burke and Philomena Harrison*

## Introduction

> The glory of the created world is its astonishing multiplicity: the thousands of different languages spoken by mankind, the proliferation of cultures, the sheer variety of the imaginative expressions of the human spirit, in most of which, if we listen carefully, we will hear the voice of wisdom telling us something we need to know. That is what I mean by *the dignity of difference*. (Sacks, 2003: 20–21; emphasis in original)

As the make-up of populations across the globe, and, in particular, in the UK, has become more diverse, value-based and contested notions of 'race', racism, identity, ethnicity and culture need to continue to be critically interrogated and challenged. The experiences of difference, individually and for communities, informs our understanding and response to the complex power relationships that exist within society, which position particular communities, groups and individuals as superior in relation to others. In order to develop any appropriate or effective response to these situations, practitioners need to create effective frameworks for these changing times and contexts, engaged as they are on a daily basis in decisions that will have an impact on the quality and future life chances for a wide range of social care and social work service users. It is therefore crucial for social work practitioners to grasp how their practice decisions and actions are informed by an understanding and appreciation of the nature of social oppressions that structure the situations, not just of the lives of service users, but also of themselves as professionals.

We propose that professional engagement in social work practice should be informed by a set of anti-oppressive ethical principles that address issues of social diversity and inequality in a world where there is clearly continuing discrimination and oppression of black and minority ethnic (BME) individuals and groups on a local, national and global scale. This designation of 'otherness' (Hill Collins, 1998) continues to pervade even where there are long-established communities of difference, who, at times, constitute the majority, in local populations. Further, this discrimination and marginalisation pervades their experiences despite notions of rights of citizenship, rights of abode, long-established bills of rights, international conventions on human rights, and clear statutes on discrimination. Racism and racialism, in its many forms, continues to blight the lives of many, especially where new global conflicts arise against a backdrop of economic crisis and national and international austerity. In this context of 'new racisms' and racist ideology, individuals and communities are being set up against each other, creating a range of further divisions based on differences rather than commonalities (Betancur, 2014).

Our thinking in general around what is necessary for developing and sustaining anti-oppressive ethical practice principles is, in essence, influenced by Gilroy's (2002) view that we should shift the focus of the impact of racism from that on specific individuals and communities to showing its impact on society as whole, in that racism and racist practices diminish us all and, furthermore, that racism produces, in this case, poor social work practice and practitioners. This acknowledgement will take professionals and service users from a position of victimology to that of a shared political and anti-oppressive analysis. In this 'standing together', we can draw on Hill Collins's development of a black feminist 'standpoint', so that, in our case, we use a 'standpoint' that explores and defines an anti-oppressive ethical positioning. Through adopting such a standpoint, the common oppressive and discriminatory experiences shared by all minority ethnic individuals and communities can be analysed and an inclusive framework for practice can be developed. This analytical framework emerges *from* the complexity of the lives and experiences of BME individuals and communities. Such a reflexive framework will enable the practitioner to face the 'complex nexus of relationships among biological classification, the social construction of race and gender as categories of analysis, [and] the material conditions accompanying these changing social constructions' (Hill Collins, 2002: 155). It also enables the collective themes of oppression, discrimination and challenges to be foregrounded in any analysis of decision-making in order to produce ethical practice. It is in and through this continuous process of reflection and reflexivity that new forms of practice and social change will emerge.

In this chapter, we aim to:

- present a definition of anti-oppressive ethics and outline values and ethical principles for practice;
- show how an understanding of anti-oppressive ethical considerations can help the worker to deconstruct the concepts, metaphors and norms embodied in modern conceptualisations of race, racism, ethnicity, culture and other aspects of social difference;
- discuss the ways in which racist discourses become embedded in policymaking at various levels and are translated into practice; and

- show how workers should respond to diversity and begin to communicate and work across the divide to achieve a measure of social justice in their everyday practice.

We provide practice guidelines to encourage workers to develop ethical practice that is anti-oppressive and socially just. The anti-oppressive ethical framework provides the practitioner with a means of knowing (everyday theorising) how their practice with the 'other' is informed and transformed by this emergent practice knowledge. Through our discussion of the challenges facing practitioners, and outlining of anti-oppressive ethical principles, we wish to bring the 'other' (Holscher and Bozalek, 2012) to centre stage and not allow anti-racist and anti-oppressive discourses to be pushed to the margins as a movement that is only seen to be deterministic and not relevant to current challenges in practice.

## Why the need for anti-oppressive ethics?

Particular judgements can be made about the moral quality of a society by how that society not only treats and cares for its most vulnerable members, but also distributes limited resources and treats the 'stranger' at its borders, as well as those who are labelled as different within its borders. Social workers witness on a day-to-day basis the obvious and not so obvious impact of the 'greed and arrogance of a society dedicated to individual self-interest' (Simey, 1996: 162). Working with people who experience discrimination and oppression, who are excluded and at the margins of society, places a moral duty on the social work profession and those who work within it to move from a position of noticing and witnessing to one of engaging in social and political action 'to resist and counteract those processes and social structures that serve to disadvantage people' (Holscher and Bozalek, 2012: 1096).

The levels of inequality, the devastating impact of poverty and the alienating experiences of oppression for many people has, within the UK context, been exacerbated by a raft of neoliberal ideologically driven and informed social policies, which firmly place responsibility for well-being on the individual (Ferguson et al, 2005; Williams and Johnson, 2010; Gray and Webb, 2013). By focusing exclusively on the individual and failing to take into account structural factors, which impact on the life chances of the individual, the government effectively distances itself from the part it plays in the development of the very policies and political practices that sustain and maintain the unequal social conditions experienced by individuals, families and communities. By engaging in the ethically suspect process of blaming individuals for their own marginalisation, the government and social institutions absolve themselves of responsibility. By prioritising the needs of the market over social welfare principles and ignoring the broader contextual factors, social welfare policies and practices become managerial and prescriptive in their focus rather than needs-led and transformative (Liebenberg et al, 2015).

There are a range of contextual factors that the practitioner or a profession attempting to be ethical in an unethical world have to strategically manage (Clifford and Burke, 2009). Responding to the 'moral imperative of caring for the neediest among us' (Bisman, 2004: 109) requires not only ethical awareness on the part of the practitioner, but also self-scrutiny of their personal and professional values. This involves a reflexive analysis of the practices that we are engaged in, or contribute to, which fail to recognise the relationship between the experiences that people have of inequality and oppression and the morality of social structures and policies as they influence both the social life and the private lives of individuals (Holscher and Bozalek, 2012; Bisman, 2014).

Ethical guidance in the form of international statements of principles developed by the International Federation of Social Workers (IFSW) and the International Association of Schools of Social Work (IASSW), as well as national codes of practice and ethics produced by the Health and Care Professions Council (HCPC), the British Association of Social Workers (BASW) and the College of Social Workers (TCSW), provide a set of values and general ethical principles to guide ethical discussion, reflection and practice decisions in a range of 'morally contentious and ambiguous situations' (Clifford and Burke, 2009: 58). These situations arise when working with conflicting interests and competing rights, or when we attempt to manage the difficult task of balancing our supportive role of protecting and empowering individuals with that of our statutory duties and obligations, which, at times, cut across and undermine people's right to be self-determining. Prioritising and managing limited resources between different service users who have different needs adds to the many ethical challenges of practice. This ethical complexity will be a fundamental part of a profession concerned with issues of human rights and social justice.

The practitioner has an ambiguous and contradictory role in relation to their true engagement in ethical anti–oppressive practices. The practitioner as a moral actor, involved in complex social situations, will be both participator and observer. Given this, there has to be an acceptance that it is not always possible to resolve difficulties in some situations, particularly when practitioners are involved in a range of interventions that are experienced by service users as disempowering and controlling. However, it is increasingly necessary to engage in practices that are responsive to the global movement of people and the consequent increasing diversity of those potentially accessing social services. Nevertheless, concerned as the profession is to be morally sensitive and true to its social justice imperative, there is a profound disjunction between its stated mission and practice when working with BME service user groups.

The profession's failure to place significance on 'race', racism and ethnicity and to systematically engage in practice that is anti-racist has been well documented (Graham, 2007; Bhatti-Sinclair, 2011; Lavalette and Penketh, 2014). The very existence of racism in its many forms (Singh, 2014) is well evidenced and has been explored in a range of research reports, academic publications and public enquiries (Macpherson, 1999; Parekh Commission, 2000; Williams and Soydan,

2005; EHRC, 2010; Williams and Johnson, 2010), where it has been demonstrated that BME individuals, families and communities are frequently pathologised and stereotyped (Williams and Soydan, 2005) and on the receiving end of punitive services rather than preventive interventions (Barn and Das, 2015). We therefore require a practice response that is informed by a theoretical and historical analysis of the political nature of racism (Singh, 2014), which moves us beyond a Eurocentric, ethnocentric, individualised and, ultimately, partial response to issues related to 'race', ethnicity and racism.

Practice that is informed by an active commitment to anti-oppressive social work values and ethics is transformative, critically reflective, reflexive and politically informed. Values, including anti-oppressive values, are contestable and fluid entities and are 'socially constructed culturally and historically specific, and open to individual interpretation' (Clifford and Burke, 2009: 51). However, we believe that a critical awareness and understanding of anti-oppressive values and principles, such as social justice, equality, working collectively and challenging unjust social conditions (Lynn, 1999; Dalrymple and Burke, 2006; Burke and Harrison, 2009; Clifford and Burke, 2009; Banks, 2012), must inform ethical practice that is ultimately transformative.

## What do we mean by anti-oppressive ethics?

In their text *Anti-oppressive ethics and values in social work*, Clifford and Burke (2009: 16) offer the following definition:

> Anti-oppressive ethics are approaches to guiding action in the light of the recognition of inequalities and powerlessness damaging to individual and collective freedom and welfare, especially in relation to groups and individuals marginalised through membership of dominated and diverse social divisions.

Anti-oppressive ethics informed by anti-oppressive values and principles, as well as key ideas from black feminist theorists and feminist ethical theorising concerned with notions of power, relational autonomy, dialogue, identity, difference and notions of care, provides an approach that is sensitive to power differentials, acknowledges the complexity of decision-making and enables practitioners to think and act ethically (hooks, 1981; Gilligan, 1982; Tronto, 1993; Held, 2006; Hill Collins, 2009; Barnes, 2012). First, the term 'anti-oppressive ethics' indicates the political and ideological position put forward by Clifford and Burke (2009: 2) regarding the importance of understanding the relationship between social diversity and inequality in relation to ethical professional practice. Second, anti-oppressive ethics offers what they consider a necessary critique of the dominant ethical discourse in social work, which derives from the liberal individualist tradition descended from Kant and Mill (Clark, 2006: 78). Deontological and consequential-based ethical theories have offered 'robust general principles of right conduct' (Clark, 2006: 76). However, Clifford and Burke argue that human relationships takes place within a range of social situations riven and complicated by the cultures, values, beliefs and biographies of the different participants. These complex social situations are also characterised by uncertainty and ambiguity and therefore require more than prescriptive ethical rules to guide understanding of the situation and direct ethical practice.

Anti-oppressive ethics, by drawing attention to oppressive social relations and the existence of social divisions such as class, gender, 'race', disability, age, sexuality and mental health status, alerts the practitioner to the structural relations, inequalities and differential powers that exist in relation to marginalised groups (Clifford and Burke, 2009). The anti-oppressive ethical approach to practice is therefore informed by an active commitment to 'oppose, minimise and/or overcome those aspects of human relationships that express and consolidate oppression' (Clifford and Burke, 2009: 16).

We are well aware that 'attempting to be ethical in an unethical world is an invitation to continual perplexity and reflection' (Clifford and Burke, 2009: 4), particularly when neoliberalism has penetrated the very fabric of social work and the daily experiences of practitioners and service users. Bureaucratic and managerialist approaches within welfare organisations push practice towards a technical activity, where practitioners feel deskilled and their professional autonomy is being eroded (Healey and Meagher, 2004; Lee, 2014; Higgins and Goodyer, 2015). High workloads coupled with staff shortages add to the levels of stress that practitioners experience. The continual implementation of reorganisation strategies and budgetary cutbacks can lead to social work practice that is depoliticised, divorced from its radical potential and morally barren. However, we would argue that despite the demanding conditions in which contemporary social work is carried out, working from an anti-oppressive ethical perspective supports practitioners to intervene in a range of situations with some degree of confidence and ethical sensitivity. Anti-oppressive ethics, by shifting thinking from a narrow concern with individual moral behaviour towards that of understanding human relationships as embedded in social and historical contexts (Clifford, 2001), enables the practitioner to fully appreciate and take account of the impacts and ramifications that discrimination, racism and marginalisation has on the daily life, well-being and agency of individuals and families within diverse communities. Importantly, it provides a framework for practitioners to view the contexts in which they work and the challenges that they face both within and external to the organisations and institutions in which they are placed. By working with the 'unintended consequences of modern organisations' (Higgins and Goodyer, 2015: 756), practitioners adopting an anti-oppressive ethical perspective can begin to explore the spaces available in which to develop practice that is not narrow, legalistic, formulaic and outcome-driven.

A number of principles can be identified in relation to an anti-oppressive approach to ethics. They are as follows: respecting and acknowledging social difference; understanding power; acknowledging the interconnections between social systems; researching and exploring personal and social histories; and engaging with reflexivity. These five interrelating and interconnected principles simultaneously help to explain social situations and to guide and support ethical practice.

## Anti-oppressive ethical practice guidelines

An anti-oppressive ethics needs to take a thorough account of *all social differences and inequalities*. The differences that divide people, beyond the major social divisions, such as mental health status or being a looked after child (LAC), need to be explored in relation to how they may shape the relationship between the practitioner and service user. Ethical implications for practice flow from the identification of the 'other' as socially different and having a range of particular experiences that define their needs and strengths. An ethical practice approach would explore how social divisions such as gender, sexuality, class, race and ethnicity interact, interconnect and mutually reinforce each other as categories of oppression and social structures. This analysis, informed by a critical understanding of intersectionality (Crenshaw, 1991), captures 'both the structural and dynamic aspects of multiple oppressions' (Harrison and Burke, 2014: 80) and avoids stereotypical and assumptive understandings of the major social divisions as homogeneous and static categories (Mattsson, 2014: 15).

*Power*, a socially structured, contested and value-laden concept that operates within the personal and public spheres of life, should be seen as multidimensional and dynamic. Structural inequalities in the distribution of power within social relationships are maintained and sustained by political, economic, historical and cultural systems, resulting in enduring social divisions. An anti-oppressive ethics alerts the worker to the variety and complexity, as well as the inequality, of power in social situations and its significant connotations for ethical action (Clifford and Burke, 2009: 34). The practitioner needs to be aware of their own personal and professional power, social location, theoretical knowledge and values, as well as the bearing that these will all have on understanding and interpreting narratives of inequality and difference (Harrison and Burke, 2014: 34–5).

Ethical decisions and discussions need to include an assessment of how different *social systems interconnect and interact* to shape a range of social relationships between individuals and groups that can be both intimate and informal, distant and official, caring and controlling. Social systems, both informal and formal, are arenas in which power is exercised and needs to be either resisted or supported if the needs of the individual are to be met (Clifford, 1998). When working with refugees and asylum seekers, for example, the practitioner has to negotiate, advocate and intervene effectively and skilfully with a range of systems in order to ensure that the rights and needs of the individual are upheld and met as the personal and psychological distress experienced is not just about pre-migration trauma, but also from their post-migration relationships with the housing, immigration, health and welfare systems (Allan, 2014; Watters, 2014).

It is important to have a holistic appreciation of the range of experiences that people have and to locate them within a broader social context. The practitioner will need to supportively explore relevant *personal and social histories* to assist their understanding of an individual's life, which may well include experiences of oppression, and their strengths and capabilities as self-determining autonomous individuals who have a specific identity. This requires the practitioner, who also has a specific personal and social history, to be able to communicate effectively across the divides of culture, language, social location, values and beliefs. Practice that is informed by an understanding of the multiple and dynamic identities of the individual is one that does not privilege a single dimension of experience as if it constituted the whole of that person.

An important skill in ethical thinking is the ability to be aware of one's own position in relation to others. To empathise with the 'other', who is very different to you, is difficult and requires the practitioner to truly and honestly engage with the 'other' in order to understand their experiences. By developing a 'deep awareness of their own beliefs, values and socio-political and cultural positioning' (Allan, 2014: 13), the practitioner has a foundation from which to fully appreciate how their particular social location will help or hinder their *reflexive engagement* with the service user. It is through 'a profoundly respectful hearing' (Simey, 1996: 124) of the position of the 'other' and being prepared to act in ways that take the humanity of others into account that the practitioner is able to engage with the ethical and political dimensions of practice. These principles provide a framework for analysing social situations and inform practice responses. Having discussed the principles, we will next explore how these principles relate to mental health practice, policy and service delivery.

## Practice matters: mental health – anti-oppressive principles in action

> When the structures of domination identify a group of people (as racist ideology does black folks in this society) as mentally inferior, implying that they are more body than mind, it should come as no surprise that there is little societal concern for the mental health care of that group. (hooks, 1993: 70)

Having discussed the relationship between anti-oppressive ethical principles and their relationship to ethical practice, what follows here is a focus on the issues and challenges arising out of practice in mental health service delivery for BME individuals, families and communities. These matters apply to social work, social care and psychiatric practice. We use the case of David 'Rocky' Bennett (which includes a reflection on aspects of this tragedy and recommendations and policymaking following the inquiry report) to explore the relevance of anti-oppressive ethical principles as they might relate to the issues and recommendations arising out of the inquiry into his death, and the subsequent recommendations made to improve and change practice with BME individuals, families and communities who use mental health services.

Discrimination and oppression experienced by BME users of mental health services is well documented (Nazroo, 1997; Bhui, 2002; Ndegwa and Dele, 2003; Sewell, 2009; Fernando, 2010; Moodley and Ocampo, 2014; CQC, 2015). In recent times, policymaking at governmental levels has attempted to address the issue of poor and inappropriate services to this group of service users (Atchenson, 1998; DH, 1998). In 2005, this action came in the form of the *Delivering race equality in mental health care (DRE)* (DH, 2005). This initiative arose specifically out of the independent inquiry report on the death of David 'Rocky' Bennett in a medium-secure unit (Blofeld, 2003) and was designed to support compliance with the Race Relations (Amendment) Act 2002. Another influential paper was the NIMHE (National Institute for Mental Health England) (2003) report titled *Inside outside: improving mental health services for black and minority ethnic communities in England*. Arising out of these initiatives, work began within health and social care agencies to develop race equality schemes and cultural competence training (Harrison and Burke, 2014).

The *DRE* was a funded five-year plan running from 2005 to 2010. Its main aims were:

- to reduce and eliminate ethnic inequalities in mental health service experience and outcomes;
- to develop the cultural capability of mental health services; and
- to engage the community and build capacity through the appointment of community development workers (see DH, 2005).

The action plan for the implementation of *DRE* was based on the aforementioned three building blocks: first, to establish better and more responsive services for BME service user groups; second, to ensure that existing services were more engaged with their local communities; and, third, to ensure that services developed better information on the delivery and effectiveness of those services. A set of 12 characteristics were developed that demonstrated need and defined the nature of successful outcomes in terms of new ways of working to improve service delivery through health and social care to minority ethnic communities. This action was designed to improve social and clinical services.

The work of *DRE* included setting up 'Focussed Implementation Sites' (FISs) across the country, which usually mapped onto regional health authorities and the relevant mental health trusts. The purpose here was to engage with the main service delivery organisations, which included the mental health trusts, third sector organisations, service users and BME communities. Leadership came at national and local levels, which included the National Health Service (NHS) Equality and Human Rights Director and the then regional Race Equality Leads established in Care Services Improvement Partnerships (CSIPs).

The regional Race Equality Leads worked closely with project managers, community development workers (CDWs), community engagement projects, clinical and social care staff in the relevant trusts, third sector organisations, and service users to develop the appropriate skills and knowledge of staff along the lines of the 10 essential shared capabilities (Hope, 2004). One further and specific aspect of the work was the development of more relevant and accurate information on the use of mental health services by BME individuals. In response to this, the *Count me in census* (CQC and National and Mental Health Development Unit, 2011), where statistics were collated every March (for the five years of the life of the *DRE* initiative) in mental health clinical services (statutory and private hospitals) – for people on mental health wards and in learning disability services – was established and information was published on a yearly basis. This collation of information has now been taken over by the Care Quality Commission (CQC) in its role in monitoring the use of the Mental Health Act 1983, as amended by the Mental Health Act 2007. The CQC usually makes specific comment on the impact of the several aspects of the legislation on BME individuals.

Overall, although the work of *DRE* identified some specific improvements (RAWOrg, no date; Wilson, 2010), to date, the picture remains much the same in terms of detention and admission rates for individuals from BME communities. The 2013/14 CQC report comments on its continued monitoring of the over-representation of BME individuals in the detained population under the Mental Health Act 1983. This has continued in the 30 years that statistics have been recorded for this particular population of patients. Generally, we continue to see a pattern of discrimination experienced by BME individuals who use the mental health system, as signalled by the Rocky Bennett case.

David 'Rocky' Bennett died in a medium-secure psychiatric unit at the age of 38. He had a diagnosis of schizophrenia. He had spent 18 years of his life experiencing the criminal justice system and the mental health system (in secure units and the community). He died in a secure psychiatric unit while pinned down beneath the bodies of four nurses. This restraint had followed an incident between 'Rocky' and another patient. It is important to note that this particular patient had racially abused Mr Bennett in the course of the incident (Blofeld, 2003).

It is useful here to explore some aspects of the report into the death of Rocky Bennett and comment particularly on some of the recommendations and their relationship to specific aspects of the anti-oppressive ethical principles outlined earlier in this chapter. We show how the recommendations relate to some of those anti-oppressive ethical principles.

The independent inquiry into the death of David 'Rocky' Bennett produced some 22 recommendations for practice in mental health. Those included here are numbered as presented in the report (Blofeld, 2003):

1. All who work in mental health services should receive training in cultural awareness and sensitivity.

2. All managers and clinical staff, however senior or junior, should receive mandatory training in all aspects of cultural competency, awareness and sensitivity. This should include training to tackle overt and covert racism and institutional racism.

4. There should be Ministerial acknowledgment of the presence of institutional racism in the mental health services and a commitment to eliminate it.

5. There should be a National Director for Mental Health and Ethnicity similar to the appointment of other National Directors, appointed by the Secretary of State for Health to oversee the improvement of all aspects of mental health services in relation to the black and minority ethnic communities.

6. All mental health services should set out a written policy dealing with racist abuse, which should be disseminated to all members of staff and displayed prominently in all public areas under their control. This policy should be strictly monitored and a written record kept of all incidents in breach of the policy. If any racist abuse takes place by anyone, including patients in a mental health setting, it should be addressed forthwith and appropriate sanctions applied.

These five recommendations all deal appropriately with changes needed at *structural levels* within the mental health services – clinical and social. They also deal with requirements in terms of the knowledge base required for ethical practice (see recommendations 1 and 2). Recommendations 4 and 5, for example, place responsibility at the highest level. This demonstrates the importance of placing such responsibility at levels in the organisation where the *power to* implement and sustain change is located. Recommendation 6 places a duty on the organisation to monitor and evaluate incidences of racist behaviour at all levels in the organisation, including that from service users. The report comments that 'Staff were not aware of the "corrosive and cumulative effect of racist abuse upon a black patient"' (Blofeld, 2003: 31). The report found that Rocky Bennett's cultural and social needs were not attended to by the institution (ie the mental health system) (Blofeld, 2003: 34) and that 'His sense of injustice together with the singularly grievous sense of insult generated by a racist taunt should not be underestimated' (comment by doctor reporting to the inquiry; Blofeld, 2003: 33).

The report also considered the issues of managing difference in the workplace. The following recommendations relate closely to the ethical principle of respecting *social difference* and the necessity of delivering relevant and appropriate services. They deal with issues concerned with both the worker and the service user, and seek to ensure that the workforce is capable of responding to difference, in this case, specifically to that of 'race'. Philomena Harrison's report on the Greater Manchester *DRE* project in 2009 (Harrison and Singh, 2009), which included an analysis of Approved Mental Health Professional (AMHP) admission forms, showed that workers ignored the section on 'culture' where the patient's ethnicity was recorded as 'white British'. This displayed poor appreciation, knowledge and understanding by practitioners, in that 'culture' and ethnicity are ascribed just to groups who are perceived as different from the majority community. There is a danger that concepts of race, ethnicity and culture are used synonymously and ascribed only to communities of difference rather than to all. Given the latter, recommendation 15 dealt with what the detail of practice should look like in relation to anti-racist practice and anti-oppressive ethical practice:

> 7. Every CPA [Care Programme Approach] care plan should have a mandatory requirement to include appropriate details of each patient's ethnic origin and cultural needs.
> 8. The workforce in mental health services should be ethnically diverse. Where appropriate, active steps should be taken to recruit, retain and promote black and minority ethnic staff.
> 15. All medical staff in mental health services should have training in the assessment of people from the black and minority ethnic communities with special reference to the effects of racism upon their mental well-being. (Blofeld, 2003: 57)

The final recommendation (number 22) – which states that 'It is vital to ensure that the findings and recommendations of this Inquiry inform all relevant parties, including the developing black and minority ethnic mental health strategy' (Blofeld, 2003: 68) – highlights how the process for change must be at both the individual and collective levels. Significant reports and inquiries arising out of tragedies in the health and social care arenas have provided guidance and strategies for developing and changing practice. The way forward beyond such inquiries must demonstrate the centrality of service user involvement in the design, planning and implementation of change and the development of new and different services. Anti-oppressive ethical principles would demand that the issues be explored at several levels, not merely at the level of the engagement of the worker with the service user. In the case of Rocky Bennett, where unchallenged racism was the core of many of the difficulties that arose, issues of power and powerlessness were clearly evident. For example, in this evidence, the racism of patients towards Rocky Bennett remained unchallenged, despite pleas from 'Rocky' himself (Blofeld, 2003: 24):

Rocky Bennett:    'Don't you know I'm black? Why do you treat me like everybody else?'

Nurse:    'Well you are no different to everybody. I do not see you as different to everybody else.'

In this exchange, the worker ignores Rocky's view on his own identity and what meaning that brought to his current situation in a medium-secure unit. The response given to him is evidence of a 'colour-blind' approach to matters of 'race' and identity. The anti-oppressive ethical principle of respecting social difference and acknowledging the specific impact of racism in the mental health system would have demanded a challenge from the workers regarding the 'everyday racism' (Essed, 2000) that existed in the secure clinic where David 'Rocky' Bennett died. The stereotypical view of dangerousness and black men (African-Caribbean men in this case) (Crichton, 1994; Fernando et al, 1998) was another contributory factor to this tragedy.

The Mental Health Act 1983, as amended by the Mental Health Act 2007, failed to place the issue of 'race' discrimination within the statute; instead, reference to it was given within the *Code of practice* (DH, 2015). It was always hoped, and argued for, that the whole matter of 'race' and mental health would receive prominent and separate consideration given the over-representation of BME individuals detained under the mental health legislation (Fernando, 2011). This *Code of practice* (the nearest to a set of ethical principles for work in mental health) provides statutory guidance to registered medical practitioners, approved clinicians, managers and staff of providers, and approved mental health professionals on how they should carry out functions under the Mental Health Act 1983. It is statutory guidance for registered medical practitioners and other professionals in relation to the medical treatment of patients suffering from mental disorder. The *Code of practice* contains a set of five principles to guide practice. However, the only place where the matter of race is referred to is under the principle of respect and dignity, alongside other major social divisions such as age, gender, disability, sex and sexual orientation, and including pregnancy and maternity. Given this weak consideration of 'race' within the mental health legislation, we strongly advocate the use of anti-oppressive ethical principles, particularly in relation to understanding the interconnections between social differences, to bolster the guidance in the *Code of practice*.

Work in the area of mental health and distress is a practice context that gives rise to many ethical dilemmas with regard to treatment and detention under the legislation. It calls into question many issues of human rights, choice, freedom and justice (Bogg, 2010; Barker, 2011). In comments from the 'Rocky' Bennett inquiry, Dr M. Lipsedge, a psychiatrist and a contributor to the inquiry on the death of Rocky Bennett, referred to Frantz Fanon's view of how 'racism objectified and made a person into a thing and that a thing, by definition, had no capacity for human relationships' (Blofeld, 2003: 49). In the tragic outcomes for David 'Rocky' Bennett, Orville Black Wood (who died in 1991 in Broadmoor) and others (Crichton, 1994), we see the product of the fears around race embodied in their lives (and deaths) and experiences in the mental health and criminal justice systems in Britain today (Athwal and Bourne, 2015). Five years has passed since the end of the implementation of the *DRE* initiative, yet we continue to see evidence of inequalities on the grounds of 'race' in the mental health system.

The recommendations from the 'Rocky' Bennett inquiry did provide a solid basis for the improvement of mental health practice with BME communities using psychiatric services. However, for change to be sustained, there needs to be an active commitment to engage in practice informed by anti-oppressive ethical principles, which we believe provide a theoretical and ethical map that will guide professionals 'in the direction of liberatory terrain' (hooks, 2013: 191).

## Conclusion

> Nothing ever happens because it is right, it happens because people fight for it. (Blight, 2015)[1]

We have put forward the argument for a systemic and systematic process where anti-oppressive ethical principles guide and support practitioners in dealing with issues of ethics and values when working with BME individuals, families and communities. These principles, which can be used by professionals within a multidisciplinary context, provide a platform to challenge practice that is based on Western Eurocentric ideas and ideologies about the human condition. The use of the proposed principles generates a number of questions regarding the quality and nature of practice interventions and the treatment of people using a range of health and social care services. This process of questioning brings to everyday practice challenges that contribute to, and capture, new and emergent knowledge that is effective and transformative.

For us, anti-oppressive ethical practice involves the practitioner and organisations making a commitment to:

- gain an informed knowledge and understanding of 'race', ethnicity, diverse cultural practices, family patterns and religious and philosophical traditions in order to know how dominant ideologies negate the complexities of difference;
- challenge existing Western and Eurocentric values (associated with individualism rather than values that stress reciprocity and communality) that drive existing service planning, delivery and practice in social work;
- critically consider the development of practice tools and assessment processes that recognise and work with the strengths of BME individuals, families and communities;
- recognise not just professional and organisational power, but also the personal power that emanates from membership of specific social divisions and the ways that that membership is implicated in the structures of oppressive practices;
- an ongoing engagement with and networking with a range of BME community-based organisations and projects; and
- continuously monitoring and evaluating practice in partnership with BME service users and service user organisations.

These commitments and the actions that derive from them will enable the practitioner to come to a deeper understanding of the complex nature of service delivery within health, social care and social work. We see these ethical commitments and principles not as bounded recipes for change, but as a dynamic framework for the development of practice that has the scope for enabling positive change at the individual, community, organisational, institutional and political levels. It is through, as well as in, the process of change that practitioners will 'seek out the contested spaces, spaces of division, and work collectively to challenge racism and all other forms of oppression' (Harrison and Burke, 2014: 84). In these times of uncertainty and demographic changes (nationally and globally/internationally), it is even more imperative for the politics of all 'colours' to come together to develop robust equality and social justice-based ethical strategies that ensure more than fairness for all individuals and communities. To achieve any semblance of equality in service delivery, our practice must be informed by an anti-oppressive ethical framework that is non-linear, creative, relational, embodied and dynamic. Anti-oppressive ethical theorising and practice will support and challenge our understanding of the complexity of the human condition, where equality, fairness and social justice are based on more than a plea for individual humanity, being grounded instead in a radical and critical analysis of the personal and the political.

## Note

[1] Professor David W. Blight, Yale University, delivered the Alistair Cooke Memorial Lecture in 2015 (Blight, 2015). This quote is taken from this lecture.

## References

Allan, J. (2014) 'Reconciling the "psych-social/structural" in social work counselling with refugees', *British Journal of Social Work*, pp 1–18 (advanced access, 23 May).

Atchenson, D. (1998) *Independent inquiry into inequalities in health report*, London: HMSO.

Athwal, H. and Bourne, J. (2015) *Dying for justice*, London: Institute of Race Relations.

Banks, S. (2012) *Ethics and values in social work* (4th edn), Basingstoke: Palgrave Macmillan.

Barker, P. (2011) 'The keystone of psychiatric ethics', in P. Barker (ed) *Mental health ethics*, Abingdon: Routledge, pp 31–50.

Barn, R. and Das, C. (2015) 'Family group conferences and cultural competence in social work', *British Journal of Social Work*, pp 1–18 (advanced access, 22 January).

Barnes, M. (2012) *Care in everyday life: an ethics of care in practice*, Bristol: The Policy Press.

Betancur, J. (2014) 'Conclusions: racism and neoracism: contributions of this book', in J.J. Betancur and C. Herring (eds) *Reinventing race, reinventing racism*, Chicago, IL: Haymarket Books.

Bhatti-Sinclair, K. (2011) *Anti-racist practice in social work*, Basingstoke: Palgrave Macmillan.

Bhui, K. (2002) *Racism and mental health*, London: Jessica Kingsley Publishers.

Bisman, C. (2004) 'Social work values: the moral core of the profession', *British Journal of Social Work*, 34(1): 109–23.

Bisman, C. (2014) *Social work: value-guided practice for a global society*, Columbia: Columbia University Press.

Blight, D.W. (2015) *Alistair Cooke memorial lecture*, 5 May, London: BBC.

Blofeld, J. (2003) *Independent inquiry into the death of David Bennett*, Cambridge: The Norfolk and Suffolk and Cambridgeshire Strategic Health Authority.

Bogg, D. (2010) *Values and ethics in mental practice*, Exeter: Learning Matters.

Burke, B. and Harrison, P. (2009) 'Anti-oppressive approaches', in R. Adams, L. Dominelli and M. Payne (eds) *Critical practice in social work*, Basingstoke: Palgrave Macmillan, pp 209–19.

Clark, C. (2006) 'Moral character in social work', *British Journal in Social Work*, 36(1): 75–89.

Clifford, D. (1998) *Social assessment theory and practice*, Aldershot: Ashgate.

Clifford, D. (2001) 'What practical difference does it make? Anti-oppressive ethics and informed consent', *Practice,* 13(3): 17–28.

Clifford, D. and Burke, B. (2009) *Anti-oppressive ethics and values in social work*, Basingstoke: Palgrave Macmillan.

CQC (Care Quality Commission) (2015) *Monitoring the use of the Mental Health Act in 2013/14*, London: CQC.

CQC and National and Mental Health Development Unit (2011) *Count me in census*, London: CQC and National and Mental Health Development Unit.

Crenshaw, K. (1991) 'Mapping the margins: intersectionality, identity politics, and violence against women of color', *Stanford Law Review*, 43(6): 1241–99.

Crichton, J.H.M. (1994) 'Comments on the Blackwood Inquiry', *Psychiatric Bulletin*, 18: 236–7.

Dalrymple, J. and Burke, B. (2006) *Anti-oppressive practice social care and the law* (2nd edn), Maidenhead: Open University Press.

DH (Department of Health) (1998) *Modernising mental health service: safe, sound and supportive*, London: DH.

DH (2005) *Delivering race equality in mental health care (DRE)*, London: HMSO.

DH (2015) *Mental Health Act 1983: code of practice*, London: TSO.

EHRC (Equality and Human Rights Commission) (2010) *How fair is Britain? Equality, human rights and good relations in 2010*, October, London: Equality and Human Rights Commission.

Essed, P. (2000) 'Everyday racism: a new approach to the study of racism', in P. Essed and D.T. Goldberg (eds) *Race critical theories*, Oxford: Blackwell Publishing Limited, pp 176–94.

Ferguson, I., Lavalette, M. and Whitmore, E. (2005) *Globalisation, global justice and social work*, Abingdon: Routledge.

Fernando, S. (2010) *Mental health, race and culture*, Basingstoke: Palgrave Macmillan.

Fernando, S. (2011) '"Race" and culture', in P. Barker (ed) *Mental health ethics*, Abingdon: Routledge, pp 250–9.

Fernando, S., Ndegwa, D. and Wilson, M. (1998) *Forensic psychiatry, race and culture*, London: Routledge.

Gilligan, C. (1982) *In a different voice: psychological theory and women's development*, Cambridge, MA: Harvard University Press.

Gilroy, P. (2002) 'The end of antiracism', in P. Essed and D.T. Goldberg (eds) *Race critical theories*, Oxford: Blackwell Publishing, pp 249–64.

Graham, M. (2007) *Black issues in social work and social care*, Bristol: The Policy Press.

Gray, M. and Webb, S.A. (2013) *The new politics of social work*, Basingstoke: Palgrave Macmillan.

Harrison, P. and Burke, B. (2014) 'Same, same but different', in M. Lavalette and L. Penketh (eds) *Race, racism and social work: contemporary issues and debates*, Bristol: The Policy Press, pp 71–84.

Harrison, P. and Singh, M. (2009) 'Enhancing Pathways Into Care (EPIC)', unpublished.

Healey, K. and Meagher, G. (2004) 'The re-professionalisation of social work: collaborative approaches for achieving professional recognition', *British Journal of Social Work*, 34(2): 243–60.

Held, V. (2006) *The ethics of care: personal, political and global*, Oxford: Oxford University Press.

Higgins, M. and Goodyer, A. (2015) 'The contradictions of contemporary social work: an ironic response', *British Journal of Social Work*, 45: 747–60.

Hill Collins, P. (1998) *Fighting words: black women and the search for justice*, Minneapolis, MN: University of Minnesota Press.

Hill Collins, P. (2002) 'Defining black feminist thought', in P. Essed and D.T. Goldberg (eds) *Race critical theories*, Oxford: Blackwell Publishing, pp 152–75.

Hill Collins, P. (2009) *Black feminist thought* (Routledge Classics edn), Abingdon: Routledge.

Holscher, D. and Bozalek, V.G. (2012) 'Encountering the other across the divides: re-grounding social justice as a guiding principle for social work with refugees and other vulnerable groups', *British Journal of Social Work*, 42(6): 1093–112.

hooks, b. (1981) *Ain't I a woman: black women and feminism*, London: Pluto Press.

hooks, b. (1993) *Sisters of the yam*, Boston: Southend Press.

hooks, b. (2013) *Writing beyond race: living theory and practice*, Abingdon: Routledge.

Hope, R. (2004) *The ten essential shared capabilities – a framework for the whole of the mental health workforce*, London: DH.

Lavalette, M. and Penketh, L. (2014) *Race, racism and social work: contemporary issues and debates*, Bristol: The Policy Press.

Lee, C. (2014) 'Conservative comforts: some philosophical crumbs for social work', *British Journal of Social Work*, 44(8): 2135–44.

Liebenberg, L., Ungar, M. and Ikeda, J. (2015) 'Neo-liberalism and responsibilisation in the discourse of social service workers', *British Journal of Social Work*, 45(3): 1006–21.

Lynn, E. (1999) 'Value bases in social work education', *British Journal of Social Work*, 29(6): 939–53.

Macpherson, W. (1999) *The Stephen Lawrence Inquiry: report of an inquiry by Sir William Macpherson of Cluny*, London: HMSO.

Mattsson, T. (2014) 'Intersectionality as a useful tool: anti-oppressive social work and critical reflection', *Affilia: Journal of Women and Social Work*, 29(1): 8–17.

Moodley, R. and Ocampo, M. (2014) *Critical psychiatry and mental health: exploring the work of Suman Fernando in clinical practice*, Hove: Routledge.

Nazroo, J.Y. (1997) *Ethnicity and mental health: findings from a national community survey*, London: Policy Studies Institute.

Ndegwa, D. and Dele, O. (2003) *Main issues in mental health and race*, Aldershot: Ashgate.

NIMHE (National Institute of Mental Health England) (2003) *Inside outside: improving mental health services for black and minority ethnic communities in England*, London: DH.

Parekh Commission (2000) *The future of multi-ethnic Britain (Parekh report)*, London: Profile Books.

RAWOrg (no date) *The end of delivering race equality: perspectives of frontline workers and service users from racialised groups*, London: RAWOrg.

Sacks, J. (2003) *The dignity of difference*, London: Continuum.

Sewell, H. (2009) *Working with ethnicity, race and culture in mental health: a handbook for practitioners*, London: Jessica Kingsley Publishers.

Simey, M. (1996) *The disinherited society: a personal view of social responsibility in Liverpool during the twentieth century*, Liverpool: Liverpool University Press.

Singh, G. (2014) 'Rethinking anti-racist social work in a neoliberal age', in M. Lavalette and L. Penketh (eds) *Race, racism and social work: contemporary issues and debates*, Bristol: The Policy Press, pp 17–31.

Tronto, J. (1993) *Moral boundaries: a political argument for an ethic of care*, London: Routledge.

Watters, C. (2014) 'Race, culture and mental health care for refugees', in R. Moodley and M. Ocampo (eds) *Critical psychiatry and mental health*, East Sussex: Routledge, pp 69–78.

Williams, C. and Johnson, M.R.D. (2010) *Race and ethnicity in a welfare society*, Maidenhead: Open University Press.

Williams, C. and Soydan, H. (2005) 'When and how does ethnicity matter? A cross national study of social work responses to ethnicity in child protection cases', *British Journal of Social Work*, 35(6): 901–20.

Wilson, M. (2010) *Race equality action plan: a five year review*, London: DH.

# Part Two
## Practice themes

---

FOUR

# Risk and safety: a strengths-based perspective in working with black families when there are safeguarding concerns

*Claudia Bernard and Shantel Thomas*

## Introduction

Engaging black families in child protection can pose a number of challenges for social workers when there are concerns about child abuse and neglect. It is widely recognised that the effective engagement of parents is central to securing the safety needs of at-risk children (Munro, 2008; Ferguson, 2011). Available evidence suggests that effectively engaging families in child protection work is challenging, not least because these families are often 'involuntary', ambivalent, hostile and highly resistant to social work intervention (Laming, 2003; Forrester et al, 2012; Platt, 2012; Turney, 2012; Tuck, 2013). A number of authors have highlighted the use of the deficit-focused approach to much practice with black families and emphasise the importance of intervention strategies that can identify and build on capacities and strengths for engaging black parents in child protection work (Genero, 1988; Chand and Thoburn, 2006; Chand, 2008). Importantly, some scholars have drawn attention to the underlying factors that are potential barriers to black families' engagement with child protection services, and suggest that factors such as fear, mistrust and stigma play a decisive role (Chand, 2005; Bernard and Gupta, 2008). Furthermore, it has been increasingly recognised that children living in families affected by factors caused by social inequalities, such as poverty, unemployment and living in economically disadvantaged neighbourhoods, are at the greatest risk of child welfare interventions (Drake et al, 2009; Bywaters et al, 2014; Bywaters, 2015). There is also a growing evidence base which shows that some minority racial groups are disproportionately affected by poverty, and are thus over-represented in the child welfare system as a consequence (Stokes and Schmidt, 2011). Thus, it is thought that a strengths-based approach, based on assets rather than deficits, is better able to capture a more nuanced understanding of the coping strategies of black parents in complex practice situations (Barn, 2007; Bernard and Gupta, 2008). Increasingly, it is being recognised that a deficit-focused approach with black families can undervalue the attributes, resources and assets of the family, and thus be an obstacle in parental engagement (Chand, 2000; Barn et al, 2006). It has been noted by some that building effective relationships can enhance the cultural assets of black parents for achieving positive outcomes for children in situations that are nuanced and complex (Soydan and Williams, 1998; Fong, 2004). In this chapter, we employ a strengths-based lens to examine a range of factors that are important for transformative practice with black families when children are at risk of harm. It uses case studies to illustrate some key elements of strengths-based practice and evaluates the benefits and challenges of strengths-based interventions. It will conclude with some suggestions of ways that the key principles of strengths-based practice can be practically applied for effective partnership work with black parents in complex practice situations.

## Strengths-based approaches

Strengths-based approaches are founded on the idea that every individual, family, group and community has inherent strengths, assets and capabilities (Rapp et al, 2005; Saleebey, 2012). A strengths-based approach takes as its starting point the notion that families are seen as the experts in solving their own problems. Thus, the social worker's task is to engage the family as a partner in order to develop a shared understanding of the presenting problem and to utilise their strengths, abilities, knowledge and resources to resolve their difficulties (McMillen et al, 2004; O'Neil, 2005; Saint-Jacques et al, 2009; Saleebey, 2012). Essentially, a strengths-based approach recognises that although families may be in crisis or dysfunctional, nonetheless, rather than overly emphasising deficits, interventions should seek a balance of harnessing families' strengths and potentials, yet, at the same time, be able to make professional judgements where children are at risk, or are being harmed (Rapp et al, 2005; Chapman and Field, 2007; Saint-Jacques et al, 2009; Keddell, 2014). Thus, partnership is at the heart of strengths-based practice and the working alliance between the social worker and service user is of paramount importance for understanding families' strengths, which can be supported by interventions (Sullivan and Rapp, 1994; Early and GlenMaye, 2000). Within the 'Signs of Safety' model, Turnell and Edwards (1997) contend that awareness of the unequal power relations between social workers and families is central to strengths-based practice in child protection processes, and making use of this awareness optimises the potential for partnership working.

There is limited empirical evidence of strengths-based practice in child protection, and what little that exists has tended to focus on family support interventions or parenting programmes for supporting children in need (Berg and Kelly, 2000; Green et al, 2004; Saint-Jacques et al, 2009; Gray, 2011). Where the thresholds for intervention require action to protect children from abuse and neglect, and in situations where families are more likely to be involuntary, antagonistic, resistant and difficult to engage, strengths-based interventions pose a more complex set of problems (Turnell and Edwards, 1997; Turnell and Essex, 2006; Alcock et al, 2009; Turnell, 2012; Bunn, 2013). It is as a result of the growing recognition of the need for strengths-based interventions in child protection work that Turnell and Edwards (1997) developed Signs of Safety, a practice model that draws on strengths-based approaches. Signs of Safety uses a solution-focused approach and there is a strong focus on developing constructive relationships with parents in order to achieve the best outcomes for vulnerable children in high-risk families (Turnell, 2012; Keddell, 2014). As Jack (2005), among others, has observed, interventions that seek to effect positive change need to be transparent and grounded in ethical principles in order to build a more collaborative approach with parents when there are safeguarding issues. More broadly, Signs of Safety scholars recognise that balancing strengths alongside making rigorous assessments of risk factors for children presents key challenges for social workers, not least because of the need to prioritise child safety needs over parental rights. Thus, this approach incorporates both problems and strengths into its framework (Turnell and Edwards, 1997; Jack, 2005; Turnell et al, 2008).

## Engaging black families in child protection work

How strengths-based practice with black families in the child protection arena is carried out is not well understood. Scholars have highlighted that adopting a strengths-based approach with resistant or 'involuntary' black families poses difficulties (Laursen, 2000; Chand, 2003; Lambert et al, 2006; Dioum and Yorath, 2013). In addition, it has been suggested that social workers may have challenges establishing effective collaborative relationships with black families because of their limited understanding of the parenting practices of black families (Harran, 2002; Okitipki and Aymer, 2003; Garrett, 2006; Gupta and Neill-McKinnell, 2009). These challenges include a lack of practice skills and knowledge for facilitating meaningful dialogues with families of different cultures, and a tendency to take a deficit-oriented focus, thus undervaluing the cultural assets of black families (Banks, 2000; Chand, 2003; Thoburn et al, 2004). The claim is made that social workers may struggle to value strengths in black families because of preconceived ideas about race that label these families as deficient and dysfunctional (Freeman and Logan, 2004). At the same time, however, child protection practitioners will need to distinguish between cultural assets that are seen as strengths in enhancing black parents' emotional and practical resourcefulness, and where parents draw on cultural practices as a justification for particular parental behaviours that may cause harm to children (Genero, 1988). Here, there is a balance between being culturally sensitive without resorting to forms of cultural relativism.

Several authors (see, among others, Bernard, 2002; Barn, 2007; Graham, 2007) contend that without an appreciation of cultural differences and of variations in black family life, it would be difficult for social workers to have a multifaceted understanding of the factors that influence how black parents navigate the adversities that they are faced with. Therefore, social workers would need to be critically aware that black families' strengths include skills for adaptability in the face of multiple adversities, nurturing extended family support networks and bi-culturality (Freeman and Logan, 2004). Importantly, advocates of strengths-based perspectives with black families point to a scrutiny of the social and cultural contextual factors that influence their child-rearing practices in order to deliver strengths-based practice (McMillen et al, 2004). An appreciation of the wider context in which black family life is taking place is fundamental to any understanding of their strengths. Ultimately, social workers will need to have some understanding of how the dynamics of racism contributes to the negative perceptions of black families' child-rearing practices, pathologises black people and stereotypes black culture and lifestyles (Bernard, 2002; Graham, 2007). Therefore, insight into the subjective experiences of black families is a crucial factor for facilitating effective working alliances with them (Laursen, 2000; Green et al, 2004; Lambert et al, 2006).

## Applying strengths-based principles

This section illustrates a strengths-based approach with the use of two case examples to highlight some key issues.

### Case example

Caribbean family: 48-year-old Mike Paterson is 36-year-old Niasha Campbell's partner and father of nine-year-old Roy, Niasha's youngest child. Niasha has four other children by three different fathers: 17-year-old Dexter, 14-year-Trish, 13-year-old Fay and 11-year-old Helen. Dexter was born when Niasha was in college. Her relationship with Dexter's father was very brief and they have had very little contact with him since he was born. Trish and Fay have the same father. He died in a car accident shortly after Fay was born. Helen's father is now married with other children and lives outside London. He tries his best to have fortnightly weekend contact with her. The family was brought to the attention of the local authority due to the high level of domestic violence incidences in the household. Mike and Niasha have been in an 'off and on' relationship for 10 years. However, he has a violent temper and continuously accuses her of infidelity. He has a fairly good relationship with all the children when he is in a good mood. He has, however, been physically violent and extremely verbally abusive to their mother in their presence, which frightens them and puts them at risk of harm. He agreed to leave the home as part of the child protection plan. However, there are concerns that he still visits, and that Niasha still sees him often. It also appears that he continues to be violent towards her, even though she denies it. She refused to let the police in the last time they visited, having received a call from a neighbour that they could hear a violent exchange of words and threats from their home. She claimed that she had walked into a door when a social worker visited and saw her bruised eye. Dexter is hardly at home and is often involved in anti-social behaviour in the area. He is a proud member of a violent local gang. Roy misses his father and his behaviour has deteriorated significantly since his father left the family home. He has begun to display aggressive and challenging behaviour towards his mother and at school. He is likely to be expelled from mainstream school if he continues to exhibit disruptive behaviour.

As we can see from the case study, the static risk factors in relation to the domestic abuse are the physical violence perpetrated towards Niasha by her current partner,

Mike, and the exposure of the children to the violence, as well as the indirect risk of injury. The social worker would be concerned not only about the harm that has been caused in the past, but also about the risk of future physical and emotional harm towards Niasha and her children.

In order to find out what is working well in this family, it is important to hear the story of each family member as this will provide clear information for the risk and safety assessment (Turnell and Edwards, 1997). Within the story, it is vital to understand the strongly held values and beliefs that inform Niasha's and Mike's views with regards to the domestic abuse and its impact on each child. This will be critical as domestic violence is a child protection issue and it is well established that children who are exposed to domestic violence have a higher risk of developing emotional and behavioural problems, such as conduct disorders, anxiety, depression, delinquency and aggression, which are common among adolescents and teenagers (McGee, 2000; Devaney, 2008; Meltzer et al, 2009; Stanley et al, 2011; CAADA, 2012). As these issues are compounded for black children who are exposed to multiple childhood adversities, assessing risks to the children and their support needs will be imperative. Once the social worker has understood Niasha's and Mike's particular 'position', they will be better aligned to establish a cooperative working relationship with the family and, in turn, enhance the cultural assets of black parents. A point to note is that the social worker does not have to agree or condone their beliefs about the domestic abuse and will have to directly address the problem with them. The risks here are that there might be an over-scrutiny of Niasha's parenting without an understanding of the challenges and difficulties of parenting in the context of domestic violence, and a lack of attention paid to Mike's parenting (Devaney, 2008; Lapierre, 2010; Alderson et al, 2013). When domestic violence is present, addressing these issues allows for an understanding of how abusive men's behaviour could undermine the mother–child relationship (Morris, 2009). With these concerns in mind, it would be important to assess Mike's understanding of the impact that domestic violence has on Niasha and the children. Engaging fathers in child protection processes and challenging them about their abusive behaviour is something that social workers often find difficult (Scourfield, 2006). However, a principal concern is to increase safety for Niasha and the children; thus, it is critical to find ways to involve Mike. Ultimately, the preferred way forward would be for the social worker to utilise their position to work alongside both parents in order to create a safer environment for all the children.

For strength-based practice, it is important to expand on the bleak picture that is often painted of a family during a child protection investigation. Exploration of the positive aspects and strengths of this family as a unit and individually, or those acknowledged by others, can assist in creating the sense that there are, in fact, aspects of family life and experiences that can be built on to resolve the abuse. The strengths-based approach is also useful as it is very likely to foster cooperation between the social worker and the family, in that they gain a sense that they are bringing a balanced perspective to the situation and are not simply fixated on what is going wrong. The basic principle of the Signs of Safety approach is the explicit and careful focus given to the goals of the two key components of the process, namely, the family members and the practitioner (Turnell, 2012; Bunn, 2013). In this case, it is clear what has to stop – the domestic abuse. Therefore, it follows that what also needs to be clearly articulated is exactly what the family will need to indicate enough safety for the case to be closed. Along with the social worker's goals, it is important to explore how Niasha, Mike and the children see how the issues should be dealt with and how they would go about creating safety for themselves.

As well as considering safety (where the abuse is acknowledged), it is also important to learn what family members want more generally. It is also often the case that people may not be willing to make changes simply to satisfy societal or governmental standards, but may be motivated to satisfy their own goal of peace from what they see as 'outside interference'. These forms of indirect motivations are useful for harnessing the energies of parents involved in child abuse investigations.

Scaling questions offer a useful mechanism for practitioners, in that they conceive the situation on a continuum of risk to safety. Therefore, throughout the working of the case, the social worker must routinely ask family members questions to gauge where they are with regards to 'ideal family functioning' and where they would hope to be in future. It is also important to acknowledge that absolute safety is never possible. Willingness to take action is also a vital sign of safety in its own right.

## Case example

African family: eight-year-old George and 10-year-old Faith are siblings. It is unclear when they moved to the UK from Africa. It appears that it was two to three years ago from the children's estimation and school records. They are currently with what appears to be their third private foster-carers. They moved from the North London area to this new 'aunt' 11 months ago. George's school brought it to the attention of the local authority that the woman he lived with was not really his aunt when he disclosed this information to them. He appears very frightened of his 'aunt' and broke down in tears when his teacher explained that a report would be sent home about his poor behaviour. The 'aunt' has only attended one school meeting and appeared quite abrupt, in a hurry and emotionally distant from the children. There are other concerns bordering on risk of significant harm. The children have reported that they have little or no contact with their birth parents and do not have contact details for them. They also appear cagey about many aspects of the information that they have given to the school and social services. Both children are generally unkempt and often come to school hungry and tired. Faith explains that their older 'cousin', who is 22 years old, frequently watches TV until late at night and as they sleep in the living room, they have to wait till he finishes before they can go to bed. Their 'aunt' will not allow social work visits. A letter has been written to her regarding the children. She responded agreeing that she did not want any social worker visits and the local authority were welcome to have the children as she was only doing their parents a favour and they were costing her a lot of time and money, as well as causing further problems. She informed the children that they will have to go into care if the local authority insists on snooping around and putting their nose in her business.

Under the Children Act 1989, the social worker will have a duty to investigate the suitability of arrangements for George's and Faith's care. It is possible that the children may have been privately fostered. It would be important to hold in mind that private fostering arrangements are not uncommon in African families, whereby a non-blood relative is enrolled to undertake a parenting role for a period of time (Olunsanya and Hodes, 2000; Shaw et al, 2010). However, the risk factors in this case example are more complex than in the first and centre on possible child trafficking and exploitation, coupled with emotional abuse and neglect. It would therefore be important to carry out a risk assessment to ascertain whether the children have been victims of trafficking. Recent focus on the safeguarding concerns facing children and young people who may have been trafficked for the purposes of sexual exploitation or domestic servitude alerts us to the need to make an assessment of risk for George and Faith (Bokhari, 2008; Rigby, 2011; Westwood, 2012; Pearce et al, 2013). Making strengths-based assessments of the care and protection needs of children who have been trafficked is not easy as this is often hidden, and there is a silence surrounding the issue (Bokhari, 2008). Therefore, the social worker would need to be sensitive and patient in order to build a trusting relationship with George and Faith to enable them to disclose if they were trafficked. Thus, the key here, again, is to gain an understanding of what it is like to be George and Faith in this family setting at this time. The focus will be on recognising their resilience, and on paying particular attention to their interests, abilities and knowledge (Lambert et al, 2006). It is thus vital to understand the 'aunt's' position and for her to feel listened to as this will form the basis of the collaborative relationship with the social worker; the key is to look at her capabilities as well as aspects of her behaviour that may be causing harm to the children. Balancing the interests of the children and their carers here might be challenging. However, it is important that George and Faith are protected from significant harm.

As with all Signs of Safety elements, information about family strengths and resources is useful in two potential directions. If a positive scenario about family life is gleaned, this could quite possibly be built on and, at the very least, offer good insight into the quality and nature of familial relationships. On the other hand, if the 'aunt' identifies little or nothing positive about the children or the situation, this may, together with other information, indicate that the severity of the problem is greater than previously perceived.

It is also important to consider ideas for action that the family has used before, or to propose ideas that make sense to them. This is achieved by incorporating their position on the problem and reflecting on their own goals. In any event, regardless of how the ideas are generated, it is imperative that the social worker enhances the readiness and confidence of all family members. A willingness to take action is also a vital sign of safety in its own right.

When exploring the issue of willingness, it is important to take into account the issue of powerlessness. For example, the children in this case example may be completely committed to doing something (anything) but feel constrained in acting because they feel powerless to change the situation. The issue of confidence is also important and, as with willingness, the social worker needs to make their own judgements with regards to the information that they have been presented with. For example, if the 'aunt' is expressing the view that she is willing to accept the assistance offered in order to make the changes to her behaviour, then that will, in turn, enhance the children's well-being. However, George and Faith might have little confidence in that action as they may have heard it all before. It would be inappropriate for the social worker to support such action in these circumstances.

When using a strengths-based perspective, the worker guides the interactions with families with structured and persistent communication and therapeutic techniques. The worker hypothesises future goals before meeting the client and uses these goals as leverage for cooperation. The idea is to influence families in such a way that they believe it is their desire and in their best interests to evoke the changes identified. This is all done through talking. The idea is to gather the information, assess the risk and exercise the authority when necessary (Munro, 2008). Attentive listening and encouragement for client self-determination are combined with clarity about the child protection concerns and honesty about the mandated authority (Turnell and Essex, 2006). It is important to be explicit about what is acceptable and what is not and to be straightforward about the consequences and expectations of engagement (Bunn, 2013; Oliver and Charles, 2015). To hold this position demands continual movement between expressing empathy and establishing the expectations of parents and carers as the worker navigates a relationship of mutuality in which there is sufficient separation to ensure that decisions are made in the children's best interests (Turnell and Essex, 2006).

The relationship relies on the worker's warmth and spontaneity as much as their skills in working with the parents' position (Keys, 2009). A key collaborative strategy is to identify the family's strength, often with the aid of solution-focused questioning techniques. Complimenting strengths encourages clients to engage and increases their motivation and self-esteem (Saleebey, 2012). The client needs consistent encouragement and workers are advised to maintain humour, hope and gratitude and not to take themselves too seriously. Even while carefully guiding the relationship for therapeutic ends, the whole worker and not just the professional persona, is required to show up.

The challenges of negotiating relationships like this in contemporary social work settings appear significant. The assumption of strength-based approaches is that most people can change their behaviour when provided with the correct support and adequate resources. However, this may not translate well in practice. In the current climate, where support and resources are scarce and the role of social workers is much more about managing 'high-risk' and 'troubled' families and being rationers of resources, this has meant less contact time with families (Ferguson and Lavallette, 2013).

In short, these case examples highlight some of the benefits of a strengths perspective for engaging with the complex dynamics of competing needs and issues that arise for vulnerable children and families, without overemphasising problems and deficits, and, most importantly, without downplaying the risks to children. Certainly, as the issues are emotionally charged and multifaceted, less experienced and less confident social workers might feel anxious and uncertain about how to intervene to assess the concerns that have been flagged and make judgements about good-enough parenting. There is more to the relationship than simply supporting client self-determination. The relationship between the worker and the family is purposeful and goal-oriented, where the worker exercises considerable power to structure and direct the work required to implement change. Strengths-based scholars highlight how important it is for the social worker to think themselves into the frame of reference of the family in order to understand the problems that are posed. In many respects, these examples highlight how a solution-focused strengths-based approach can enable social workers to grapple with the complex layers of risks and challenges that are interwoven through the cases.

## Conclusion

This chapter has explored a strengths-based perspective to interventions for safeguarding and promoting the welfare of black children, and, in doing so, has attempted to illuminate some particular tensions and contradictions for families with complex needs. Such an approach starts from a recognition of the power differentials that exists between social workers and service users, and, thus, provides a set of tools and strategies to engage with families' strengths and resources. An important aspect of strengths-based interventions is the notion that families are seen as experts of their own lives. The social worker's task is to build on family knowledge and emotional resources to generate solutions to the problems that may pose risks to children (Rapp et al, 2005).

As has been highlighted with the case examples, while there are many positive benefits of a strengths-based approach, nevertheless, there are some challenges to utilising such an approach in situations where children are at risk of harm. Without question, keeping a clear focus on the safety needs of at-risk black children is paramount. As we have argued, interventions are about assessing parental capabilities to achieve positive outcomes for children; therefore, validating parental strengths is important for engaging parents as partners in the work. In the main, where children are harmed as a direct result of parental behaviour, social workers will need to have a strong belief that change is possible in order to avoid the danger of compromising the safety needs of black children by silencing their voices and marginalising their experiences. In cases involving child protection where the concern is to increase safety and minimise risk, a strengths-based approach provides social workers with the means to engage resistant parents. Advocates of strengths-based practice make the point that in situations where there are dilemmas and tensions, using such an approach allows for assessments that can value and enhance care-giving practices, and are thus better able to foster an environment conducive for attempting partnerships with black parents (Thoburn, 2009).

However, while the benefits of strengths-based practice are widely recognised, there are difficulties and challenges for partnership working with parents. Some of the difficulties posed are in maintaining a balance between working alongside parents to assess the needs of the child but without letting their responses and circumstances take precedence over children's needs. As such, it is important to note that there may be avoidance, ambivalence and disguised or partial compliance that hamper the helping process (Brandon et al, 2008). Of course, it should not be assumed that interventions that are effective for one family would work for all black families. It will be vital to take into consideration the individual child's needs, as well as the family circumstances. As noted previously, professional assumptions about risks for black children may be influenced by stereotypical deficit-focused views of black families (Banks, 2000; Thoburn et al, 2005). Given the increasingly heterogeneous nature of black communities in the UK, with differentiated cultural practices and beliefs about child-rearing, engaging strengths-based intervention efforts to assess and manage risks is bound to pose considerable challenges for social workers (Bernard and Gupta, 2008; Dustin and Davies, 2007). Thus, addressing these challenges requires social workers not only to be empathic and reflexive, but also to have the skills and confidence to facilitate difficult conversations in order for transformative practice to take place. Ultimately, social workers intervening in black families to safeguard children need a clear child-centred focus if they are to make sound assessments of risks for children's and parents' capacity to respond to concerns.

## References

Alcock, H., Wilcockson, S., Donaldson, G. and Barnes, J. (2009) *Does the Signs of Safety social work model focus upon highlighting strengths as well as difficulties, improve the participation of and outcomes for children and their families whilst ensuring that agencies adopt integrated, common approaches?* Children's Workforce Development Council, London: HMSO.

Alderson, S., Westmarland, N. and Kelly, L. (2013) 'The need for accountability to, and support for, children of men on domestic violence perpetrator programmes', *Child Abuse Review*, 22(3): 182–93.

Banks, N. (2000) 'Assessing children and families who belong to minority ethnic groups', in J. Horwath (ed) *The child's world: assessing children in need*, London: Jessica Kingsley.

Barn, R. (2007) 'Race, ethnicity and parenting: understanding the impact of context', *ChildRIGHT*, no 233.

Barn, R., Ladino, C. and Rogers, B. (2006) *Parenting in a multi-racial Britain*, London: National Children's Bureau.

Berg, I.K. and Kelly, S. (2000) *Building solutions in child protective services*, New York, NY: Norton.

Bernard, C. (2002) 'Giving voice to experiences: parental maltreatment of black children in the context of societal racism', *Child and Family Social Work*, 7(4): 239–51.

Bernard, C. and Gupta, A. (2008) 'Black African children and the child protection system', *British Journal of Social Work*, 38(3): 476–92.

Bokhari, F. (2008) 'Falling through the gaps: safeguarding children trafficked into the UK', *Children and Society*, 22(3): 201–11.

Brandon, M., Belderson, P., Warren, C., Howe, D., Gardner, R., Dodsworth, J. and Black, J. (2008) *Analysing child deaths and serious injury through abuse and neglect: what can we learn? A biennial analysis of serious case reviews 2003–2005*, CSF-RB023, London: Department of Children, Schools and Families.

Bunn, A. (2013) 'Signs of Safety in England: an NSPCC commissioned report on the Signs of Safety model in child protection', available at: www.nspcc.org.uk/Inform/research/findings/signs-of-safety-pdf_wdf94939.pdf (last accessed 2 February 2014).

Bywaters, P. (2015) 'Inequalities in child welfare: towards a new policy, research and action agenda', *British Journal of Social Work*, 45(1): 6–23.

Bywaters, P., Brady, G., Sparks, T. and Bos, E. (2014) 'Child welfare inequalities: new evidence, further questions', *Child and Family Social Work*, first published online, 8 May. DOI: 10.1111/cfs.12154.

CAADA (Co-ordinated Action Against Domestic Abuse) (2012) *CAADA insights 1: 'a place of greater safety'*, Bristol: CAADA.

Chand, A. (2000) 'The over-representation of black children in the child protection system: possible causes, consequences and solutions', *Child and Family Social Work*, 5(1): 67–77.

Chand, A, (2003) '"Race" and the Laming Report on Victoria Climbié: lessons for inter-professional policy and practice', *Journal of Integrated Care*, 11(4): 28–37.

Chand, A. (2005) 'Do you speak English? Language barriers in child protection social work with minority ethnic families', *British Journal of Social Work*, 35(6): 807–21.

Chand, A. (2008) 'Every child matters? A critical review of child welfare reforms in the context of minority ethnic children and families', *Child Abuse Review*, 17(1): 6–22.

Chand, A. and Thoburn, J. (2006) 'Research review: child protection referrals and minority ethnic children and families', *Child and Family Social Work*, 11(4): 368–77.

Chapman, M. and Field, J. (2007) 'Strengthening our engagement with families and increasing practice depth', *Social Work Now*, 38: 21–8.

Devaney, J. (2008) 'Chronic child abuse and domestic violence: children and families with long-term and complex needs', *Child and Family Social Work*, 13(4): 443–53.

Dioum, M. and Yorath, S. (2013) 'Safeguarding vulnerable children: the role of the Victoria Climbié Foundation', *Journal of Health Visiting*, 1(2): 80–5.

Drake, B., Lee, S.M. and Jonson-Reid, M. (2009) 'Race and child maltreatment reporting: are blacks overrepresented?', *Children and Youth Services Review*, 31(3): 309–16, doi: http://dx.doi.org/10.1016/j.childyouth.2008.08.004

Dustin, M. and Davies, L. (2007) 'Female genital cutting and children's rights: implications for social work practice', *Child Care in Practice*, 13(1): 3–16.

Early, T. and GlenMaye, L. (2000) 'Valuing families: social work practice with families from a strengths perspective', *Social Work*, 45(2): 118–30.

Ferguson, H. (2011) *Child protection practice*, Basingstoke: Palgrave Macmillan.

Ferguson, I. and Lavalette, M. (2013) 'Critical and radical social work: an introduction', *Critical and Radical Social Work*, 1(1): 3–14.

Fong, R. (ed) (2004) *Culturally competent practice with immigrant and refugee children and families*, New York: Guilford Press.

Forrester, D., Westlake, D. and Glynn, G. (2012) 'Parental resistance and social worker skills: towards a theory of motivational social work', *Child and Family Social Work*, 17(2): 118–29.

Freeman, E.M. and Logan, S.L. (eds) (2004) *Reconceptualizing the strengths and common heritage of black families: practice, research and policy issues*, Illinois, IL: Charles C. Thomas Publisher Ltd.

Garrett, P.M. (2006) 'Protecting children in a globalized world: "race" and "place" in the Laming Report on the death of Victoria Climbié', *Journal of Social Work*, 6(3): 315–36.

Genero, N.P. (1988) 'Culture, resiliency and mutual psychological development', in H.I. McCubbin, E.A. Thompson, A.I. Thompson and J.A. Futrell (eds) *Resilience in African-American families*, California, CA: Sage.

Graham, M. (2007) *Black issues in social work and social care*, Bristol: The Policy Press.

Gray, M. (2011) 'Back to basics: a critique of the strengths perspective in social work', *Families in Society*, 92(1): 5–11.

Green, B.L., McAllister, C.L. and Tarte, J.M. (2004) 'The strengths-based practices inventory: a tool for measuring strengths-based service delivery in early childhood and family support programmes', *Families in Society*, 85(3): 327–34.

Gupta, A. and Neill-McKinnell, M. (2009) 'The wider family and community', in H. Cleaver, P. Cawson, S. Gorin and S. Walker (eds) *Safeguarding children: a shared responsibility*, Chichester: Wiley.

Harran, E. (2002) 'Barriers to effective child protection in a multicultural society', *Child Abuse Review*, 11(6): 411–14.

Jack, R. (2005) 'Strengths-based practice in statutory care and protection work', in M. Nash, R. Munford and K. O'Donoghue (eds) *Social work theories in action*, London: Jessica Kingsley.

Keddell, E. (2014) 'Theorising the Signs of Safety approach to child protection social work: positioning codes and power', *Children and Youth Services Review*, 47(1): 70–7.

Keys, M. (2009) 'Determining the skills for child protection practice: emerging from the quagmire!', *Child Abuse Review*, 18(5): 316–32.

Lambert, M.C., Rowan, G.T., Longhurst, J. and Kim, S. (2006) 'Strengths as the foundation for intervention with black youth', *Reclaiming Children and Youth*, 15(3): 147–54.

Laming, L. (2003) *The Victoria Climbié Inquiry*, Cm 5730, London: TSO.

Lapierre, S. (2010) 'More responsibilities, less control: understanding the challenges and difficulties involved in mothering in the context of domestic violence', *British Journal of Social Work*, 40(5): 1434–51.

Laursen, E. (2000) 'Strength-based practice with children in trouble', *Reclaiming Children and Youth*, 9(2):70–5.

McGee, C. (2000) *Childhood experiences of domestic violence*, London: Jessica Kingsley Publishers.

McMillen, J.C., Morris, L. and Sherraden, M. (2004) 'Ending social work's grudge match: problems versus strengths', *Families in Society*, 85(3): 317–25.

Meltzer, H., Doos, L., Vostanis, P., Ford, T. and Goodman, R. (2009) 'The mental health of children who witness domestic violence', *Child and Family Social Work*, 14(4): 491–501.

Morris, A. (2009) 'Gendered dynamics of abuse and violence in families: considering the abusive household gender regime', *Child Abuse Review*, 18: 414–27.

Munro, E. (2008) *Effective child protection* (2nd edn), Los Angeles, CA: Sage Publications.

Okitipki, T. and Aymer, C. (2003) 'Social care with African families and their children', *Child and Family Social Work*, 8(3): 213–22.

Oliver, C. and Charles, G. (2015) 'Enacting firm, fair and friendly practice: a model for strength based child protection relationship?', *British Journal of Social Work*, first published online, 4 March, DOI: 10.1093/bjsw/bcv015.

Olunsanya, B. and Hodes, D. (2000) 'West African children in private foster care in City and Hackney', *Child Care, Health and Development*, 26(4): 337–42.

O'Neil, D. (2005) 'How can a strengths approach increase safety in a child protection context?', *Children Australia*, 30(4): 28–32.

Pearce, J., Hynes, P. and Bovarnick, S. (2013) *Trafficked young people: breaking the wall of silence*, London: Routledge.

Platt, D. (2012) 'Understanding parental engagement with child welfare services: an integrated model', *Child and Family Social Work*, 17(2): 138–48.

Rapp, C., Saleebey, D. and Sullivan, P.W. (2005) 'The future of strengths-based social work practice', *Advances in Social Work*, 6(1): 79–90.

Rigby, P. (2011) 'Separated and trafficked children: the challenges for child protection professionals', *Child Abuse Review*, 20(5): 324–40.

Saint-Jacques, M., Turcotte, D. and Pouliot, E. (2009) 'Adopting a strengths perspective in social work practice with families in difficulty: from theory to practice', *Families in Society*, 90(4): 454–61.

Saleebey, D. (2012) *Strengths perspective in social work practice* (6th edn), Boston, MA: Allyn & Bacon.

Scourfield, J. (2006) 'The challenge of engaging fathers in the child protection process', *Critical Social Policy*, 26(2): 440–9.

Shaw, C., Brodie, I., Ellis, A., Graham, B., Mainey, A., De Sousa, S. and Willmott, N. (2010) 'Research into private fostering', DCSF-RR229, London: DCSF.

Soydan, H. and Williams, C. (1998) 'Exploring concepts', in C. Williams, H. Soydan and M.R.D. Johnson (eds) *Social work with minorities: European perspectives*, London: Routledge.

Stanley, N., Miller, P. and Richardson Foster, H. (2011) 'Engaging with children's and parents' perspectives on domestic violence', *Child and Family Social Work*, 17(2): 192–201.

Stokes, J. and Schmidt, G. (2011) 'Race, poverty and child protection decision making', *British Journal of Social Work*, 41(6): 1105–21.

Sullivan, W.P. and Rapp, C. (1994) 'Breaking away: the potential and promise of a strengths-based approach to social work practice', in R. Meinert, J. Pardeck and W. Sullivan (eds) *Issues in social work*, Westport, CT: Auburn House.

Thoburn, J. (2009) *Effective interventions for complex families where there are concerns about, or evidence of, a child suffering significant harm*, Briefing 1, London: Safeguarding.

Thoburn, J., Chand, A. and Proctor, J. (2004) *Child welfare services for minority ethnic children: the research reviewed*, London: Jessica Kingsley Publishers.

Thoburn, J. Chand, A. and Proctor, J. (2005) *Review of research on child welfare services for children of minority ethnic origin and their families*, London: Jessica Kingsley Publishers.

Tuck, V. (2013) 'Resistant parents and child protection: knowledge base, pointers for practice and implications for policy', *Child Abuse Review*, 22(1): 5–19.

Turnell, A. (2012) 'The Signs of Safety: comprehensive briefing paper', Resolutions Consultancy. Available at: http://vidensportal.dk/filer/born-unge/omsorgssvigt/signs-of-safety-breifing-paper-april-2012.pdf

Turnell, A. and Edwards, S. (1997) 'Aspiring to partnership: the Signs of Safety approach to child protection', *Child Abuse Review*, 6(3): 179–90.

Turnell, A. and Essex, S. (2006) *Working with 'denied' child abuse: the resolutions approach*, Buckingham: Open University Press.

Turnell, A., Lohrbach, S. and Curran, S. (2008) 'Working with the "involuntary client" in child protection: lessons from successful practice', in M. Calder (ed) *The carrot or the stick? Towards effective practice with involuntary clients*, London: Russell House Publishing, pp 104–15.

Turney, D. (2012) 'A relationship-based approach to engaging involuntary clients: the contribution of recognition theory', *Child and Family Social Work*, 17(2): 149–59.

Westwood, J. (2012) 'Constructing risk and avoiding need: findings from interviews with social workers and police officers involved in safeguarding work with migrant children', *Child Abuse Review*, 21(5): 349–61.

# FIVE

# Rapid appraisal in practice assessment: an example of work with Muslim youth in Scotland

*Lena Robinson and M. Rafik Gardee*

## Introduction

This chapter focuses on the power of narrative when working with young people from minority ethnic backgrounds and examines the value of *telling my story* and the lessons that narrative and storytelling indicate for assessment. It examines how the rapid appraisal method can be used to facilitate conversation without judgement with Muslim youth, which is useful for discovering opinions that are not swayed by pre-judgement or a concrete set of guiding questions. Furthermore, the chapter explores the ways in which we, as practitioners, can bring these perspectives together for practice assessment. While we operate in an increasingly ethnically and culturally diverse world, many of the theories and models available to social work practitioners fail to reflect or respond appropriately to that diversity. For this reason, the practitioner research presented in the chapter presents opportunities to better understand practice and improve its effectiveness.

The chapter begins with a description of Islam in the UK and the cultural identity issues faced by Muslims, particularly youth. Next, it explores some of the issues related to the integration and adaptation of Muslim youth to their host societies, with a focus on the concepts of radicalisation and acculturation. Factors examined in relation to adaptation include cultural identity, the role of religion in daily life and self-identity, attitudes about acculturation, and perceived discrimination. An example is drawn from work with Pakistani Muslim youth in the UK to illustrate the application of theory to practice and provide suggestions for practical action. Finally, recommendations for the future expansion of practitioner research in this field are discussed.

## Context

The constructs of acculturation and radicalisation are the primary components of the conceptual framework used in exploring the issues facing young Muslims in the UK. Muslims constitute a significant and growing percentage of young people in Western societies and are the largest religious minority group in the

UK. The 2011 UK Census reported Christians as the largest religious group in England and Wales, with 33.2 million people (59% of the population). The second largest religious group was Muslims, with 2.7 million people (5% of the population). In 2001, 0.84% (42,557) of Scottish residents reported that they were Muslim; by 2011, this number had risen to 1.4% of the population (77,000). The majority of Scotland's Muslim population is based in the west of Scotland and is of Pakistani Punjabi background (UK Office of National Statistics, 2010, 2011).

While nearly half of all Muslims in the UK were born in the country, they are ethnically diverse as a group. Two thirds of Muslims (68%) have an Asian background, including Pakistani (38%) and Bangladeshi (15%). Nearly four in 10 Muslims reported their ethnicity as Pakistani, and this group increased from 658,000 in 2001 to over a million in 2011. During the same period, the number of Bangladeshi Muslims grew from 260,000 in 2001 to 402,000 in 2011. The number of Muslims in all ethnic groups, particularly Asians, increased during this period (Statistics UK, 2012). This large, varied population is also increasingly young. Muslims have the youngest age profile of the main religious groups in the UK. In 2011, nearly half of Muslims (48%) were aged under 25 (1.3 million) (Statistics UK, 2013). As demonstrated by these demographic figures, the number of Muslims in the UK is expanding rapidly, and followers of the religion are ethnically diverse.

Young Muslims who are at least second-generation immigrants in the UK are likely to be well acquainted with mainstream culture but may face conflicting demands due to differences between mainstream values and those of their ethnic culture. They must resolve the issue of how to combine these competing identities. Two theoretical approaches to the study of immigrants' ethnic identity development are prominent: ethnic identity formation theory and acculturation theory. 'Cultural identity' is a broad term used in this chapter to include both ethnic and national identity. The first approach takes a developmental focus in that it examines individual change, and was originally based on ego identity formation theories. The second approach examines the extent to which ethnic identity is maintained when a minority ethnic group is in contact with another dominant group (Phinney, 2003).

## Acculturation strategies

The construct of acculturation has been used by psychologists to describe within-group cultural differences. Acculturation refers to the interaction between a dominant and a non-dominant culture, where one is affected much more profoundly than the other. Acculturation theory is concerned with the extent to which ethnic identity is maintained when an ethnic group is in continuous contact with a dominant group (Phinney, 1990).

Berry (1990) suggested that the acculturation strategies of minority ethnic groups can best be described in terms of two independent dimensions: (1) the retention of cultural traditions; and (2) the establishment and maintenance of relationships within the larger society. When these two central dimensions are considered simultaneously, a conceptual framework is generated that posits four modes of acculturation: assimilation, integration, separation and marginalisation. *Assimilation* occurs when an individual does not wish to maintain their cultural identity and seeks daily interaction with other cultures. In contrast, *separation* occurs when an individual from a non-dominant group places value on holding onto their original culture and, at the same time, wishes to avoid interaction with others. 'Separation' is an appropriate term when this mode of acculturation is pursued by a dominant group with respect to a non-dominant group. *Integration* occurs when an individual has an interest in both maintaining their original culture and interacting on a daily basis with other groups. In this mode of acculturation, some degree of cultural integrity is maintained while, at the same time, an individual participates as an integral part of a larger social network. Finally, *marginalisation* occurs when there is little possibility of or interest in cultural maintenance and only slight interest in relationships with other groups. Attitudes towards and actual behaviours regarding these four strategies constitute an individual's acculturation strategy.

While acculturation is a neutral concept in principle (ie change may take place in either or both groups), in practice, it tends to induce more change in immigrant (non-dominant) groups. There are vast individual differences in how people attempt to deal with acculturative change (Berry, 1997). Acculturation has become a core issue in managing human relationships in culturally diverse societies (Berry, 2005). Three questions are often posed by acculturation researchers:

• How do individuals seek to acculturate following migration?
• How well do they adapt to their new circumstances?
• Is there a significant relationship between how they acculturate and how well they adapt?

## Religion and identity

An expanding body of literature has studied the importance of religion in the identity of Muslims (Hutnick, 1985; Knott and Khokher, 1993; Jacobson, 1997; Saeed et al, 1999; Modood, 2004, 2005; Abbas, 2005; Robinson, 2008). One of the earliest studies on the topic (Hutnick, 1985) examined the self-reported importance of religion in the identity of South Asian Muslims in the UK. A total of 80% of respondents listed religion as an important aspect of their identity (Hutnick, 1985). Among a group of second- and third-generation Pakistani Muslims in Glasgow, aged 14–17, 'Muslim' and 'Pakistani' identities were the top two categories mentioned on a self-identification survey, with Muslim (85%) being chosen nearly three times as often as Pakistani (30%) (Saeed et al, 1999). Modood et al (1997) found that Muslims (74%) were more likely than Hindus (43%) and Sikhs (46%) to say that religion was very important in the way they lived their lives.

## Perceived discrimination

While some immigrants are perceived positively (Ward and Stuart, 2009), others find themselves in a community that is negatively embedded within political and cultural discourse. Biased portrayals in the media and government policies of surveillance in Muslim communities for potential extremist activities, which creates 'suspect' communities (Githens-Mazer, 2011; Hickman et al, 2011; Awan, 2012), indicate that this is often the case for young Muslims in the UK. Post-9/11, Muslims in Britain have become primary targets of racist antagonism ('Islamophobia') based on ethno-religious and cultural difference (Parekh, 2000).

There is considerable evidence of discrimination against Asians in education, employment, health care and the criminal justice system (Jones, 1993; Modood et al, 1997). Muslims in the UK are the most disadvantaged group (as measured by income, housing, occupation and education) among South Asians (Modood et al, 1997). Experiences of prejudice and discrimination are factors that make the acculturation process potentially stressful (Berry, 1997). In Robinson's (2008) study of the adaptation and integration of South Asian youth in Britain, most Indian adolescents felt that they were not at all or only rarely discriminated against, while their Pakistani Muslim peers perceived more discrimination. The majority of Pakistani Muslim youth in the study adopted a separation strategy.

Modood et al (1997: 133) noted that: 'there is now a consensus across all groups that prejudice against Asians is the highest of any ethnic, racial or religious group; and it is believed by Asian people themselves that the prejudice against Asians is primarily a prejudice against Muslims.' The wars in Iraq and Afghanistan (perceived by some as West versus East or Christianity versus Islam) have brought to the surface and increased people's awareness of issues of identity and religious allegiance (Abbas, 2005).

## Radicalisation

Radicalisation has been defined in many ways but is generally used to describe a phenomenon that leads to home-grown terrorism, which is commonly known as terrorist acts perpetrated by those who live in the country that they wish to attack (King and Taylor, 2011). However, in this chapter, we use it in a broader context to refer to adherence to extremist ideology that may in the future lead to the aforementioned behaviour. While the term radicalisation is applicable in many political and religious contexts, in this case, we use it to refer to the radicalisation of the religious and political views of Muslims. Radicalisation is an important consideration for young Muslims living in Western countries in light of the fact that religion plays an important role in their self-identity (Abbas, 2005).

Many frameworks have been used to describe radicalisation. Radicalisation has been defined by scholars as a process that moves along a continuum from pre-radicalisation through stages of self-identification, indoctrination and, finally, jihadisation (Silber and Bhatt, 2007). Similarly, Borum (2003) described a pathway that allows for the development of a justification for terrorism. Moghaddham's (2006) terrorism 'staircase' includes six stages, or 'floors', at which specific factors influence an individual in terms of their journey towards radicalisation. Wiktorowicz (2005) outlined a course of radicalisation based on a case study of the Islamist Al-Muhajiroun movement in the UK. His trajectory includes four linear processes, namely, cognitive opening, religious seeking, frame alignment and socialisation. Cognitive opening can be correlated with a pre-radicalisation stage in which an individual makes the first of many decisions leading to radicalisation (King and Taylor, 2011). The process of cognitive opening is often the result of personal crisis due to an issue such as discrimination or the end results of discrimination such as job loss or social stigma.

While the meaning of radicalisation has been discussed extensively in the academic community, there is no universally accepted definition of the term. It is important to consider radicalisation from an academic perspective, as well as how it is used in the media and by politicians. To properly assess the concept, it should be considered in regard to mainstream political thought and its co-optation by the media and frequent use in a manner that indicates negative connotations. Highly saturated media coverage of terrorism-related activities has resulted in the use of radicalisation as a buzzword in terrorism-related news items, meaning that it is used in contexts different from those it is intended to describe (for an overview of the causes of the radicalisation of young Muslims, see Francis, 2012).

## Conversations with Muslim youth

Conversations with Pakistani Muslim youth in Scotland were conducted from October to December 2014 to examine these radicalising agents and the factors contributing to their acculturation strategies. The objective of the conversations was to determine how respondents dealt with these agents in the course of their daily lives. Respondents participated voluntarily in the interviews. Due to the nature of the research, no ethical approval was required. As long as research does not formally involve any National Health Service institution or university and is performed on a purely personal or professional basis, there is no need for formal ethical approval (UK Department of Health, 2011). Prior to the conversations, participants were briefed about the objectives of the research and how the collected data would be used. Respondents were selected from both large and small cities to examine the role of geography. Their relationships with religious leaders and imams and participation in masjid activities were part of conversations in an attempt to determine the role that religion plays in their lives and the degree to which it is involved with self-identity. Discussion of school experiences and feelings about current events were helpful in appraising respondents' acculturation strategies.

## Methodology

A qualitative approach was employed and a series of brief exploratory conversations were conducted using a rapid appraisal approach with 13 male and two female respondents. Each conversation lasted a minimum of 90 minutes to allow sufficient time for respondents to share their opinions. Rapid appraisal is a qualitative method that is participative and provides generalisable data through informal conversations or discussions (Chambers, 1994).

All respondents resided in Scotland and were third- or fourth-generation Muslims of Pakistani descent. Nine lived in Glasgow, while the rest lived in other smaller cities, including Edinburgh (3), Dundee (2) and Motherwell (1). The sample was purposively selected to include youth identified by the author during the course of previous work and participation in mosque/masjid activities. While some respondents were in key leadership positions, with frequent interaction with imams, committee members at masjids and elders in the community, at least five respondents had social or health-related problems – two had been treated for minor drug abuse and three had intergenerational problems – which involved borderline conflict resulting in isolation and depression. During his work in the communities, the author encountered mainly male subjects, thus accounting for the gender bias in the sample.

Informal conversations using prompts (as opposed to semi-structured questions) were conducted. Respondents were asked to respond to a set of eight open-ended prompts about the issues they face, with no time limit or additional prompts given. Prompts were centred on the perceptions and attitudes of respondents regarding Islamic learning institutions and imams, particularly the teaching methodology and attitudes they encountered during lessons, experiences at school and their understanding of global current events. The prompts were designed to elicit responses on daily life and issues encountered by respondents and included the deliberately chosen terms 'integration' and 'radicalisation' in an attempt to provoke responses closely corresponding to the themes of acculturation and radicalisation. Responses were transcribed and respondents were asked to approve the notes taken.

Conversation topics included:

- Attitudes towards the environment within masjids. As religion is a key aspect of the lives of many young Muslims, attitudes towards masjids and the programmes they offer for youth were explored. The direct link of radicalisation to the attitudes and beliefs of imams makes this topic particularly salient. This prompt was considered essential to elicit respondents' views on acculturation, integration and radicalisation as community places of worship are generally regarded as safe and neutral.
- Admittance of women to masjids. This topic is of particular relevance because religious services (and, to a lesser extent, other programmes) often do not include women, generally due to a lack of facilities. This excludes young

women from one of the main components comprising their identity, potentially making them exceptionally vulnerable in terms of radicalisation (Wiktorowicz, 2005). For a review of female involvement in extremist activities and terrorism, including motivation and recruitment and environmental determinants, see Jacques and Taylor (2010).

- Attitudes on current affairs and the response of imams and elders. This prompt was included to establish if respondents are discussing current events with friends who are part of the majority society and to determine attitudes about specific current events.
- Experiences at school. Discussion about daily experiences was included to yield insight into the practical application of acculturation strategies and the issues encountered by Muslim youth as they interact with peers in the host society. Responses to this prompt are important in determining the level of acculturation and the degree to which respondents are comfortable interacting in the larger society.

## Responses

A summary of respondents' responses, categorised by the main themes, is provided here.

### Masjids

Respondents were asked to talk about their experience of masjids and responses included (often critical) comments about the management committees that run the masjids, imams, religious services and programmes for youth.

### Management committees

Management committees wield considerable power as they conduct fundraising and thus control much of a masjid's finances. To a large extent, imams are perceived as being "under the control of the committees" as they are the paymasters, and there is a perception of "hidden conflict".

### Imams

Views expressed regarding older imams were generally negative and revealed concerns about communication (sometimes due to poor English-language abilities on the part of imams) and a clear lack of bridging between the youth and the older religious leaders. Responses to this prompt are important because they reveal respondents' attitudes about their religious leaders, which, as discussed previously, is an important component of their identity in many cases. Responses included the following:

- The older imams, mostly from their respective countries of origin, do not speak the English language properly and are sometimes "incomprehensible".
- "If we do not understand them and ask questions, we are treated as 'scum' and we think some of them border on lunacy because their understanding of cultural attitudes is so negative."
- "They do not know how to relate to us or how to mix with us. They are not really interested in our problems at school or at home."
- Elders who assist imams "often make us feel as if we are not wanted there".
- "We are told Islam is tolerant and peaceful and we must respect our teachers and the elders, but most of them do not reciprocate."

Imams who spoke English and were born in the UK were perceived as more accessible but were perceived as "officious", which is a justifiable view since many are busy with activities outside the masjids and a number work part-time to supplement their income. There was an impression that "they don't pay them enough to pay attention to their work".

### Khutbahs (Friday sermons)

Communication issues and imams' inability to relate to youth were further reinforced by respondents' views of khutbahs, or Friday sermons:

- "Most of the time is spent on damnation, hell and fire. When the imam is in a good mood, he tells about paradise and what we are going to get in it."
- "Why don't they talk about the problems of young people, the community at large and how they can help? How can we be made more welcome into the House of Allah?"
- "Why don't they speak about the problems Muslims are encountering in our area and the world, as well as how we can help?"

Some respondents stated that they wanted information or wanted to ask an imam a question about Islamic rules and rights as they affect them or the community but felt too intimidated to do so. These responses further reveal the gap between the youth and religious leaders. On the other hand, two respondents in Glasgow were complimentary about their masjid and stated that there were many activities for young children, older children, women and the elderly. Furthermore, there were meetings with committee members who were individually approachable and a number of designated older persons with whom they felt they could relate.

### Admittance of women to masjids

Five of the respondents expressed concerns that no women were allowed in the masjids and there were no adequate facilities for them. The two female respondents were particularly critical, commenting that they felt that they should have a place where they could go and read their prayers with like-minded females in a safe environment. They wondered what was wrong with this idea – "it would make the best use of facilities".

## Current affairs

When the subject of current global problems was raised, specifically atrocities committed by extremists, all respondents stated that they were opposed to the torture or beheadings that extremist groups have inflicted on others (referring particularly to ISIS or other extremist groups). Ten respondents expressed concern about the perception of Muslims as a result of these acts and were unhappy about the term 'jihadists'. One asked what they should do when the "whole Western world is against us as Muslims – tell us how must we protect ourselves from their views about us?"

There was evident distress about recent images and stories regarding supposed jihad activities. A majority of the youth talked about media bias regarding Muslims:

- "We see those awful images, and it makes us feel sad and shameful."
- "They only write or speak about extremists ... they never mention what the goras [white people] have done to our people in the past, especially the historical aspects of the Western countries' terror on a global scale."

There were references to Israel and its blockade and the destruction of the homes of the people of Gaza, as well as concerns about Muslims killing one another. All of the respondents expressed that they felt that it was not right to kill or hurt their "oppressors", but one respondent's response was representative of the opinions expressed by a few others: "What can we do when none of our so-called leaders are prepared to speak out or defend the defenceless people?" Some respondents referred to older imams and a number of first- and second-generation immigrant parents and elders whom they felt did not understand how badly Muslims were being treated.

The respondents were very critical of current political events. One stated:

> "Islamic dictators are using the wealth of the people for their own gains! Even in the Muslim countries, especially the Middle East, they treat Muslims from other countries badly and keep them as slaves. Why don't the Muslim leaders speak about it openly?"

However, despite negative opinions regarding the actions of other Muslims, particularly those in powerful positions, respondents expressed the belief that Islam meant peace: "We have to be kind and get involved in helping people in need." Some respondents expressed concern over the hypocritical way some Muslims, particularly members of their own communities, treated other Muslims.

There was criticism of Muslim leaders at the local and national levels. One respondent stated that "a lot of them who are interviewed cannot speak the language properly and it makes us a laughing stock". They also felt that there was a lack of criticism of Muslim despots and leaders: "The political leaders are afraid of upsetting them." Several respondents made the connection to the arms trade and said that there was a fear within Western leadership that this profitable trade would be decreased if certain leaders were criticised: "Why are they selling arms to countries that oppress their own people?"

Responses clearly indicate that while respondents were largely acculturated in terms of their views on current events, they acutely sense bias in how Muslims as a group are represented and feel that they may not be accurately portrayed in terms of their views and acculturation strategies.

## Acculturation and radicalisation

All respondents stated that they identified with their peers and easily engaged in conversations about shared interests, but many expressed that they felt there was "no respect or understanding" by the wider community, which they attributed to the media and some politicians that they felt had the "wrong impression about us generally". All of the respondents regarded themselves as Scottish and British but were also proud of their heritage, identity and religious beliefs. The respondents generally expressed that they felt aggrieved about radicalisation:

- "No one asks us how we feel about our concerns."
- "We see on the social media, on the news and the print media, the awful scenes of war, bombs, people getting shot and maimed, people living in such terrible circumstances in camps, and it makes us feel helpless. We also have feelings."
- "We are not radicals, but we have views. Why can we not sensibly discuss our feelings about current affairs?"
- "If we disagree on how we see the world and what is happening globally, the authorities will regard us as against them, especially with all the wars and insecurity around the world."

## Experiences at school

Statements made regarding school experiences clearly indicated that discrimination had been experienced by a majority of respondents. This is an important issue because this type of discrimination can be considered as the personal crisis that Wiktorowicz (2005) referenced as the initial step on the radicalisation trajectory. Despite experiences of bullying and discrimination, on the whole, respondents indicated that they were satisfied with their school experiences and had a positive experience. However, some of the more negative statements are included here as these are the ones that indicate problems areas. Views expressed include:

- "Nowadays, they treat us differently and call us names and tell us we are terrorists! We get sort of bullied, and it makes us angry and resentful. We feel the atmosphere has changed … the teachers keep quiet or ignore us."
- "We are subject to awful jeering and comments."
- "They tell us we have to be like them with their values, British values. Why should we be like them? We do not drink, go to wild parties, have girlfriends, go out in gangs and be rude to people. They have no respect for our beliefs."

### Experiences with social and community workers

Support available from professional staff, especially social workers, was also discussed. Some respondents mentioned verbal abuse from imams, elders and some of the second-generation parents, which could be minimised if there were identified professionals such as social or community workers who could act as advocates for youth experiencing social problems in times of difficulty. One respondent mentioned: "If only there were professional social workers or community people with experience who can understand our frustration and lack of politeness and help us to overcome some of our issues and socially related problems."

## Implications for practice

The suggestions we provide for practical action in the future are guided by the preventive approach found in public health in which antecedents to future illness or risk behaviours are the targets of intervention. Brownlee's (1978) work on the role of culture in community care is an apt model for the situation. She studied the epidemiological implications of culture on health and posited that culture is the most relevant social determinant of community health, including its social aspects. As behavioural determinants of health and social problems are often part of a causal chain or network, networks should be investigated as a whole as action at this level is often effective in controlling the causal conditions and hence preventing disease (in this case, radicalisation stemming from potential radicalising factors) (Kark, 1974). Previous work has suggested that preventive measures should be implemented to address the 'pre-radicalisation' phase, which is the period when individuals begin to develop sympathies for extremist ideas or terrorist movements without becoming directly involved (Bhui et al, 2014). The following suggestions are focused on the use of social services in immigrant communities, addressing the masjid environment, including training for imams and the diversification of management committees, and ensuring support for multiculturalism in schools.

A particular concern when dealing with immigrant groups is that the government-sponsored social services that are available in developed countries are largely non-existent or poorly developed in emerging countries or economies. In the country of origin for many Muslims, the use of social services is not a priority because extended families act as a social support network. Immigrants from developing countries may find the activities of social workers, and, indeed, those of public health nurses, unfamiliar and threatening. Hence, the use of social services is considered a last resort (Chambers and Ganesan, 2005). Effective partnership between the National Health Service and local authorities providing social care is a prerequisite for achieving good outcomes. Since 2002, the focus in Scotland has been on achieving better outcomes through partnerships and redesigning and developing integrated clinical and care pathways that consider both health and social care.

Many of the youth expressed that they felt deterred by and aggrieved at the harsh discipline they receive from imams practising within their communities. As the conversations revealed, imams, especially those who are older or from outside the UK, often do not understand the psychology of teaching or the importance of education. As previously mentioned, religion (and hence religious leaders) plays an important role in the lives of young Muslims, so appropriate training is an effective intervention within the network of these young people. The development of specialised courses on teaching and educational psychology during training may be one way to address this issue. Increasing fluency in English and encouraging exposure to different cultures are additional suggestions.

Inclusion of a more diverse cross-section of communities on management committees, including activists and social workers interacting with youth and the elderly, would create more diversity of opinion and less autocracy and would also place more focus on community outreach at the grass-roots level. One of the most striking outcomes of the conversations was the adoption of an integration strategy by all respondents. Most respondents clearly expressed that they feel affinity with society at large and popular culture (markers of their Scottishness included their accent, consuming Scottish products such as the non-alcoholic drink Irn-Bru and appreciating football and the natural environment); however, at the same time, they also have a desire to uphold their religious beliefs. In schools where teachers come from different cultures and religion receives minimal attention, there may not be an understanding of students for whom religion forms an integral part of their self-identity. Teachers and social workers should have some knowledge of the religious groups present in their community and how they function. Again, there is a need for multidisciplinary learning and teaching. Social workers should liaise and develop integrated educational programmes with community organisations, including representatives from masjids, in order to support multicultural societies.

The UK government has taken a preventive approach to extremism, which is defined as 'vocal or active opposition to fundamental British values, including democracy, the rule of law, individual liberty and mutual respect and tolerance of different faiths and beliefs' (Her Majesty's Government, 2011; UK Prime Minister's Office, 2013). Many have argued that this approach comes at the expense of maintaining a common national identity, stemming from the belief that being Muslim and British are mutually exclusive. The government has come under intense scrutiny for what some call a failure to implement policies guided by a comprehensive understanding of radicalisation (Ansar, 2014) and the role that acculturation plays in the process. Some researchers have made the argument that this strategy, by treating all Muslims as at risk of becoming radicalised and creating 'suspect' communities, actually hinders multicultural integration (Githens-Mazer, 2011; Hickman et al, 2011; Awan, 2012).

## Conclusion

This chapter explored the ways in which we, as practitioners, can incorporate differing perspectives and cultures in the practice of transformative social work. The rapid assessment approach used for conducting the conversations is helpful in practitioner research for acquiring a snapshot of a particular situation. Advantages of this type of research include a research agenda driven by direct knowledge of the context and users of services, as well as practical and immediate results that can be used directly to improve practice and impact policies. This methodology could be expanded in the future to include a cross-sectional group of professionals, community representatives and other categories of youth. Further practitioner research could explore the identified radicalising agents for Muslims from different countries or different groups based on factors such as immigration status (first-versus second-generation) and geographical location (urban versus suburban setting). Further investigation would be useful in identifying the requirements for capacity building within the Muslim youth community and assisting in the development and delivery of culturally appropriate support services, especially in shaping integrated social care, and community facilities based within their masjids.

### References

Abbas, T. (2005) *Muslim Britain: Communities under pressure*, London: Zed Books Ltd.

Ansar, M. (2014) 'Self-interest, sycophancy and strategic failure – how Britain lost the war on Muslim radicalisation', *Huffington Post*, 25 August.

Awan, I. (2012) '"I am a Muslim not an extremist": how the prevent strategy has constructed a "suspect" community', *Politics & Policy*, 40(6): 1158–85.

Berry, J.W. (1990) 'Psychology of acculturation', in R.W. Brislin (ed) *Applied cross-cultural psychology*, Newbury Park, CA: Sage, pp 232–53.

Berry, J.W. (1997) 'Immigration, acculturation and adaptation', *Applied Psychology*, 46: 5–68.

Berry J.W. (2005) 'Acculturation: Living successfully in two cultures', *International Journal of Intercultural Relations*, 29: 697–712.

Bhui, K., Warfa, N. and Jones, E. (2014) 'Is violent radicalisation associated with poverty, migration, poor self-reported health and common mental disorders?', *PLoS ONE*, 9(3).

Borum, R. (2003) 'Understanding the terrorist mindset', *FBI Law Enforcement Bulletin*, pp 7–10.

Brownlee, A.T. (1978) *Community, culture, and care: a cross-cultural guide for health workers*, St. Louis, MO: The C.V. Mosby Company.

Chambers, N. and Ganesan, S. (2005) 'Refugees in Canada', in N. Waxler-Morrison (ed) *Cross-cultural caring: a handbook for health professionals*, Vancouver: UBC Press, pp 289–322.

Chambers, R. (1994) 'Participatory Rural Appraisal (PRA): analysis of experience', *World Development*, 22(9): 1253–68.

Francis, M. (2012) 'What causes radicalisation? Main lines of consensus in recent research'. Available at: http://www.radicalisationresearch.org/ (accessed 28 August 2015).

Githens-Mazer, J. (2011) 'Club Britain: access denied', *Al Jazeera*, 12 September.

Her Majesty's Government (2011) *Prevent strategy*, London: The Stationery Office.

Hickman, M., Thomas, L., Silvestri, S. and Nickels, H. (2011) *Suspect communities: counter-terrorism policy, the press and the impact on Irish and Muslim communities in Britain*, London: City University London.

Hutnick, N. (1985) 'Aspects of identity in multi-ethnic society', *New Community*, 12(1): 298–309.

Jacobson, J. (1997) 'Religion and ethnicity: dual and alternative sources of identity among young British Pakistanis', *Ethnic and Racial Studies*, 20(2): 238–56.

Jacques, K. and Taylor, P. (2010) 'Female terrorism: a review', *Terrorism and Political Violence*, 21(3): 499–515.

Jones T. (1993) *Britain's ethnic minorities: An analysis of the labour force survey*, London: Policy Studies Institute.

Kark, S. (1974) *Epidemiology and community medicine*, New York, NY: Appleton-Century-Crofts.

King, M. and Taylor, D. (2011) 'The radicalization of homegrown jihadists: a review of theoretical models and social psychological evidence', *Terrorism and Political Violence*, 23(4): 602–22.

Knott, K. and Khokher, S. (1993) 'Religious and ethnic identity among young Muslim women in Bradford', *Journal of Ethnic and Migration Studies*, 19(4): 593–610.

Modood, T. (2004) 'The place of Muslims in British secular multiculturalism', in N. Ghanea (ed) *The challenge of religious discrimination at the dawn of the new millennium*, Netherlands: Springer, pp 223–43.

Modood, T. (2005) *Multicultural politics: racism, ethnicity, and Muslims in Britain*, Minneapolis, MN: University of Minnesota Press.

Modood, T., Berthoud, R., Lakey, J., Nazroo, J., Smith, P., Beishon, S. and Virdee, S. (1997) *Fourth national survey of ethnic minorities in Britain: Diversity and disadvantage*, London: Policy Studies Institute.

Moghaddam, F.M. (2006) From the Terrorists' point of view: What they experience and why they come to destroy. Westport: Praeger Security International .

Parekh, B. (2000) *The future of multiethnic Britain*, London: Profile Books.

Phinney, J. (1990) 'Ethnic identity in adolescents and adults: review of research', *Psychological Bulletin*, 108: 499–514.

Phinney, J. (2003) 'Ethnic identity and acculturation', in K. Chun, P. Organista and Marin, G. (eds) *Acculturation: Advances in theory, measurement and applied research*, Washington, DC: American Psychological Association, pp 63–81.

Robinson, L. (2008) 'Cultural identity and acculturation preferences among South Asian adolescents in Britain: an exploratory study', *Children and Society*, DOI: 10.1111/j.1099-0860.2008.00179.x

Saeed, A., Blain, N. and Forbes, D. (1999) 'New ethnic and national questions in Scotland: post-British identities among Glasgow Pakistani teenagers', *Ethnic and Racial Studies*, 22(5): 821–44.

Silber, M. and Bhatt, A. (2007) *Radicalization in the West: the homegrown threat*, New York City, NY: New York City Police Department.

Statistics UK (2012) *Religion in England and Wales 2011*, London: United Kingdom Office of National Statistics.

Statistics UK (2013) *What does the Census tell us about religion in 2011?*, London: United Kingdom Office for National Statistics.

UK Department of Health (2011) *Governance arrangements for research ethics committees*, www.dh.gov.uk.

UK Office of National Statistics (2010) 'Data resources: people and society', https://www.ons.gov.uk/.

UK Office of National Statistics (2011) 'People and places data tables for 2011 Census', https://www.ons.gov.uk/census/2011 census.

UK Prime Minister's Office (2013) *Tackling extremism in the UK: report from the Prime Minister's task force in tackling radicalisation and extremism*, London: UK Government.

Ward, C. and Stuart, J. (2009) 'The many faces of identity: Ethnic and religious identities as buffers of discrimination and predictors of psychological well-being in Muslim youth in New Zealand', Eight Biennial Conference of the Asian Association of Social Psychology, December, Delhi, India.

Wiktorowicz, Q. (2005) *Radical Islam rising: Muslim extremism in the West*, Oxford: Rowan & Littlefield.

# SIX

# Interpreting: one size fits all? English language as an essential component of social work

*Siân E. Lucas*

## Introduction

This chapter focuses on spoken language interpreting in social work and the role of the English language. First, national and global language practices are considered, with particular focus on England. Throughout the chapter, languages other than English are referred to as 'minority languages', regardless of the prevalence of the language and the number of speakers. In the second section, language practices and their relevance for social work are considered; this is followed by a discussion about the phenomenon of interpreting and its relevance to social work. In the third section, a case study is presented to illustrate a social worker's experience of using interpreting provision in his work with service users who have limited English-language proficiency (referred to as 'LEP service users'). The case study is informed by research that involved in-depth interviews with child and family social workers in England (Lucas, 2014). The purpose of the research was to gain an understanding of social workers' experiences of supporting LEP service users with the use of spoken language interpreters (referred to as 'interpreters' throughout the chapter). In the fourth section, the case study is discussed and the challenges that the social workers faced when working with LEP service users are identified, this includes the ramifications of an absent interpreter and the latent power of the English language. To conclude, implications and opportunities for interpreting provision for LEP services users in social work practice and policy are considered. Through uncovering a disjuncture between rhetoric and practice, the chapter highlights language and language rights as fundamental features of social work.

## Language practices

Language is a central aspect of humanity; it is a marker of belonging and acts as a vehicle for communication (Labov, 1977; Lippi-Green, 1997; Calvet, 1998; Pavlenko and Blackledge, 2004). Contact between people who speak different languages has occurred throughout the course of history, through expeditions, industrial and economic trading, international travel, communication technologies, and migration (Crystal, 2003; Wei, 2007). There are two broad trends in language practices across the globe. The first is the diversification of the linguistic landscape, as evidenced by the multiple languages that are used and a revival of spoken minority languages. The second trend is the decline of spoken minority languages across the globe and, concurrently, an increase in the number of people who speak global languages such as English (Crystal, 2012). The latter trend relates to the phenomenon of 'language deaths': the process in which languages develop, alter, merge and, in some cases, become extinct (Crystal, 2003). 'Language deaths' occur when the prestige or legitimacy of a particular language is contested, often as a result of the domination of a global or 'official' language (Calvet, 1998; Trudgill, 2000; Schmid, 2001; Mohanty, 2010; Jaspers, 2011; Crystal, 2012). Later in the chapter, the relevance of the dominance of the English language in relation to the social work profession is considered.

From a statistical point of view, English is understood as the dominant language of the UK since it is spoken by the majority of residents. While the exact number of spoken languages in England is unknown, there is evidence to suggest that England has been and continues to be a nation of linguistic diversity. It is estimated that over 200 languages are spoken in Manchester alone (Long, 2013), and that over 300 language varieties[1] are spoken among schoolchildren in England (Baker and Eversley, 2000; CILT, 2005; Eversley et al, 2010). There are a number of autochthonous minority languages spoken in England, such as Welsh, Cornish and Scots Gaelic, in addition to more recent minority languages. Up until the 2004 enlargement of the European Union, the main minority languages and varieties used in England were those of the Indian subcontinent: Panjabi, Urdu, Bengali, Guajarati and Hindi. Since 2004, there has been an increase in Eastern European languages, and in the 2011 Census, Polish was found to be the most prevalent minority language, followed by Punjabi and Urdu (ONS, 2012).

The linguistically diverse profile of England is comprised not only of different languages, but also of different accents and language proficiencies. In 2011, the Census for England and Wales asked for the first time how well residents could speak English when it was not their main language. The data show that a small proportion of residents had limited English-language proficiency, English was the main language for 92% of the population[2] and the remaining 8% had a different main language. Of this 8% who had a different main language, 17% (726,000) could speak 'limited English' and the remaining 3% (138,000) 'could not speak English at all'. While these statistics offer a useful dimension to the linguistic profile of England and Wales, for the purposes of this chapter, it is important to note that a person's capacity to speak English does not necessarily correspond with their need for interpreting provision. Contact between persons who speak different languages may occur with and without interpreting provision. In addition, a minority-language speaker may be bilingual and able to speak English, and therefore may not require interpreting provision.

This section has presented two main points in relation to the linguistic profile of England: first, a variety of languages are spoken on a daily basis; and, second, a relatively small number of the population speak no or limited English language. The following section considers language practices and their relevance for social work.

## Language practices and social work

Communication occurs in multiple ways: in person, with the use of technologies and through the mediums of written, spoken and signed language varieties. Communication is a significant feature of social work education, theory, legislation, policy and practice (Lishman, 2009; Koprowska, 2010; Woodcock Ross, 2011) and social workers employ a range of communicative forms in their work with individuals, families and groups as they generate, gain and transfer information, knowledge, facts and feelings. Social workers often work in contexts in which they need to tread carefully and to explain sensitive and complex matters, which require detailed and lengthy discussion. In such cases, clear and accurate communication is paramount (Woodcock Ross, 2011). Pugh (2004) argues that linguistically sensitive practice is informed by an awareness of the social, psychological, political and sociological significance of language, particularly as different languages sustain and embody different social arrangements (see, eg, Hale, 2001; Temple, 2010). Hence, communication is more than the exchange of a message between speakers.

The social work profession operates in relation to the surrounding social and geographic space, including the changing and emerging linguistic landscape. Given the multiple languages that are used in England, social workers may work with individuals, families and groups who possess varying degrees of English language, and, in some cases, interpreters may be used to facilitate communication. Data concerning the number of recipients of social work services who require interpreting provision are unknown and not routinely collected by local authorities. These practices can be located within the politicised terrain, in which concerns prevail about social cohesion and the inclusion and exclusion associated with a person's knowledge and use of the English language. While it can be assumed that the majority of social work services in England are provided in English, there are a number of services that operate in particular minority languages. There are no data to determine the number of social work services that operate in languages other than English. Similarly, there are no data to determine the number of bilingual social workers who communicate in minority languages or who provide interpreting support, although reference is made to bilingual social workers by multiple authors (Pugh, 1996; Harrison, 2007; Dominelli, 2010; Sawrikar, 2013a). In recognition of this dearth of data, Pugh (1996) argues that issues about language difference are subsumed under issues of 'race', ethnicity and cultural difference. With this in mind, there is need to examine social workers' experiences and viewpoints about working with interpreters during their involvement with LEP service users. Before presenting a case study to illuminate a social worker's experience of working with interpreters, the practice theme of interpreting is discussed, with consideration of its relevance to social work practice and the political terrain in which these practices are embedded.

## Interpreting

Interpreting can take place in person, online, on the phone or via interpreting technologies (Alexander et al, 2004), and in-person interpreting can be carried out by both trained and untrained interpreters (Pérez-González and Susam-Sarajeva, 2012). There are debates about whether interpreters adopt an 'invisible' or 'active' presence when they interpret. Traditional understandings of interpreting allude to the 'invisibility' of the interpreter, in which the presence of the interpreter is minimised (Wadensjö, 1998; Mason, 1999; Miguélez, 2001). There is however, a literature that has alluded to the 'active presence' of interpreters (Meyer, 2001; Wadensjö, 2001; Baraldi and Gavioli, 2012). Meyer has shown how untrained interpreters in medical settings make strategic renditions or additions in which they alter interlocutors' talk and move away from the source message. Musser-Granski and Carrillo (1997) argue that interpreters have the tendency to take over the therapeutic element of the session and dialogue unilaterally with the client. Wadensjö (2001) has highlighted the active presence of trained interpreters in therapeutic encounters. Wadensjö (1998) argues that interpreters perform 'coordinating functions' as they direct and instruct speakers to pause, continue and to clarify meaning. Later in the chapter, the significance of interpreters' active or invisible presence in relation to social work is considered.

### Interpreting and social work practice

There are direct and indirect references to minority-language speakers in legislation and policy. The Equality Act 2010, in addition to national guidance ('London child protection procedures' [HMSO, 2011] and 'Working together to safeguard children' [HM Government, 2010]), stipulates that service providers must offer services in a person's preferred language. The Children Act 1989 states that due attention should be paid to the language of children and families (section 22(5)(c) and section 1(3)).

There have been a number of attempts to promote the accessibility and delivery of social work services for minority-language speakers, including: the use of outsourced interpreting provision; the appointment of bilingual employees; and initiatives for employees to learn specific minority languages spoken in the communities that they work in. Interpreters provided by outsourced translation and interpreting services may or may not be trained interpreters and there is no legal duty for social work organisations to employ trained and registered interpreters. However, trained and registered interpreters must be used in the courts of law (see Tipton, 2014b).

The discrepancy between rights and needs is a perennial concern of the social work profession and this also applies to matters of interpreting and minority-language speakers. A person's use of interpreting provision does not exclusively correlate with their linguistic proficiency, and there may also be an assumption that a LEP person will choose to use interpreting provision. A person's use of interpreting provision can be associated with the political, emotional and socio-psychological dimensions of language, particularly in encounters when people attempt to speak in a language other than their main language (Murray and Wynne, 2001; Pugh, 2004; Sue, 2006; Temple, 2006; Tribe and Keefe, 2009; Maiter and Stalker, 2010). Research by Villaneuva and Buriel (2010) reported that adults who spoke English as an additional language were reluctant to communicate in English given their self-perceived 'heavy English accent'. Tse (2001) argues that a person's capacity to speak in a language other than their main language is related to multiple factors, including the person's self-perceived linguistic proficiency, their year of entry to the country and their immigration status. The specific context and setting of the encounter has been found to impact upon people's confidence to speak the majority language and their subsequent use of interpreting provision. For example, Lucas (2014) suggests that a LEP person may require interpreting provision in 'high-context' interaction, where communication and the accuracy of communication is paramount (see Robinson, 2004), such as social work, but may not require an interpreter during a 'low context' interaction at the local shops, which can be driven by minimal, outcome-informed interaction.

Lack of consideration about linguistic need is thought to result in stereotypes and assumptions, for example, the assumptions that interpreting provision deters people from learning English and that minority-language speakers could communicate in English if they tried (Department for Communities and Local Government, 2012), these points will be explored in the following section.

The difficulties that social workers experience during involvement with LEP service users is often related to interpreting provision. Despite legal statute concerning the rights of minority-language speakers, few public bodies have detailed language policies and strategies for implementation, and Rennie (1998) argues that minority-language speakers may not receive the same quality of service as English speakers because they are unaware of their right to request interpreting provision. There appears to be a lacuna between legislation, which promotes the importance of communicating with service users in their preferred language, and the realisation of this in practice. As Farr (2011: 1168) argues: '[while a] multicultural ideology is promoted explicitly in public policy, a multilingual ideology is not'. Writing after the Welsh Language Act 1993, and before the Welsh Language (Wales) Measure 2011[3] and Social Services and Well-being (Wales) Act 2014,[4] Drakeford and Morris (1998) considered the 'minoritised' status of the Welsh language. They highlight the challenges of making genuinely free language choices, despite public bodies' duty to ensure that services are equally available in Welsh and English. Drakeford and Morris argue that the provision of interpreting services in Wales contradicts traditional demand-led public administration; they argue that the view that 'they can have it if they ask for it' or that interpreting services are 'available on request' (Drakeford and Morris, 1998: 106) is not sufficient and adds to service users' burden. There is, therefore, concern about the disjuncture between principle and practice, namely, how legislation and policy that pronounce linguistically sensitive services are exercised in practice.

Further concerns about interpreting provision have related to the unavailability of interpreters (Rennie, 1998; Cohen et al, 1999; Masocha, 2013), intra-professional conflict between interpreters and interlocutors (Edwards et al, 2006; Kriz and Skivenes, 2010; Tipton, 2014a), and practitioners' and service users' concern about interpreters' accuracy, bias and confidentiality in interpreting encounters (Chand, 2005; Maiter and Stalker, 2010; Sawrikar, 2013a, 2013b; Tipton, 2014b).

## Political discourse

Despite the fact that relatively small numbers of the population have limited English-language proficiency (ONS, 2012), there is pervasive media discourse that stigmatises the use of interpreting provision for LEP persons (Alexander et al, 2004; Spolsky, 2012; Tipton, 2012). The preoccupation with social cohesion and integration has had an impact on policy and practice. Interpreting provision is considered to be a burden on the economic climate as it discourages migrants from learning English and presents a threat to an 'imagined' monolingual country (Blackledge, 2002). The perceived burden of interpreting provision was most notably evident in the document '50 ways to save: examples of sensible savings in local governments' (Department for Communities and Local Government, 2012), and subsequent commentary from the then commissioning MP and Secretary of State for Communities and Local Government, Eric Pickles. A direct reference to translation is found within the document, and interpreting provision is depicted as an unnecessary burden and subsequently pinpointed as a way for councils to reduce spending. 'Stop translating documents into foreign languages: Only publish documents in English. Translation undermines community cohesion by encourage [sic] segregation' (Department for Communities and Local Government, 2012: s 35).

The instruction to stop the translation of documents can be associated with an assimilation outlook, in which minority-language speakers are pressured to conform and assimilate by gaining acquisition of the English language, and interpreting provision is conceptualised as an unnecessary burden and deterrent for people to learn English. These arguments conjure up an often cited, but poorly evidenced, claim that immigrant communities 'hold on' to their minority language at the expense of learning English (Tse, 2001). Following this thread, Pickles implies that minority-language speakers are assumed to be in some way responsible for segregation. This point is indicative of linguistic discrimination, based upon the implicit resentment that is projected towards people who require interpreting provision and the prestige placed on the English language. A consequence of this instruction is that minority-language speakers may not receive interpreting provision due to fiscal priorities and political rhetoric that determines who is and is not deemed eligible for services. These policies reproduce means of exclusion and marginalisation as minority-language speakers are identified as 'Other' (Amin, 2010; Harries, 2014) or the 'incomprehensible Other' (Subtirelu, 2015). As Solomos (2003) argues, the ubiquity of terms such as 'integration', 'inclusion' and 'exclusion', which are commonplace in policy and media outlets, prevents any need for a discussion of their meaning; 'Hence in the government's view it is "obviously" desirable and in "everybody's" interest that everyone speaks English' (Solomos, 2003: 254).

In this section, the practice of interpreting provision was introduced, this included legislation that relates to interpreting practice and some of the practical, emotional and political difficulties that characterise the phenomenon of interpreting and the people who use interpreting provision. In the following section, the role of the English language is considered in relation to social work.

## The English language: an essential component of social work?

The English language garners political and cultural dominance, in addition to statistical dominance, given the increasing number of people who speak English. The benefits associated with the acquisition of English-language proficiency have been identified by government policymakers, not only as a way to reduce the costs of interpreting provision, but also a remedy to facilitate positive relationships between different communities and to enable participation in society. In this regard, the English language is regarded as a 'right of passage' to the receiving society (Wiley and Lukes, 1996: 520), and as a way to facilitate a person's integration into British society (Aspinall and Hashem, 2011). This process has been referred to as the 'centre–periphery metaphor', based upon an asymmetrical 'us versus them' discourse, looking upon 'them' (non-native speakers) as a problem that 'we' (native speakers) have to find a solution for' (Weber and Horner, 2012: 153).

Command of the English language is associated with British identity. For example, the 31st British Social Attitudes survey reported that 95% of those surveyed thought that being able to speak English is important to being 'truly British' (Park et al, 2014). Gilroy (1987, 2004) and Blackledge (2004) point to the tacit racial connotations in the symbols of perceived 'Britishness'. Ideas about the 'naturalness' of English are infiltrated by an ethnocentric outlook towards other languages in which English is 'the normal unmarked standard against which other languages are contrasted, usually less favourably' (Pugh, 2004: 49). Not speaking the English language is viewed as problematic and confused as a matter of inferiority and unintelligence (Scheffer, 2011). Subtirelu (2013) and Gumperz (1982) have shown how monolinguals from the dominant language group construe difficulties in communication with LEP persons or minority speakers as indicative of their social and intellectual inadequacy and Robinson (1995) states that viewing alternative varieties of English as deficient highlights the stigma attached to non-standard dialects. In a similar vein, Lippi-Green (2012: 335) argues that 'discrimination on the basis of language has not to do with the language itself, but with the social circumstances and identity attached to that language'.

In this section, outlooks towards minority languages have been explored in relation to the status and dominance of the English language. It has been suggested that ideas about language membership are closely associated with ideas about belonging, and such ideas may be embedded at a political level and infiltrated at a social level. The English language can therefore be placed at the top of a hierarchical scale and is privileged and legitimised as the official language of England. Concurrently, deficit assumptions about linguistic difference lead to the minoritisation of minority-language speakers (Gunaratnam, 2003), this may result in group stereotyping and outlooks that delegitimise and discourage the use of interpreting provision.

In the following section, a case study is presented to illuminate a social worker's experience of working with interpreters in his involvement with LEP service users. The case study is informed by an in-depth interview with one social worker that took place as part of doctoral research focused on interpreting in social work practice and child language brokering (Lucas, 2014). All identifying details have been changed to protect the participant's confidentiality. At the end of the case study, key issues for social work policy and practice are discussed.

## Case study

Adrian is a white British monolingual male who speaks English. He has worked as a social worker for a local authority children's services team for eight years. Multiple languages are spoken in the local authority and interpreting provision is provided by a local translation and interpreting service. All employees within the local authority have been instructed to save money wherever possible: refreshments cannot be offered to visitors, car sharing is advised, printing documents is restricted and appointments with interpreters have been highlighted as a significant expense for the agency. Due to the expense of interpreting provision, social workers must seek approval from management before they use this provision.

Adrian does not particularly enjoy working with interpreters, this is due to three main reasons: first, he has concerns about the time and additional work required when an interpreter is needed, for example, there have been occasions when interpreters have not turned up for prearranged appointments and this has delayed Adrian's intervention; second, he is concerned about the cost of interpreting provision; and, third, he is concerned about the accuracy of interpreters' input and how this affects his and service users' understanding.

Adrian is conscious that interpreting provision is extremely expensive and he tries to save money for the organisation by avoiding or limiting the use of interpreting provision wherever he can. He tries to fit appointments into one-hour sessions (as the interpreting agency charge an hourly rate), or he avoids using an interpreter and gets by with the use of body language and the service users' limited English. On some occasions, he uses family members to interpret. Adrian is suspicious that interpreters may extend his questions or omit his and service users' responses. Adrian recognises that it is difficult to build rapport with service users and to allow conversations to digress. This leads him to believe that interpreters take over his role and, in some cases, may prevent service users from asking questions or challenging decisions. Due to these reasons, Adrian prefers to avoid working with service users who require interpreters. He finds work with English-speaking service users comparatively less complicated and time-consuming.

## Discussion

The points raised in this case study are representative of the views that were shared among the sample of social work participants, each of whom conceptualised interpreting as a difficult area of social work practice. To discuss the case study and the implications it raises for social work practice and policy, the discussion focuses on the three concerns raised: the time that interpreting entails; the cost of interpreting provision; and concern about the accuracy of translated content. The discussion is drawn together by considering the ramifications of an absent interpreter and the role of the English language.

In the case study, there appear to be difficulties both when interpreters are used and when they are not used. The interpreter can therefore be understood as a pragmatic instrument who can alleviate the linguistic gap. However, the interpreter is also positioned as an insipid threat whose actions may generate difficulties, such as expense for the local authority, added time constraints that will impede Adrian's workload and uncertainty about meaning.

Adrian raises concerns about the time that work with interpreters entails, this includes time for logistical tasks, such as arranging provision, time for content to be translated between parties during the interpreting encounter and unanticipated delays if the interpreter does not attend planned appointments or if an interpreter is sent who does not speak the preferred language of the individual or family. Although outsourced interpreting provision is available to Adrian, he attempts to avoid straining resources and, where possible, elects to get by without an interpreter or attempts to reduce costs by restricting appointments to one hour. While it is tenuous to suggest that Adrian's decision not to use an interpreter is unequivocally attributable to his attempts to reduce costs, this example illuminates a felicitous predicament in which fiscal pressures and the retrenchment of the welfare state shape and prevent his use of interpreting provision. This resonates with the idea of 'ambivalent assimilation' (Williams and Graham, 2014), a term used to describe the structures that deploy and/or hinder social workers' attempts to promote social justice. Adrian appears to act as a gatekeeper of interpreting provision and attempts to avoid or restrict the use of interpreting provision to save costs for the local authority. Adrian's autonomy therefore appears to be guided by neoliberal priorities to save resources rather than the individual's or family's need for interpreting provision.

Adrian is concerned about the accuracy of the translated content. This concern is based upon a pessimistic supposition influenced by Adrian's awareness of the possibility that the interpreter may proffer inaccurate or incomplete renditions. This uncertainty is compounded by Adrian's inability to verify the accuracy of the content that is translated, which means that Adrian's speculation remains unsubstantiated. The interpreter's performance is scrutinised by Adrian and this appears to be connected to the devolution of responsibility, and disruption of Adrian's expert disposition as a social worker. Adrian recognises that his role as a social worker is, to some extent, replaced by the interpreter, as he assumes that the interpreter may expand his instructions and curtail opportunities for the service user to ask Adrian questions or to challenge him. This concern is indicative of the idea of the active presence of interpreters (Wadensjö, 1998). The interpreter's presumed autonomy is problematic for Adrian, and highlights that Adrian is absent from the meaning-making process, as Adrian only hears what the interpreter says but not the exact words and the delivery of the service user's content. Moreover, Adrian is unable to recognise the emotional, social and psychodynamic dimensions of language (Pugh, 2004).

The general uncertainty corresponds with Edwards, Alexander and Temple (2006), who highlight the political and conceptual process of trust in interpreter-mediated encounters. Similar findings were reported by Tipton (2014a, 2014b), who found a lack of intra-professional understanding between social workers and interpreters, and problems that related to the transferability of professional values across roles. Tipton (2014b) found that social workers were concerned about interpreters needing to rush off to the next assignment and unsolicited opinions given by interpreters.

### Ramifications of an absent interpreter

The case study indicates that although interpreting provision is available, it remains 'out of reach' for Adrian. Organisational pressures deter him from using the services and, consequently, interpreting provision is demarcated as an extravagance rather than a need. This resonates with research that has reported the difficulties of working with service users who speak limited English language, for example, Kriz and Skivenes (2010) reported a social worker who referred to working with a family who spoke limited English and who used interpreting provision as a 'bloody nightmare'. The litany of concerns presented about work with interpreters influences Adrian's outlook to social work with LEP service users, this illuminates how minority-language speakers become actively minoritised (Gunaratnam, 2003) or positioned as an institutional construct (Drennan and Swartz, 2002).

The non-use of an interpreter to facilitate communicate across linguistic difference neglects legislation and policy (Children Act 1989; 'Working together to safeguard children' [HM Government, 2010]; Equality Act 2010) that asserts the importance of available 'language provision' and a person's 'preferred language'. The importance of interpreters' input in social care was revealed in the Serious

Case Review of Daniel Pelka (DfE, 2013). Daniel was a four-year-old boy of Polish descent who was murdered by his mother and her partner while several agencies were involved with the family. The inquiry reported that the linguistic faculties of the family were unknown and that interpreting provision was used inconsistently among the various public services involved; moreover, interpreting provision was offered to Daniel's care-givers rather than to Daniel himself and there was an assumption that the use of interpreters would be ineffective. The inquiry states that 'an interpreter should have been regularly used to aid communication' (DfE, 2013: 52, s 6.62).

This section has highlighted the importance of interpreters and the uncertainty that work with interpreters includes. These difficulties imply that LEP people are subject to marginalisation, which is exacerbated by resource deficiencies.

### The English language

The English language plays a latent role in the case study. Adrian compares and contrasts work with LEP service users with service users who speak English and do not require an interpreter, and he notes that the use of interpreters adds an extra layer of complexity to intervention with LEP service users which creates concerns about communication, time and costs. This comparison creates and reinforces a dichotomy between English-speaking families and non-English-speaking families. Following this outlook, it can be argued that social workers inadvertently contribute to the superiority and dominance of the English language as the preferred language of social work. This highlights the potential for marginalisation of LEP persons. The following section draws upon the preceding discussion and highlights ways that social work can transform practice with interpreters and LEP service users.

## Transformatory practice

Social workers are expected to work with the changing and diverse profile of service users as they respond to shifts and changes in social structures (Negi et al, 2010). As stated at the start of the chapter, communication between people who speak different languages is not a new phenomenon given continued migration patterns and the linguistically diverse profile of England.

Despite hindrances and movements by political legislation or the state, interaction between people who do not speak a mutual language will continue. As Calvet (1998: 17) asserts, linguistic frontiers do not correspond to state and national frontiers and 'it is the destiny of humanity to be confronted not by one language but by several'. In light of the prevalence of linguistic diversity, the activity of interpreting should not be treated as a peripheral issue as it has relevance to social work in all locations and social work settings. Moreover, as Anthias (2012: 105) states, 'diversity is not just about the other', and, thus, it is important for social workers, whatever their linguistic capacity, to engage with interpreters, to examine their language practices and to find ways to improve services for LEP service users. In addition, it would be useful to ascertain how many social workers are bilingual and speak multiple languages in their practice.

Two broad recommendations can be made for social work practice. First, social workers can be thought of as gatekeepers of interpreting provision since they have the jurisdiction to implement or deny the practice. It is important that social workers are attuned to legislation and policy, welfare entitlements, and entitlements to interpreting provision and ethical responsibilities (Cox and Giesen, 2014; Williams and Graham, 2014). Moreover, interpreting, akin to communication, is more than the exchange of language, and as Hunter, Lepley and Nickels (2010) argue, social work practice must go beyond competencies such as language and knowledge of specific cultures and social work must work towards addressing human rights, justice and power relationships. It is incumbent upon social workers to recognise the importance of communication in the pursuit of social justice and to reject tendencies to associate a LEP person as not entitled to services. Moreover, it is important to explore how language proficiency can differentiate and marginalise people, for example, the negative conceptualisation of work with interpreters is likely to affect outlooks towards the people who require interpreting provision. A corollary of this association is that work with LEP service users takes on an undesirable quality.

Second, social workers need to develop confidence and competence to work with interpreters and to support service users with different linguistic faculties. There needs to be a context in which the quality of the interpreting provision has priority over the costs of provision. Taking this thesis forward, it may be appropriate to draw upon a narrative about the economic value of language, particularly the positive economic contribution of interpreting provision, in order to show how interpreting provision ameliorates future costs and deters and prevents marginalisation and the future use of remedial services. For example, O'Donnell et al (2013) counsels that cuts to interpreting provision will lead to the low uptake of preventive services and entry into the health service at crisis point, with the use of the more permeable parts of public services.

## Conclusion

This chapter is intended to enhance understandings of the key issues that face social workers in their work with interpreters. The findings offer insight into one social worker's subjective reality. It is important to treat the findings in this case study with caution given the incomplete and partial presentation of the participant's experience (Holstein and Gubrium, 1995) and the complex and multifaceted nature of social work. The case study is not representative of all social workers and their experiences of using interpreting provision. Since the research focuses exclusively on social workers' experiences, it is unclear if the identified issues correspond with interpreters' and service users' experiences and viewpoints. It is also important to note that miscommunication and uncertainty is not restricted to social work with LEP persons and that such difficulties are known to occur when people share a mutual language. Nevertheless, the case study is instructive as to an understanding of the practice issues encountered.

Interpreting is necessary to facilitate communication between people who do not share a mutual language; this means that the interpreter plays a crucial role in the social work involvement. However, as this chapter has illuminated, the use of interpreting provision in social work involves a myriad of tensions. There is need for social work to critically engage with interpreting practice and it is important to craft an approach that combines an awareness of and mutual respect for the respective roles of interpreters and social workers in the anticipation of improving partnership working and service delivery. Further inquiry is needed to consider whether the active presence of interpreters is welcomed, in which interpreters offer autonomous additions or cultural insight. Finally, it can be argued that 'one size' of interpreting does not necessarily 'fit'. In order to facilitate transformatory social work practice, there is need to examine language practices, to highlight the relative power of particular language varieties, to bridge language gaps and to promote linguistic diversity.

## Acknowledgements

This research was sponsored by the Economic and Social Research Council. I would like to thank the social workers who participated in this study. My thanks go to the editors of this collection for their helpful comments on an earlier draft of this chapter.

## Notes

[1] 'Variety' refers to the use of language in a particular situation. 'Accent' refers to spoken pronunciation, which tends to signal where a speaker is from. 'Dialect' refers to vocabulary and grammar, which identifies a speaker's regional or social background (see: www.davidcrystal.com).

[2] The population of England and Wales on the day of the Census (27 March 2011) was 56,075,912.

[3] The Welsh Language (Wales) Measure 2011 gave the Welsh language official status in Wales and established the principle that the Welsh language should be on an equal footing to the English language.

[4] The Social Services and Well-being (Wales) Act 2014 will require a range of care and support services to be provided in Welsh from 2016.

# References

Alexander, C., Edwards, R., Temple, B., Kanani, U., Zhuang, L., Miah, M. and Sam, A. (2004) 'Access to services with interpreters: user views', Joseph Rowntree Foundation.

Amin, A. (2010) 'The remainders of race', *Theory, Culture and Society*, 27(1): 1–23.

Anthias, F. (2012) 'Transnational motilities, migration research and intersectionality; towards a translocational frame', *Nordic Journal of Migration Research*, 2(2): 102–10.

Aspinall, P.J. and Hashem, F. (2011) 'Responding to minority ethnic groups' language support needs in Britain', *Equality, Diversity and Inclusion: An International Journal*, 30(2): 45–162.

Baker, P. and Eversley, J. (2000) *Multilingual capital: the languages of London's school children and their relevance to economic, social and educational policies*, London: Battlebridge.

Baraldi, C. and Gavioli, L. (eds) (2012) *Coordinating participation in dialogue interpreting*, Amsterdam: John Benjamins Publishing Company.

Blackledge, A. (2002) 'The discursive construction of national identity in multilingual Britain', *Journal of Language, Identity & Education*, 1(1): 67–87.

Blackledge, A. (2004) 'Constructions of identity in political discourse in multilingual Britain', in A. Pavlenko and A. Blackledge (eds) *Negotiation of identities in multilingual contexts*, Clevedon: Multilingual Matters, pp 68–92.

Calvet, L.J. (1998) *Language wars and linguistic politics*, Oxford: Oxford University Press.

Chand, A. (2005) 'Do you speak English? Language barriers in child protection social work with minority ethnic families', *British Journal of Social Work*, 35(6): 807–21.

CILT (2005) 'Language trends survey'. Available at: www.cilt.org.uk/home/research_and_statistics/language_trends_surveys.aspx

Cohen, S., Moran-Ellis, J. and Smaje, C. (1999) 'Children as informal interpreters in GP consultations: pragmatics and ideology', *Sociology of Health and Illness*, 21(2): 163–86.

Cox, P. and Geisen, T. (2014) 'Migration perspectives in social work research: local, national and international contexts', *British Journal of Social Work*, 44(1): 157–73.

Crystal, D. (ed) (2003) *The Cambridge encyclopedia of the English language* (2nd edn), Cambridge: Cambridge University Press.

Crystal, D. (2012) *English as a global language* (2nd edn), New York, NY: Cambridge University Press.

Department for Communities and Local Government (2012) '50 ways to save: examples of sensible savings in local government', Crown Copyright.

DfE (Department for Education) (2013) 'Coventry Safeguarding Children Board (2013) 'Daniel Pelka – serious case review'. Available at: http://www.coventry.gov.uk/download/downloads/id/17081/daniel_pelka_-_serious_case_review_overview_report.pdf

Dominelli, L. (2010) *Social work in a globalizing world*, Cambridge: Polity.

Drakeford, M. and Morris, S. (1998) 'Social work with linguistic minorities', in C. Williams, H. Soydan and M.R.D. Johnson (eds) *Social work and minorities: European perspectives*, London: Routledge, pp 93–209.

Drennan, G. and Swartz, L. (2002) 'The paradoxical use of interpreting in psychiatry', *Social Science & Medicine*, 54(12): 1853–66.

Edwards, R., Alexander, C. and Temple, B. (2006) 'Interpreting trust: abstract and personal trust for people who need interpreters to access services', *Sociological Research Online*, 11(1). Available at: http://www.socresonline.org.uk/11/1/edwards.html

Eversley, J., Mehmedbegović, D., Sanderson, A., Tinsley, T., Von Ahn, M. and Wiggins, R.D. (2010) *Language capital: mapping the languages of London's schoolchildren*, London: Central Books Ltd.

Farr, M. (2011) 'Urban plurilingualism: language practices, policies, and ideologies', *Journal of Pragmatics*, 43: 1161–72.

Gilroy, P. (1987) *'There ain't no black in the union jack': the cultural politics of race and nation*, London: Hutchinson.

Gilroy, P. (2004) *After empire: melancholia or convivial culture?*, London: Routledge.

Gumperz, J.J. (1982) *Language and social identity*, Cambridge: Cambridge University Press.

Gunaratnam, Y. (2003) *Researching 'race' and ethnicity*, London: Sage.

Hale, S. (2001) 'How are courtroom questions interpreted? An analysis of Spanish interpreters' practices', in I. Mason (ed) *Triadic exchanges: studies in dialogue interpreting*, Manchester: St. Jerome Publishing, pp 21–50.

Harries, B. (2014) 'We need to talk about race', *Sociology*, 48(6): 1107–22.

Harrison, G. (2007) 'Language as a problem, a right or a resource? A study of how bilingual practitioners see language policy being enacted in social work', *Journal of Social Work*, 7(1): 71–92.

HM Government (2010) 'Working together to safeguard children: a guide to inter-agency working to safeguard and promote the welfare of children', Department for Children, Schools and Families. Available at: http://webarchive.nationalarchives.gov.uk/20130401151715/https://www.education.gov.uk/publications/eOrderingDownload/00305-2010Dom-EN-v3.pdf

HMSO (Her Majesty's Stationery Office) (2011) 'London child protection procedures', London Safeguarding Children Board. Available at: www.londonscb.gov.uk/procedures/

Holstein, J.A. and Gubrium, J.F. (1995) *The active interview*, Thousand Oaks, CA: Sage.

Hunter, C.A., Lepley, S. and Nickels, S. (2010) 'New practice frontiers: current and future social work with transmigrants', in N.J. Negi and N. Furman (eds) *Trans-national social work practice*, New York, NY: Columbia University Press, pp 222–42.

Jaspers, J. (2011) 'Talking like a "zerolingual": ambiguous linguistic caricatures at an urban secondary school', *Journal of Pragmatics*, 43(5): 1264–78.

Koprowska, J. (2010) *Communication and interpersonal skills in social work*, London: Sage.

Kriz, K. and Skivenes, M. (2010) 'Lost in translation: how child welfare workers in Norway and England experience language difficulties when working with minority ethnic families', *British Journal of Social Work*, 40(5): 1353–67.

Labov, W. (1977) *Language in the inner city: studies in the black English vernacular*, Oxford: Blackwell.

Lippi-Green, R. (1997) *English with an accent: language, ideology, and discrimination in the United States*, London: Routledge.

Lippi-Green, R. (2012) *English with an accent: language, ideology and discrimination in the United States* (2nd edn), London and New York, NY: Routledge.

Lishman, J. (2009) *Communication and social work*, Basingstoke: Palgrave Macmillan.

Long, J. (2013) 'Polyglot picture of multilingual Manchester'. Available at: http://ontheplatform.org.uk/article/polyglot-picture-multilingual-manchester

Lucas, S.E. (2014) 'Social work in a multilingual world: interpreter mediated encounters', unpublished doctoral dissertation, University of Salford, UK.

Maiter, S. and Stalker, C. (2010) 'South Asian immigrants' experience of child protection services: are we recognizing strengths and resilience?', *Child & Family Social Work*, 16(2): 138–48.

Masocha, S. (2013) 'We do the best we can: accounting practices in social work discourses of asylum seekers', *British Journal of Social Work*, 44(6): 1621–636.

Meyer, B. (2001) 'How untrained interpreters handle medical terms', in I. Mason (ed) *Triadic exchanges: studies in dialogue interpreting*, Manchester: St. Jerome Publishing, pp 87–106.

Miguélez, C. (2001) 'Interpreting expert witness testimony: challenges and strategies', in I. Mason (ed) *Triadic exchanges: studies in dialogue interpreting*, Manchester: St. Jerome Publishing, pp 3–20.

Mohanty, A.K. (2010) 'Languages, inequality and marginalization: implications of the double divide in Indian multilingualism", *International Journal of the Sociology of Language*, 205: 131–54.

Murray, C.D. and Wynne, J. (2001) 'Using an interpreter to research community, work and family', *Community, Work and Family*, 4(2): 157–70.

Musser-Granski, J. and Carrillo, D.F. (1997) 'The use of bilingual, bicultural paraprofessionals in mental health services: issues for hiring, training, and supervision', *Community Mental Health Journal*, 33(1): 51–60.

Negi, N.J., Furman, N. and Salvador, R. (2010) 'An introduction to transnational social work', in N.J. Negi and N. Furman (eds) *Trans-national social work practice*, New York, NY: Columbia University Press, pp 3–19.

O'Donnell, C., Burns, N., Dowrick, C., Lionis, C. and MacFarlane, A. (2013) 'Health-care access for migrants in Europe', *The Lancet*, 382(9890): 393.

ONS (Office for National Statistics) (2012) '2011 Census for England and Wales'. Available at: www.ons.gov.uk/ons/guide-method/census/2011/index.html

Park, A., Bryson, C. and Curtice, J. (eds) (2014) *British social attitudes: the 31st report*, London: NatCen Social Research. Available at: www.bsa-31.natcen.ac.uk

Pavlenko, A. and Blackledge, A. (2004) *Negotiation of identities in multilingual contexts*, Clevedon: Multilingual Matters.

Pérez-González, L. and Susam-Sarajeva, S. (2012) 'Non-professionals translating and interpreting: theoretical and methodological perspectives', *The Translator*, 18(2): 149–65.

Pugh, R. (1996) *Effective language in health and social work*, London: Chapman & Hall.

Pugh, R. (2004) 'Preparing for linguistically sensitive practice', in M. Robb, S. Barrett, C. Komaromy and A. Rogers (eds) *Communication, relationships and care: a reader*, London: Routledge, pp 139–47.

Rennie, S. (1998) *Interpreting and access to public services: a textbook for public service interpreters and trainers*, Shipley: SEQUALS.

Robinson, L. (1995) *Psychology for social workers: black perspectives*, London: Routledge.

Robinson, L. (2004) 'Beliefs, values and communication', in M. Robb (ed) *Communication, relationships and care: a reader*, London: Routledge, pp 110–20.

Sawrikar, P. (2013a) 'A qualitative study on the pros and cons of ethnically matching culturally and linguistically diverse (CALD) client families and child protection caseworkers', *Children & Youth Services Review*, 35(2): 321–31.

Sawrikar, P. (2013b) 'How effective do families of non-English-speaking background (NESB) and child protection caseworkers in Australia see the use of interpreters? A qualitative study to help inform good practice principles', *Child & Family Social Work*, 20(4): 396–406.

Scheffer, P. (2011) *Immigrant nations*, Cambridge: Polity Press.

Schmid, C.L. (2001) *The politics of language: conflict, identity, and cultural pluralism in comparative perspective*, Oxford: Oxford University Press.

Solomos, J. (2003) *Race and racism in Britain* (3rd edn), Basingstoke: Palgrave Macmillan.

Spolsky, B. (2012) 'Family language policy – the critical domain', *Journal of Multilingual and Multicultural Development*, 33(1): 3–11.

Subtirelu, N.C. (2013) '"English … it's part of our blood': ideologies of language and nation in United States Congressional discourse', *Journal of Sociolinguistics*, 17(1): 37–65.

Subtirelu, N.C. (2015) '"She does have an accent but …": race and language ideology in students' evaluations of mathematics instructors on RateMyProfessors. com', *Language in Society*, 44(1): 35–62.

Sue, D.W. (2006) *Multicultural social work practice*, Hoboken, NJ: Wiley.

Temple, B. (2006) 'Representation across languages: biographical sociology meets translation and interpretation studies', *Qualitative Sociology Review*, 2(1): 7–21.

Temple, B. (2010) 'Feeling special: language in the lives of Polish people', *The Sociological Review*, 58(2): 286–304.

Tipton, R. (2012) 'Public service interpreting and the politics of entitlement for new entrants to the United Kingdom', *Language and Politics*, 11(2): 1569–2159.

Tipton, R. (2014a) 'Investigating intersubjectivity as a discursive accomplishment in relation to interpreter mediation: building a conceptual and analytical framework', *Journal of Foreign Language Teaching and Applied Linguistics*, 1: 219–42.

Tipton, R. (2014b) 'Perceptions of the "occupational other": interpreters, social workers and intercultures', *British Journal of Social Work*, DOI: 10.1093/bjsw/bcu136.

Tribe, R. and Keefe, A. (2009) 'Issues in using interpreters in therapeutic work with refugees. What is not being expressed?', *European Journal of Psychotherapy and Counselling*, 11(4): 409–24.

Trudgill, P. (2000) *Sociolinguistics: an introduction to language and society*, London: Penguin.

Tse, L. (2001) *'Why don't they learn English?' Separating fact from fallacy in the U.S. language debate*, New York, NY: Teachers College Press.

Villanueva, C.M. and Buriel, R. (2010) 'Speaking on behalf of others: a qualitative study of the perceptions and feelings of adolescent Latina language brokers', *Journal of Social Issues*, 66(1): 197–210.

Wadensjö, C. (1998) *Interpreting in interaction*, London: Longman.

Wadensjö, C. (2001) 'The interpreter's position in therapeutic encounters', in I. Mason (ed) *Triadic exchanges: studies in dialogue interpreting*, Manchester: St. Jerome Publishing, pp 71–86.

Weber, J.J. and Horner, K. (2012) *Introducing multilingualism: a social approach*, London: Routledge.

Wei, L. (ed) (2007) *The bilingualism reader*, London: Routledge.

Wiley, T.G. and Lukes, M. (1996) 'English-only and standard English ideologies in the U.S.', *TESOL Quarterly*, 30(3): 511–35.

Williams, C. and Graham, M. (2014) 'A world on the move: migration, mobilities and social work', *British Journal of Social Work*, 44(1): 1–17.

Woodcock Ross, J. (2011) *Specialist communication skills for social workers: focusing on service users' needs*, Basingstoke and New York, NY: Palgrave Macmillan.

# SEVEN

# Co-production: workers, volunteers and people seeking asylum – 'popular social work' in action in Britain

*Rhetta Moran and Michael Lavalette*

## Introduction

> I don't believe in charity; I believe in solidarity. Charity is vertical, so it's humiliating. It goes from top to bottom. Solidarity is horizontal ... I have a lot to learn from other people. Each day I am learning. *Soy un curioso.* (Galeano, 2004 [1999]: 147)

In this chapter, we look at the possibilities of 'co-production' informing our social work theories and practices. By 'co-production', we mean the direct involvement of social workers – both academics and practitioners – and service users and activists in the generation of knowledge about the social situation of workers and the users of services (understanding and interpreting the 'public causes of private pain', to apply an insight from C. Wright Mills [1959]), and developing the appropriate forms of practice that arise as a result.

We do this by means of a case study of a 'popular social work' organisation (Refugee and Asylum Participatory Action Research [RAPAR][1]) operating with refugees and people seeking asylum. RAPAR is based in Manchester in the north of England and brings service users, volunteers with a range of skills, a small number of qualified social workers and other *pro bono* professionals together to research, campaign and address service user needs. It does this through casework, community-based organising and development, and participatory action research. It exists outside of the statutory sector and, on principle, refuses to take money and resources from the UK Home Office.

RAPAR is a campaigning human rights organisation. It developed out of a close engagement with social movements against war and racism, and in defence of refugee and asylum-seeker rights. It is not, we acknowledge, a 'mainstream' social work organisation. However, we would suggest, historically, some of the most progressive developments in social work have not been generated 'internally' from within the profession, but have come about through engagement with social movements and what we term 'popular social work' initiatives within movements (Jones and Lavalette, 2011, 2013; Lavalette, 2011).

By using the term 'popular social work', we are referring to current debates about social work activities provided by alternative, politically conscious providers of services (Jones and Lavalette, 2011). There is a rich history of popular social work projects, linked with social movement activity, whose history has been 'hidden from history' (Jones and Lavalette, 2013). Popular social work projects: are 'organic' and develop in response to particular community needs; avoid notions of professional hierarchy, distance and ego; are determinedly partisan (in the sense of identifying their work with the liberation of the oppressed); and are built on notions of trust between coequal participants in social work movements. They stand in sharp contrast to current developments in 'official' social work in England, for example, where programmes like Think Ahead, Frontline and Step Up are promoted by the government and are based on a narrow definition of social work as being specialist, 'statutory work' carried out in state agencies ('state social work') or under contract in private or voluntary sector organisations ('state-directed social work').

If social work wants to develop and enrich its work with service user communities, it is, we suggest, popular social work projects like those offered by RAPAR that offer us the most valuable lessons to take into practice.

## Co-production

Social work theory and practice has long been committed to the need to take cognisance of service user perspectives in decisions about their lives (Beresford and Croft, 2004). In Britain, the most recent models of working alongside service user communities developed out of the demands of the social welfare movements that emerged in the 1980s and 1990s. Self-organised, vociferous and militant groups of disability activists challenged medical models of disability – drawing a distinction between the impact of physical impairment and the social construction of disability (UPIAS, 1974). They campaigned against government attacks on a range of disability benefits and services and demanded that those services should be shaped primarily by the needs, interests and demands of disabled people themselves and not by a range of professional experts – and social work, alongside the medical professions, was very much in the activists line of fire – who took decisions about disabled people without their direct involvement in the process (Slorach, 2014).

The demand for service user voice and engagement, therefore, came from the social welfare movements and challenged dominant social work theory and practice – such developments were not inherent within the profession itself. As such, this was the latest in a long line of social movements that have, historically, challenged (either directly or indirectly) social work theories to adapt and change to reflect social movement demands for a more equal and diverse world and, as a consequence, the demand for a more humane social work (Lavalette, 2013; Barker and Lavalette, forthcoming). It was the demands of the women's movement in the late 1960s and 1970s that posed a challenge to social work theories about stable families and ideal mothers (Langan, 1998, Penketh, 2011); it was the black liberation movement that sowed the seeds that, within social work, produced the move towards anti-racist practice (Penketh, 2000, Williams, 2011); and it was the Gay Liberation Front that set the terrain to challenge psychological theories about the 'abnormality' of homosexuality or, more recently, transgendered communities (Miles, 2011).

RAPAR, as a campaigning popular social work organisation, has developed reflexive work about the needs, ideas and activities of service users that derives from its engagement with a range of social movements connected to displacement and anti-racism. RAPAR's work is based on the concepts of the co-production of knowledge and practice, solidarity, conscientisation, and anti-dependency (on the theoretical framework framing RAPAR's work, see Moran, 2003; Moran et al, 2006).

The co-production of knowledge and practice deepens the relationship between social work and service users. It requires more than simply taking account of service user perspectives. In internal working relationships, it involves service users as equal co-participants, and, through practice, rejects notions of 'professional distance' and any hierarchy between service users, academics and practitioners. Co-production involves a melting of the distinctions between practitioners, volunteers and service users. Each has an important role in setting agendas, developing casework, identifying campaign priorities and engaging in research processes. It is built upon the ethical values of respect, solidarity and mutuality; a set of values that reflect the collective needs of the dispossessed and marginalised.

The emphasis on solidarity is important. As a network, RAPAR is built on concepts of mutual support in the struggle to obtain, defend and extend social, political and human rights. People commit to engage as activists and coequal partners, and through that conscious approach, intrinsically undermine the potential for dependent relationships to take root. As such, this anti-dependency is an overt rejection of the assistentialism (Freire, 1970) that both populates and is a function of much of the third sector, especially within the refugee field. Active human agency is at the heart of the organisation's philosophy, and every member must have an element of agency intact.

Freire's (1970) treatment of conscientisation is also central. The purpose of research and campaigning work is partly so that participants develop their understanding about their situation within wider relationships and structures of oppression and exploitation. This is important because people seeking asylum are too often pathologised – treated as failures or as individuals with problems. Conscientisation helps to clarify how political and social relations perpetuate oppression in society. It can also aid the process of identifying some of the ways to challenge those oppressive relations.

If social work is to develop models of working based on ideas of co-production, then RAPAR's modus operandi offers valuable insights, we believe, that can inform debate on future directions in social work.

## RAPAR

In 2001, RAPAR's initiator (at the time, a researcher at the University of Salford) was approached for help by community health and social work practitioners in North-West England who were confronted with a new population service user group: forcibly dispersed refugees (Moran, 2003).

Before its election in 1997, the Labour Party said little about asylum and immigration; there were only six lines in their 1997 election manifesto that directly dealt with the question (Labour Party, 1997). However, over the following three years, as the Labour government introduced and implemented the Immigration and Asylum Act 1999, four critical legislative developments occurred:

- First, in 1999, claiming to be 'redistributing' people arriving for asylum more evenly throughout the country, the government introduced a policy of forced dispersal. At the same time, while accommodation continued to be available to people failed by the asylum system, cash payments were stopped and replaced by vouchers, which limited and restricted people's ability to purchase essential goods. Voucher payments were given at a rate lower than benefit levels, enforcing desperate poverty on forcibly dispersed peoples (Asylum Support Partnership, 2010).
- Second, the asylum system was privatised in 2000 when the quasi-autonomous non-governmental organisation (quango) the National Asylum Support Service (NASS) took over responsibility for asylum, at arm's length, from the Home Office (Local Government Sourcing, 2007). The consequence was less accountability of services and greater abuse in the system (Temple and Moran, 2005).
- Third, with the spectre of the 'overflowing' French detention centre at Sangatte near Calais as his backdrop in 2001, the then Home Secretary Jack Straw mooted 'overhauling' the 1951 UN Declaration of Human Rights (Straw, 2001). At this time, an administrative distinction began to be systematically implemented between refugees and people seeking asylum. The consequence was that people designated with 'asylum seeker' status began to be treated as an exceptional category that could, legitimately, be placed outside of access to mainstream services (Moran, 2003) and dehumanised in the press (Mollard, 2001).
- Finally, in March 2002, people seeking asylum were prohibited from working (Liberty, no date). This effectively made legal entry to claim asylum impossible and legitimated the concept of an asylum seeker being 'illegal'.

These developments occurred in tandem with the political fallout from 9/11. The post-9/11 world has witnessed increasing levels of Islamophobia and anti-migrant racism, described by Liz Fekete (2014) as 'xeno-racism' – targeting new communities in ways that utilise all the 'old' racist stereotypes and racist forms of political action. In political and media debates, asylum seekers became labelled as the problematic 'other' and their treatment at the hands of the state became increasingly punitive (Dean, 2011).

It was against this backdrop that RAPAR developed. From the beginning, RAPAR's intention was to establish an organisation where academics, practitioners and refugees would work together on individual casework, community campaigns and relevant research to establish facts about the reality of life for those who were forcibly dispersed, and to promote constructive social action.

By 2003, RAPAR began to reach the national media with its research about what was happening to people seeking asylum from both Iraq (McFayden, 2003) and Somalia (Asthana, 2004) and to their local communities in Britain. However, partly as a consequence of its media profile, during 2004–05, the organisation faced highly concentrated – and highly placed – efforts to stop its work and force it to close down (Hatton, 2011). These efforts were resisted and the organisation remains dedicated to its original aspiration of continuously developing and delivering action-oriented research, community development, individual casework and campaigns about and with – as opposed to on and for – displaced people and their surrounding communities.

When dispersed people choose RAPAR, they join the organisation and become full and equal members. The majority of people that join RAPAR face a range of challenges relating to citizenship, housing, deportation, employment, education, personal safety, personal trauma and other problems. It enables people to access the services they need, and it releases their abilities to find effective solutions to the challenges they face.

There are three ways in which RAPAR develops work: casework, community organising and development and research. In what follows, we look at work in each area in turn, drawing on specific cases (which are already in the public sphere) to highlight the organisation's work.

## Casework

A central part of the organisation's work is individual support and casework. The casework combines 'Action and Compassion with Tenacity' (ACT) to support the human rights needs of individuals and families who come to the organisation looking for support, help and solidarity. On average, there are 20 active cases at any one time and these will involve a variety of individual and family cases, ranging from relatively straightforward aspects, and therefore short-term, to the more complex and correspondingly long-term (RAPAR, no date).

To give an example, let us look at the 'short-term' case aspect of Mohammad Al Halengy (RAPAR, 2014a). When he joined RAPAR, Mohammad had already been accepted by the British state as a survivor of torture. When his lawyer submitted a fresh claim for asylum, Mohammad, who had been 'sofa surfing', now wanted to apply for accommodation, under Section 4(1) of the Immigration and Asylum Act 1999. This section of the Act allows accommodation to be provided for persons with Temporary Admission, those released from immigration detention and those on immigration bail (UK Visas and Immigration, 2015). Thus, Mohammad made his claim for accommodation while his fresh claim for asylum was being considered. Like many other asylum-related organisations, RAPAR worked alongside Mohammad (who had become a member of RAPAR once his case had been accepted) to submit the necessary paperwork through which he could be allocated accommodation. However, unlike other organisations, RAPAR insisted that he was housed within a reasonable distance of his torture survival support services. This necessitated directly challenging the custom and practice of the Home Office Caseowner allocated to his case, who would ordinarily reserve the right to disperse him to accommodation wherever they saw fit – including a city some considerable distance from his present 'home' town. In the process of working this case, it also became necessary to expose the fact that other organisations in the sector, in their adaption to the Home office directive to move him far away, were not acting with him or in his best interests. Eventually, RAPAR's work enabled Mohammad to live in his chosen city, close to his torture survival services. However, as we will discuss later, this approach did (and does) has both strengths and limitations for both Mohamed and to RAPAR.

Conversely, to give an example of a more complex case, we could look at RAPAR's work with the Olatunde family (RAPAR, 2012). This case involved a family of three teenagers and their mum who fled Nigeria six years earlier to avoid their surviving daughter being forced to undergo female genital mutilation (FGM). When this family joined RAPAR, they had been disbelieved by the British state and were at immanent risk of deportation. In this case, the complexities included addressing the development of acute mental health needs that arose out of the state's rejection of their case, negotiating gendered and relative power relationships within the community, and enabling the responsible adults surrounding this family, including teachers, to become usefully supportive. It is the range of interlinked issues that RAPAR has to deal with that marks out its complexity. At the time of writing, this case is ongoing.

Whether the cases are relatively straightforward or more complex, RAPAR members record problems and start to consider ways to begin to solve them. In this way, members are supported to directly involve themselves and acquire decision-making power about how to tackle the problems that have presented. They learn through the experience that each member involved in any case brings something to the problem-solving process and, collectively, learn about how systems actually work and what scope exists to change those systems' responses to members' needs.

## Community organising and development

RAPAR members with specific issues may decide to develop campaigns as a part of the process of securing lasting solutions. In other instances, the process of creating a case or a campaign leads to community development initiatives where groups and networks form to advance their own project ideas towards becoming real, engaged and active citizens over time. Using RAPAR's office space, and offering travel costs and childcare when possible, activists within the organisation who have relevant skills or experience, for example, community development or journalism, become involved.

For example, in 2008, a member of the Somali community joined RAPAR and brought to the organisation the mother of a 14-year-old boy who had been excluded from school for almost a year. This was initially a straightforward piece of casework that involved RAPAR members advocating on the boy's behalf to the Education Department in Manchester. However, this intervention became known about within different Somali community circles and RAPAR was then approached to work inside and with community members grappling with the problem of a disproportionate number of young men who were not in school. RAPAR then accessed local funds to investigate the scale of the problem and published research exposing the nature and extent of the problem (Moran and Mohamed, 2012). The publication of the research prompted the school at the heart of the issue to set up a parents' forum, which brought parents from Somalia into direct negotiation with the school. At that point, RAPAR withdrew; the Somali parents' forum continues to operate in Manchester.

## Research

A central part of RAPAR's purpose is to develop and deliver research. RAPAR encourages people to participate in the generation of research and knowledge based on their lived experiences. It is the generation of this research that provides the evidence that can inform casework, community organising and development, and the various campaigning strategies adopted by the organisation and its members.

In the ideal, given the commitment to action research, all individuals and/or groups should be involved in the researching process. For example, in the Somali research cited earlier, it was necessary to involve everyone: the excluded children, parents, teachers, youth service workers and local government officers.

However, there are often power differences between participants within the research process. These differences are expressed through actual human behaviours within physical environments that are situated inside structural and organisational hierarchies (Wright Mills, 1967), and these differences can both inhibit and/or complicate participatory processes. Recognising this is important; it means that RAPAR builds research in ways that are designed to interrogate, challenge and even alter those power relations within the researching processes themselves.

For example, in the Somali research, through respecting cultural frameworks and social mores – which is possible when some of the RAPAR members are from those communities – and by continuously reflecting back and then affirming and developing the data as they emerge, various power relations can be confronted, and research approaches reflected upon. This grows individual and group confidence in the value of what is being researched because the community is the co-producer of the knowledge and data that are now being used to 'speak truth to power'. It is these commitments that underpinned RAPAR's work and led to the publication of 'Doing research with refugees' (Temple and Moran, 2006), which included a set of research guidelines for future researchers to follow.

## Strengths and limitations

Having outlined RAPAR's work in these three areas, we now proceed to look at some of the strengths and limitations of this approach as part of an evaluation of the organisation's activities. In the sections that follow, questions about strengths and limitations are illustratively, rather than exhaustively, discussed and, where appropriate, we refer to the RAPAR examples introduced earlier.

### Strengths

#### Casework and campaigning

The individuals or families who join RAPAR and decide to develop their cases within the organisation immediately confront a conscious anti-dependency model. For the first time since becoming a dispersed person, RAPAR members may experience feelings of empowerment that arise from being at the centre of the processes that they are trying to find solutions to. They become self-conscious actors and agents for change, rather than passive participants in processes that act upon them.

Take the example of Mohammad Al Halengy, discussed earlier, who went on to successfully 'work' his case (RAPAR, 2014a). For Mohammad, there is the fundamental 'benefit' that he is still physically safe and has not been deported back to torture, imprisonment or death at the hands of those from whom he fled in the first place. Further, after his successful casework and campaign, Mohammad was eventually able to live in the city near his support networks and with good access to the torture survival resources that he needed.

Alternatively, for the families of people who are already dead, there may be some comfort – such as it is – to be gleaned from experiencing some form of recognition that what happened to their loved one was wrong. Also, the knowledge that their efforts to expose what happened may help to avoid a future repetition can be a benefit.

For example, in the summer of 2014, RAPAR was joined by the family of Jordan Begley to draw public attention to the death of their son 'following a Greater Manchester Police (GMP) officer's use of a Taser weapon at Jordan's home in Gorton [Manchester]' (RAPAR, 2014b). Through mounting the campaign, the family came to experience a degree of control over the justice campaign being run about the case and were able to counter the unfounded conjecture that was being published concerning Jordan's death. The campaign for justice for Jordan was about discovering what happened and why, allowing the family to achieve appropriate closure, and working to ensure that such events are not repeated and that other families will not have to go through such anguish (RAPAR, 2014b).

Another, alternative, benefit scenario is where a case is ongoing but participants know that, so far, they have protected their children from grave harm, or, similarly, where their case is ongoing but because of the steps that they have already taken to resist attempts to degrade their humanity, they remain relatively securely placed, for example, with a roof over their head, to continue their struggle. This is the situation for the Olatunde family involved in the ongoing FGM case discussed earlier (RAPAR, 2012).

More generally, being in control of their own case can have a range of benefits. Self-esteem may rise. People who have become used to being disbelieved and rejected, and who are very often destitute, undocumented and/or without recourse to any form of public funds when they reach RAPAR's door, regularly express very deep appreciation of the simple act of being welcomed into a warm, clean, safe and mutually respectful space.

For some, that growing self-esteem and confidence translates into a growing role within RAPAR. For the last 10 years, the elected chair has always been a displaced person who has uncovered their own capacities to take on such a role inside of the organisation. Also, since it began, at least 50% of its elected 'leadership group' have been displaced, and that group always contains at least one person who is outside any asylum system whatsoever, being undocumented and officially destitute.

The organisation's management structure demands that everybody is working with – and never for or on – the person who has become a new member. Therefore, the committee structure reflects the organisation's commitment to individual and collective agency (Callinicos, 1987) and to the active involvement of all members in the co-production of knowledge, theory and practice.

Practically, new skill bases may develop, which can include: how to compose a team of casework volunteers; how to research; how to store and manage relevant material; how to communicate effectively within and across different sectors (including legal, health, education, housing, voluntary and media); and how to prepare and post webpages. If members go on to develop campaigns that support their cases, these skills may also extend to public speaking, making structured presentations, contributing to press releases and even participating in live reporting and performances about their cases.

Partnered, external, service providers can also benefit directly from the work that RAPAR undertakes. Sometimes, an external organisation who has partnered with RAPAR through a campaign or casework finds itself with positive publicity and exposure (Bachelor, 2014). In other instances, RAPAR's acceptance of a referral from an external organisation may result in that organisation taking a complex and time- and labour-intensive case off their books. This is often the situation when it involves people without recourse to public funds. They have presented to a statutory agency and been advised that they cannot be helped within the law. At that point, a statutory worker may contact RAPAR and ask for help.

However, where and when it is possible, RAPAR does what it can to consciously avoid undertaking work that should be provided by statutory or state services – an important issue in Britain at a time of significant welfare transformation.

At the organisational level, the benefits that RAPAR experiences from doing successful casework and campaigns are multiple. First, some RAPAR members have taken what they have learned and moved into higher education or other services as paid workers. Second, when a case or campaign succeeds, through the organisation's own mechanisms and structures, the sense of empowerment expands. Such successes strengthen the resolve to continue with tenacity.

Further, as a learning organisation, every step of every case worked and every campaign launched and driven through is a potential learning opportunity in its own right. Every time RAPAR engages externally, it finds out more and more about how systems work and, simultaneously, how RAPAR should or should not communicate about and with them. Actions also reveal internal strengths and weaknesses.

Does the state benefit from RAPAR's independent casework and campaigning? In so far as RAPAR's work exposes the failings of the state to adhere to its own laws, processes, responsibilities, rules and agreements, its work presents opportunities for evidence-based improvements to be developed by the state in these areas. However, to date, the state has not used the evidence presented to significantly change its policies and procedures.

## Community organisation and development

Often, the decision to develop a campaign creates traction within the local community and/or communities of interest further afield. Public awareness can develop. When this occurs, a group that is community-based may begin to grow, as was the case in the Somali example cited earlier.

RAPAR members already part of the Somali communities found each other and shared their common issue (around the exclusion of their children from schools). They then started to define themselves as a group by reaching out into the communities. In addition to the preliminary benefit of 'naming the problem', such groups can, sometimes very quickly, begin to formalise their presence and, in the process, locate themselves within their specific historical context. The Somali parents who organised around the issue of school exclusion constituted themselves in that process and, consequently, became part of a wider collective that was beginning to address policing problems in the inner city. The launch of the Northern Police Monitoring project in 2012 enabled this group to connect a 21st-century permutation of the policing problem that was described by C.L.R. James (1982) in his writing about the Manchester Moss Side riots of 1981.

In relation to the more obvious and traditional forms of 'benefit', such as formal and positive recognition by superordinate or mainstream bodies, RAPAR's sole experience was in 2009, when it received the Elspeth Kyle National Award for Best Community Impact, awarded by Novas Scarman UK, in recognition of the impact that RAPAR's work has made, on the ground, within the communities of Manchester.

## Research

In contrast to research that is derived from within academically located sites, RAPAR's autonomy creates relatively unencumbered projects. Not being market-driven, or shaped by any university's research priorities, RAPAR offers continuous opportunities to develop action research processes that are driven by members' ideas and cases. As creators and owners, they decide every aspect of the researching process: from what research questions to ask, through what methodologies to employ, to how to analyse findings and what to disseminate, when and to whom (Moran and Butler, 2001: 60–4). Of course, new members are not simply left to make these decisions on their own. There is structured support in place from experienced members who offer the mentoring and educational/research 'scaffolding' (Vygotsky, 1986; Daniels, 2008) to ensure that projects are viable, doable and match the members' action-directed goals.

RAPAR's reflexive (Gouldner, 1970) approach prioritises applied research processes that aim for constructive changes within the time frame of the research itself – as well as afterwards. In the Somali case study, the case revealed a hitherto hidden problem of school exclusions in the Somali community. The local education authority decided to undertake research. The commissioned research completed by RAPAR contributed to the formation of the Somali Forum and further enhanced effective community organisation and development. As a result, in addition to its intrinsic value as a contribution to research, RAPAR's report enabled positive changes to take place in the relations between the secondary schools in the catchment area and the parents of affected pupils.

However, there was an important element established by RAPAR when undertaking the commissioned research. RAPAR only ever undertakes research that will remain the intellectual property of the generators. In this way, the organisation seeks to avoid research 'cleansing' processes (Medawar, 1967) and is free to use and share its research material in any way it sees fit. Therefore, the co-production of knowledge that comes through participatory action research processes establishes co-generated data that are then re-presented to sites of power to demonstrate why change in processes, policies and resources are necessary.

## Limitations

RAPAR's mode of working also brings certain difficulties and pressures that need to be considered. In this section, we consider the limitations associated with RAPAR's approach in each of the three areas: casework/campaigns, community development and research. However, rather than exploring the limitations discretely in each area, this section is written with the recognition that each type of activity harbours the potential for the organisation and members involved to experience these limitations and it will not cite individual case examples on ethical grounds.

When members begin to confront problems through casework, or if they start a campaign, they are either going to re-immerse themselves into the memories of their prior traumas or they are going to be witnessing alongside other members inside of the process. These problems may involve events that are either immediately life-threatening or are about events that promote physical, emotional and mental distress or anxiety. To even begin this process involves confronting fears and mustering enough courage to overcome any sense of helplessness or internal self-doubt. As a small, membership organisation, RAPAR does not always have the resources to fully support those who are reliving earlier traumas, and though well connected to support services, the organisation can struggle when members are going through periods of extreme distress.

There is the constant risk of failure and its attendant emotional, mental, physical, relational and organisational consequences. Failure has an immediate impact on the individual, or family, at the heart of the case. It can mean that an individual is imprisoned or deported, tortured, injured or killed. However, failure also has an impact on the people who worked with this individual or family, and, of course, it has an impact on the organisation as a whole. Deep upset, anger, frustration and helplessness are aroused by failure. To date, where the decision to publicly campaign has been sustained, RAPAR has not lost a single case. However, throughout its existence, there have been a number of cases where people have been deported, disappeared, imprisoned or died. Given the huge investment that members put into each case, such losses are deeply felt.

The nature of RAPAR's work is such that, sometimes, casework, community organising and development or participatory action research finds itself exposing bad practice in other organisations. That exposure may stimulate enquiries into the way some services are working. It may improve them in the longer term. For example, RAPAR's initial casework led to a report in the magazine *Inside Housing* about the section 4 housing system operated by the Border and Immigration Authority, third sector service delivery, and housing providers in the Greater Manchester area (Nadeem, 2009). While this led to marked physical improvements in the homes of a large group of single-parent women seeking asylum, it also brought those same women to the attention of authorities that exercised real power and control over where they were living and, relatedly, their individual asylum claims.

As a by-product, the gaps in service delivery that had not been previously addressed by a range of agencies, including other third sector agencies within the field, were exposed. When this happened, it placed an additional layer of stress upon RAPAR. The organisation does not set out to expose failings inside other organisations, but when it does, it tests the quality of RAPAR's relationship with those organisations. It may result in improved relations; it can just as easily stimulate resentment and anger.

Further, the impact of negative responses is largely conditioned by the power wielded by the exposed organisation. Most recently, RAPAR has been involved in highlighting the gap between the findings of an inquest relating to a death in detention (at Pennine House Detention Centre, which is owned by Manchester Airport plc, a holding company for the 10 boroughs of Greater Manchester) and the report of that same death by the Police and Prison Ombudsman (RAPAR, 2015). In the process, RAPAR confronted both local authorities and the Coroner's Office. The tension introduced between RAPAR and statutory organisations, in particular, makes it difficult for RAPAR to obtain funding contracts despite repeated attempts.

When a case or a campaign moves forward strongly, the volume of information that becomes newly available about what is going wrong is not inevitably matched by a commensurate rate of learning. The risk of people feeling overwhelmed by their new knowledge and the challenge of communicating about it in ways that are effective is ever present, and can be paralysing at times.

For members who take on the leadership of a community organising development, the process of sustaining the group up to the point where it can secure discrete sources of support for its continuation can create significant, and sometimes even insupportable, strain. Once it has become live, so too has the challenge of grappling with the complexity of group dynamics, political schisms, hidden agendas and even infiltration. The leaders may risk burnout, but where RAPAR has succeeded in enabling individuals to recognise this intrinsic and potential problem, continuous dialogue and reflection-in-action can help people to self-manage their level of engagement.

Once a group becomes established, the potential for disruption and co-option is ever present and grows. It is tiring to maintain a constant vigilance against attempts to co-opt or shut down the organisation. The repertoire of interference ranges from false flattery and/or job offers directed towards specific members to the targeted intimidation of others.

Unlike the context that surrounds the statutory sector, front-line delivery entities or large central- and local government-funded charities – a social work department, a school, a hospital, a prison cell, a primary care setting or a hostel – there is no overarching, procedural, relatively distant and established infrastructure to which RAPAR can refer when the going gets tough. It has had to carve out its own administration, financial systems and a range of policy processes and procedures with regard to risk reduction and assessment, children and vulnerable adults, complaints, volunteer support, casework and campaign algorithms, and research ethics processes and procedures. These procedures must exist in a robust form but the process of creating and regularly updating them is time- and energy-consuming and is not what most people join the organisation to do.

RAPAR survived a trial by fire during 2004–06 when the organisation as a whole came under direct and sustained attack by a combination of local, regional and national bodies (Hatton, 2011). Since that time, at different historical points, RAPAR has received reports of the organisation as a whole and individuals within it being exposed to ridicule, defamation and slander. These attacks are a result of RAPAR's continuing exposure of institutional racism and a range of examples of very bad, and in some instances deadly, practices in the maltreatment of forcibly displaced peoples, which places the organisation in direct conflict with police forces and statutory, private and third sectors.

## Conclusion

In highlighting the work of RAPAR, we have intended to show how the concept of 'co-production' of knowledge, theory and practice can develop. RAPAR structures itself as a 'membership' organisation, where dispersed people seeking asylum work as coequal partners with a range of volunteers, lawyers, academics and social workers to work on their cases, engage in campaigning activity and undertake research about their own – and their colleagues' – social situations. It offers a model built upon the concepts of anti-assistentialism, conscientisation and solidarity. Anti-assistentialism and conscientisation are derived from the work of Friere (1970). Anti-assistentialism is the conscious rejection of dependency: the requirement that members who choose to join RAPAR still have agency, can work their own case and engage, at least to some extent, in the political struggle for rights for displaced people. Conscientisation relates to the organisation's emphasis on the transformative learning processes that arise from campaigning and participatory action research: that members work to reveal the historical and contemporary relations of oppression and exploitation that impact on their – and their colleagues' – situations and take action to challenge and change these relations wherever possible. Solidarity, as expressed by Galeano (2004 [1999]), is the 'horizontal support' for equals that reveals and expresses our common humanity.

The fact that RAPAR is constructed as a membership organisation based on the concepts of anti-assistentialism, conscientisation and solidarity means that those whose cases are taken up by the organisation have full participatory rights in the running and the practice of the organisation. The leadership structure is formed to ensure full representation from all networks within the organisation. Members are directly involved in setting the goals of RAPAR and identifying the strategies to be pursued in individual cases and campaigns. Co-production means challenging notions of professional hierarchy, or campaign or political 'leaders'. It is recognised that all members have skills and background experiences that can enhance and enrich the work of the organisation. RAPAR creates an open but self-controlled space where people actively choose to engage, to lead and to follow (all of which are active social processes) in the organisation's work. These processes, we suggest, create an organisation that is 'trusted' by participants – an important value in a field where there is so much room for suspicion and distrust by dispersed people of the state and its networks.

Co-production, in the sense described here, is an active, participatory concept that can enrich and develop a trusted social work practice: a practice that is prepared to 'speak truth to power' and defend the rights and activities of the oppressed and dispossessed. Of course, such an approach can bring difficulties: it can create tension with statutory and other social welfare organisations; it is demanding of time and energy; and it is sometimes not without personal cost for those involved. These difficulties have to be managed and this can create tensions. However, honesty in appraisal, openness with members, space for collective reflection and an active commitment to being reflexive as much as possible are some of the tools that can aid the self-management process.

We are sure that there are many organisations who work along similar lines to RAPAR. However, the pressures of working in such open ways mean that one of our limitations is that we often do not create or protect the time to share our experiences or write our histories. This chapter is a small contribution to the growing debate on co-production within social work organisations, one that emphasises that this is not an abstract, academic concept, but one that can enrich and shape our social work engagement with the world.

## Note
[1] See: www.rapar.org.uk

## References

Asthana, A. (2004) 'Living in fear: my week with the hidden asylum seekers', *The Observer*, 28 March. Available at: http://www.theguardian.com/uk/2004/mar/28/immigration.immigrationandpublicservices (accessed 24 May 2015).

Asylum Support Partnership (2010) 'The Azure Payment Card and the need for cash support for refused asylum seekers', Parliamentary Briefing, November. Available at: http://www.refugeecouncil.org.uk/assets/0001/5899/1011_Azure_card_briefing.pdf (accessed 20 May 2015).

Bachelor, L. (2014) 'HSBC accused of closing UK bank accounts held by Syrians', *The Guardian*, 8 August. Available at: http://www.theguardian.com/money/2014/aug/08/hsbc-accused-closing-bank-accounts-syrians (accessed 20 May 2015).

Barker, C. and Lavalette, M. (forthcoming) 'Welfare changes and social movements', in D. Della Porta and M. Diani (eds) *The Oxford handbook of social movements*, Oxford: Oxford University Press.

Beresford, P. and Croft, S. (2004) 'Service users and practitioners reunited: the key component of social work reform', *British Journal of Social Work*, 31(1): 53–68.

Callinicos, A. (1987) *Making history: agency, structure and change in social theory*, Cambridge: Polity Press.

Daniels, H. (2008) *Vygotsky and research*, London: Routledge.

Dean, M. (2011) *Democracy under attack*, Bristol: The Policy Press.

Fekete, L. (2014) 'The growth of xeno-racism and Islamophobia in Britain', in M. Lavalette and L. Penketh (eds) *Race, racism and social work*, Bristol: Policy Press.

Friere, P. (1970) *Pedagogy of the oppressed*, London: Continuum Publishing Company.

Galeano, E. (2004 [1999]) 'Interview with David Barsamian', in D. Barsamian (ed) *Louder than bombs: interviews from* The Progressive Magazine, Cambridge, MA: Southend Press.

Gouldner, A.W. (1970) *The coming crisis of Western sociology*, London: Heinemann.

Hatton, J. (2011) 'How and why did migration and refugee studies (MARS) facilitate migration control?', unpublished PhD thesis, University of Oxford, UK.

James, C.L.R. (1982) 'Free for all: the nine year old leader', *Race Today* 14(3). Available at: https://www.marxists.org/archive/james-clr/works/1982/free-for-all.htm (accessed 20 May 2015).

Jones, C. and Lavalette, M. (2011) 'Popular social work in the Palestinian West Bank: dispatches from the front line', in M. Lavalette and V. Ioakimidis (eds) *Social work in extremis*, Bristol: The Policy Press.

Jones, C. and Lavalette, M. (2013) 'The two souls of social work: exploring the roots of "popular social work"', *Critical and Radical Social Work*, 1(2): 147–66.

Labour Party (1997) 'The Labour Party manifesto, 1997', in I. Dale and I. Dale Nfa (eds) *Labour Party general election manifestos 1900–1997*, London: Routledge.

Langan, M. (1998) *Women, oppression and social work: towards a radical democratic politics*, London: Verso.

Lavalette, M. (2011) 'Introduction: social work in extremis – disaster capitalism, "social shocks" and "popular social work"', in M. Lavalette and V. Ioakimidis (eds) *Social work in extremis*, Bristol: The Policy Press.

Lavalette, M. (2013) 'Neformalno Socialno delo, Uradno Uocialno delo in Druzbena Gibanja' ('Social work and social movements'), *Socialno Delo*, 52(March–June): 113–27.

Liberty (no date) 'Asylum support and the right to work'. Available at: https://www.liberty-human-rights.org.uk/human-rights/asylum-and-borders/asylum-support-and-right-work (accessed 20 May 2015).

Local Government Sourcing (2007) 'Home Office National Asylum Support Service'. Available at: https://www.localgovsourcing.co.uk/web/customers/customerDetail.jsp-LANG=EN&ID=9177.htm (accessed 20 May 2015).

McFayden, M. (2003) 'A cold shoulder for Saddam's victims', *The Guardian*, 22 March. Available at: http://www.theguardian.com/world/2003/mar/22/iraq.immigrationandpublicservices

Medawar, P.B. (1967) *Art of the soluble: creativity and originality in science*, London: Heinemann Young Books.

Miles, L. (2011) 'LGTB oppression, sexualities and radical social work today', in M. Lavalette (ed) *Radical social work today*, Bristol: The Policy Press.

Mollard, C. (2001) 'Asylum. The truth behind the headlines', Oxfam. Available at: http://policy-practice.oxfam.org.uk/publications/asylum-the-truth-behind-the-headlines-111959 (accessed 20 May 2015).

Moran, R.A. (2003) 'From dispersal to destitution: dialectical methods in participatory research with people seeking asylum', conference proceedings from 'Policy and Politics in a Globalising World', 24 July, University of Bristol.

Moran, R.A. and Butler, D.S. 'Whose health profile?', *Critical Public Health*, 11(1): 59–74.

Moran, R.A. and Mohamed, Z. (2012) 'Who's around NEET – and why? Young men from Somali backgrounds', Commissioned by the Central Collegiate of Manchester in partnership with Focussing First on People . Available at: http://www.rapar.org.uk/uploads/4/6/8/7/4687542/moran__mohamed_whos_around_neet__and_why.pdf (accessed 20 May 2015).

Moran, R.A., Mohamed, Z. and Lovel, H. (2006) 'Breaking the silence: participatory research processes about health with Somali refugee people seeking asylum', in R. Moran and B. Temple (eds) *Doing research with refugees*, Bristol: The Policy Press.

Nadeem, B. (2009) 'Refugees suffer as homes run out', *The Guardian*, 20 February.

Penketh, L. (2000) *Tackling institutional racism*, Bristol: The Policy Press.

Penketh, L. (2011) 'Social work and women's oppression today', in M. Lavalette (ed) *Radical social work today*, Bristol: Policy Press.

RAPAR (Refugee and Asylum Participatory Action Research) (no date) 'Action compassion tenacity'. Available at: http://www.rapar.org.uk/about-casework.html (accessed 20 May 2015).

RAPAR (2012) 'Olayinka and her family MUST stay in Britain!'. Available at: http://www.rapar.org.uk/olayinka-and-her-family-must-stay-in-britain.html (accessed 20 May 2015).

RAPAR (2014a) 'Sudanese Beja solidarity campaign: keep Mohammed safe in the UK'. Available at: http://www.rapar.org.uk/beja-solidarity-campaign.html (accessed 20 May 2015).

RAPAR (2014b) 'Why did Jordan Begley die?'. Available at: http://www.rapar.org.uk/why-did-jordan-begley-die.html (accessed 20 May 2015).

RAPAR (2015) 'Death in detention: ombudsman's report criticises care of Tahir Mehmood'. Available at: http://www.rapar.org.uk/news--views/death-in-detention-ombudsmans-report-criticises-care-of-tahir-mehmood (accessed 20 May 2015).

Slorach, R. (2014) 'Out of the shadows: disability movements', *Critical and Radical Social Work*, 2(2): 159–73.

Straw, J. (2001) 'An effective protection regime for the twenty-first century', speech to IPPR, 6 February, *The Guardian*, 6 February. Available at: http://www.theguardian.com/uk/2001/feb/06/immigration.immigrationandpublicservices3 (accessed 20 May 2015).

Temple, B. and Moran, R. (2006) *Doing research with refugees*, Policy Press: Bristol.

Temple, B. and Moran, R., with Fayas, N., Haboninana, S., McCabe, F., Mohamed, Z., Noori, A. and Rahman, N. (2005) 'Developing communities containing dispersed refugee people seeking asylum', Joseph Rowntree Foundation. Available at: https://www.jrf.org.uk/report/developing-communities-containing-dispersed-refugee-people-seeking-asylum (accessed 20 May 2015).

UK Visas and Immigration (2015) 'Asylum support, section 4 policy and process'. Available at: https://www.gov.uk/government/uploads/system/uploads/attachment_data/file/414232/Asylum_Support_Section_4_Policy_and_Process_v4.pdf (accessed 20 May 2015).

UPIAS (Union of the Physically Impaired Against Segregation) (1974) 'Aims and declaration'. Available at: http://pf7d7vi404s1dxh27mla5569.wpengine.netdna-cdn.com/files/library/UPIAS-UPIAS.pdf (accessed 20 May 2015).

Vygotsky, L. (1986) *Thought and language*, Cambridge, MA: MIT Press.

Williams, C. (2011) 'The jester's joke', in M. Lavalette (ed) *Radical social work today*, Bristol: The Policy Press.

Wright Mills, C. (1959) *The sociological imagination*, New York, NY: OUP.

Wright Mills, C. (1967) *The power elite*, New York, NY: OUP.

# EIGHT

# Consultation and civic engagement

*Tue Hong Baker and Charlotte Williams*

## Introduction

In recent decades, government bodies and a wide range of policymakers have been concerned to establish greater levels of engagement with the publics they service. This 'consultative turn' in policy and practice is driven by the need to design and deliver more responsive services, to provide investment in, and legitimacy for, policy decisions and policy implementation, and to bolster the notion of citizen engagement with greater levels of democratic participation. Policy information, consultation and feedback are seen as the key to better practice. The ambition is to improve the transparency of government deliberative processes, increase the accessibility of policy-based information and increase uptake by citizens of government programmes. In this endeavour, government and associated organisations have become concerned with those segments of the population that do not readily or easily participate, among these, minority ethnic groups.

Many organisations and local councils have identified so-called '*hard to reach*' populations using largely demographic definitions, such as young people, rural dwellers, disabled people and minority ethnic groups, but have also defined populations as hard to reach by virtue of attitudinal barriers. For example, those who believe that services are not for them or that the council is not interested in their view, those ignorant of policy and practices, and those who do not have the 'know-how' to engage. A number of practical obstacles also prohibit engagement, such as transport difficulties, health barriers and cultural and language diversity, among others, which work to hamper engagement in specific constellations. In addition, stigma or discrimination can deter groups from engaging with public bodies.

Rural areas present very different challenges than, for example, areas of population concentration. These barriers are not particular to black and minority ethnic (BME) groups alone, but these groupings, in particular, have come under the policy lens following the mandated requirement for consultation under the Race Relations (Amendment) Act 2001, being further boosted by the equality duties under the Equalities Act 2010. Across the UK, no public authority can neglect proactively engaging and consulting with members of minority ethnic communities in the design and delivery of services. This chapter reports on a collaborative action research project undertaken between a minority ethnic non-governmental organisation (NGO) (the North Wales Race Equality Network [NWREN]) and a university-based academic during 2006–08. Utilising an inductive method, the project aimed to capture the processes of engagement from both sides of the public service counter in an attempt to enhance the practices of major government departments when reaching out to minority ethnic groups. It opens by summarising key messages from the literature on consulting with minority groups. It reports on the experiences of five selected organisations and the accounts of minority ethnic residents in rural Wales involved in the process of civic engagement. It concludes by identifying the emergent messages that arise from this encounter that may provide lessons to places elsewhere.

## Policy context and messages from the literature

In recent years, the relationship between public bodies and the communities they serve has been transformed by a range of policy initiatives. In Wales, 'Making connections' (WAG, 2004), 'Getting on together – a community cohesion strategy for Wales' (WAG, 2009) and the Equalities Act 2010 (Statutory Duties (Wales) Regulations 2011) put citizen focus at the heart of public policy and placed clear duties on public bodies to both know the extent and nature of their minority ethnic populations and consult with them on the range of policy issues. The value of good consultation cannot be overstated. It not only ensures the incorporation of the valuable insights and experiences of marginal groups and individuals, but also ensures buy-in for decisions, policy implementation and practice. It can also foster trust and thereby increase the uptake of services. Organisations need to know if their service is relevant, what impacts it is having, what service needs are and more.

Nevertheless, it is acknowledged that establishing good practices and capturing the views of minority groups in rural areas presents particular challenges (Dhalech, 1999; Devon Race Equality Council, 2003; NWREN, 2003, 2006; Garland et al, 2006; Brackertz, 2007; Craig and Lachman, 2008). The diversity and dispersal of minority individuals and households in such areas means that they are too often considered 'hard to reach' and many of the traditional methods of consultation prove ineffective. Public bodies are obliged to deal with a moving rather than a static picture of ethnic diversity in their areas as communities are rapidly changing, and they need to develop strategies of engagement that capture this dynamic. It is also increasingly recognised that approaches that essentialise communities by categorising them by ethnic group alone are largely out of step with the diversity of the local demographic. In rural areas, in particular, it may be difficult to establish any significant ethnic group as a collective; rather, these areas are characterised by individuals and families with very diverse status.

While a comprehensive literature exists on models and approaches to community engagement, and specifically with 'hard to reach' groups (see, eg, UK Community Participation Network, 1999; Russell et al, 2001; Hashagen, 2002; Scottish Executive Involving People Team, 2002; Dunlop, 2004; HSE,

2004; Community Action Hampshire, 2006; Cabinet Office, 2008; COSLA, 2008; Participation Cymru, 2011), there has been relatively little work aimed at tapping into models in use with minority ethnic groups in rural areas (Devon Race Equality Council, 2003; BEN, 2006; Cynwys Project, 2007). In too many instances, public bodies have fallen back on frameworks that are too rigid to engage with diverse populations or have had to rely on approaches developed where there are concentrations of minority individuals and/or organisations.

A review of the literature (Scottish Executive, 2002; Devon Race Equality Council, 2003; NWREN, 2003; Caust et al, 2006; Boag-Munroe and Evangelou, 2012) on the common issues identified by public bodies suggested key barriers to effective consultation to be:

- lack of time and capacity;
- restricted funding and other resource issues;
- poor track record in building relationships;
- lack of transparency of the process;
- being tied to traditional or mainstream methodologies;
- relying on a single methodology;
- the geographical dispersal of minority ethnic households and individuals;
- low minority ethnic population density;
- lack of demographic knowledge;
- lack of awareness of cultural issues/engagement 'literacy';
- being overambitious – seeking quantity not quality; and
- varying levels of commitment from the top.

The literature identifies a variety of approaches. More traditional models include the use of consultation documents, public consultation events, focus groups, questionnaires and face-to-face interviews, as well as the use of telephone interviews and case studies (see, eg, Brackertz, 2007). Where there were more innovative models identified in the literature, useful case studies exist, if not always specifically applied to minority ethnic groups in the rural context, for example, peer/community researchers (Stonewall Cymru, 2007; Saltus and Folkes, 2012), film-making (Taylor, 2005; Wellcome Trust, 2011), Web-based forums/platforms (Northern Ireland Forum, 2008; Twitchen and Adams, 2011) or mobile phone technology (LifeSwap, 2007). As an alternative to methods that rely on literacy and articulation skills, visual and creative techniques, such as 'Planning for Real' (Browne et al, 2005), participatory diagramming and mapping (Ahmad and Pinnock, 2007), were cited as effective tools for 'showing' opinions and ideas, while recruitment methods, such as snowballing, utilising gatekeepers and piggybacking on other events (Holder and Lanao, 2002; Groundwork East London, 2005; Brackertz and Meredyth, 2007; Dean et al, 2012), were helpful for gaining access to 'hard to reach' groups and individuals.

Typically, minority ethnic groups in rural areas lack the political clout to exercise voice and participate fully in local affairs. They are poorly represented on local boards, committees and other decision-making bodies or in positions of public office. It is well documented that their service needs are often overlooked or marginalised and there are considerable barriers for them in accessing services and gaining advice and information. In addition, they face racism and discrimination in their communities (Jay, 1992; Derbyshire, 1994; Agyeman and Spooner, 1997; Kenny, 1997; Neal, 2002; De Lima, 2004; Pugh, 2004; Robinson and Gardner, 2004; Ray and Reed, 2005; MEWN Cymru 2006; Williams, 2006). Minority ethnic organisations, groups and individuals report a sense of 'over-consultation' and 'consultation fatigue' as the policy mandate pushes public bodies to engage with them.

## Background to the study

The following case study is based on an action research project funded by the Carnegie UK Trust under the Rural Research Action Programme. It was designed and delivered through a partnership between what was then the 'North Wales Race Equality Network' (now North Wales Regional Equality Network) and Professor Charlotte Williams, Keele University, Staffordshire. The overall aim of the project was to explore the nature of the engagement between minority ethnic groups and public service bodies and to seek to enhance consultation strategies. This followed a far-reaching push by the newly devolved Welsh government for policy to be more citizen-focused and inclusive.

North Wales comprises six local authority areas, Ynys Mon, Gwynedd, Conwy, Denbighshire, Flintshire and Wrexham. Large expanses of the region can be described as rural, with population concentrations in small towns along the coastal strip. At the time of the study, the last census data showed that all six authorities had a minority ethnic presence of under 2%, ranging in number from as little as 481 'non-white' people in Ynys Mon to 1,400 people in Gwynedd. These figures do not include all ethnic groups or transient populations such as students or workers, and do not allow for the changes to the area brought on by the influx of new economic migrants from the accession countries of the European Union post-2004.

The minority ethnic population of North Wales is extremely diverse, geographically scattered and in a state of flux and change. Available census data at the time showed that no concentrated pockets of minority ethnic groups of more than 200 people could be found in any one ward across the region. There are no geographically based minority ethnic communities in the area, the more usual profile being isolated individual households or family groups. The largest minority groups by ethnic category are the Chinese and Mixed groupings. The typical profile is of a relatively young economically active minority population with a strong emphasis on employment in public sector organisations, catering and small businesses (BEST Partnership, 2004). Previous surveys have characterised the nature of needs among these households and the experience of racism and discrimination (NWREP, 2004; Crew et al, 2007; Cynwys Project, 2007), and other studies in the area have illustrated the changing profile of rural communities with the influx of economic migrants from the accession countries (NWREN, 2005; Hold et al, 2007). The minority ethnic population is highly differentiated and rapidly changing, but as this study illustrates, there is a core of 'settled' households that have been in the area over a large period of time.

## Methods

The research included a literature review, a survey of selected public authorities ($n$ = 18) in the area to assess their consultation strategies in use and the facilitation of consultation processes with three public bodies. An action research project was undertaken with the selected organisations aimed at enhancing their current practices. In addition, a questionnaire survey of minority ethnic individuals ($n$ = 90) resident in the region and a series of focus group interviews ($n = 6$) were conducted contemporaneously to assess four key aspects of rural living: belonging; family, friends and community association; getting involved; and influencing decisions.

## Living and working in rural areas: minority ethnic views

The research team sought out the views from the grass roots with the aim of providing a two-sided account of the engagement conundrum. The responses of over 90 individuals and three focus groups produced a rich account of minority views of living and working in the North Wales area. By far the greater number of participants had been resident in the area for over five years and a third for over 20 years. Respondents valued many of the traditional features of rural living, including the beauty, peace, quiet and environmental benefits, a feature consistent with other studies in the area (Robinson and Gardner, 2004). People were seen to be contributing to a variety of activities in their community, motivated by a sense of 'duty' and 'putting back into society'. Key barriers to engaging with public authority consultations included lack of time and carer responsibilities, but also language and culture barriers and concerns about discrimination and racism. In confirmation of the literature on rural racism, it is clear that the noted constellation of factors of isolation, conspicuousness, fear of racism and discrimination overlay an individual's ability to participate meaningfully at the local level (Campbell and McLean, 2002; Robinson and Gardner, 2004).

The findings of this study suggest a picture of individuals with high investment in their locality and good levels of integration against a broad range of non-political indicators. However, there was an apparent low sense of attachment or engagement with the local state and an apparent weak sense of being able to influence and shape decisions. Representation on local (public service) bodies in the area is notably low.

The issue of consultation was pursued for further exploration in the focus group interviews. All participants had had some involvement in consultation processes in the previous 12 months. Themes of consultation overload identified in previous research (BEST Partnership, 2004) characterised several of the responses:

- "sometimes I try to deflect a consultation … I feel as if I'm in danger of becoming a usual suspect."
- "just too many. Different agencies asking the same thing over and over again."

The difficulty of engagement often resulted in individuals being targeted repeatedly once they became known to organisations. They sometimes bore the brunt of unrealistically excessive expectations:

- "sent questionnaire in English and asked me to get it out to my friends … asked me to organise meetings and collect information and people's views to bring to the event. I had no time … felt guilty for not doing these things … feel obligation not just to [organisation who asked me], but to community."
- "again and again, we're expected to give up our time, go to a place they pick, at a time they choose just so they can fulfil their targets, tick their box … not because they want to do anything … it's abusive."
- "I'm not a representative of the … community, there are no … community leaders … it's just my viewpoint, I can't speak for the others."

There was also caution about involvement related to whether it would make a difference to outcomes. Lack of feedback, action or meaningful change was cited by all respondents:

- "I ask them for what purpose they are consulting. I will refuse if don't see it as relevant or as tokenistic."
- "If I bring people to a consultation, I feel responsible. If it doesn't go well or [the organisation] don't do what they've promised, it reflects on me."
- "Nothing changes, no action is taken. Sometimes, I find myself repeating what I said many years ago. The issues are still the same, nothing has changed. There is a lack of effectiveness in the whole process."

Participants also identified a number of negatives or things that they felt might have improved the consultation experience. Language issues featured large, with the lack of translation facilities seen as a drawback by some participants. Consultation documents that were not available in languages other than English and Welsh could inevitably limit participation. One respondent recounted how they had been told that there was no money for translation when requesting an alternate language, despite consultation papers claiming to have other languages and formats on request:

- "because of language issues, there were people there who didn't really know 100% what the consultation was about."

- "When I need to translate as well … it's hard to participate myself. It's very tiring … bit frustrating."

Poor facilitation and inadequate methodologies were also identified by the participants, including particularly long speeches or presentations that were too dry or too technical in language:

- "told that we would be recorded … not really asked for permission … no mention of confidentiality or how recording was going to be used."
- "Whilst some organisations go out of their way to do all the right things in a general consultation, when a crisis occurs, all the lessons they had apparently learnt goes out the window. They're apologetic afterwards but they don't seem to learn from the experience."

Lack of preparation or thought in planning events was noted by participants, with issues such as poor or inappropriate food, lack of labelling facilitators, and unsuitable times or venues. Many of the issues resonate with the findings of other studies and reflect the poor 'consultation literacy' of public bodies. However, some of the comments also revealed some of the difficulties posed by the consultation process for individuals living in rural and remote locations, which relate to their sense of conspicuousness and the risks that consultation may have for their standing in their own community:

- "sometimes we talk about quite difficult … controversial problems … I feel that how I behave at consultations may have an impact on my private life; how I'm perceived by others in the community."
- "there are conflicts … issues within the community. Sometimes, [people] lack courage to express their views … they want to avoid conflict or [they are] trying to be diplomatic … not many of us … everyone knows everyone else … can be difficult."
- "Some organisations also have a way of selecting people. Sometimes, they just want people who will not oppose or challenge their ideas."

These comments illustrate the heavy emotional investment that the consultation process may demand of minority ethnic people in such areas, not only in terms of the risks to their status and regarding the confidentiality of their views, but also in terms of compromising their views.

Participants made a number of constructive recommendations for improving consultation. Utilising expertise at NGO/grass-roots level was a recurring theme, with suggestions that the statutory sector should "go out into the community" or work with BME-focused organisations, perhaps paying to "'farm out" for consultation on an organisational basis'. Making consultation issues and events relevant, of interest and meaningful were frequently cited, but varied as to individual priorities and preferences. Food was seen as very important by many as an incentive, not only from a practical perspective, but also as an acknowledgement of respect and cultural awareness, as were factors like payment of travel expenses and appropriate 'freebies'.

Acquiring new skills, knowledge or experience (aside from a better knowledge of services) was also seen as an intrinsic benefit of involvement for minority individuals and groups. Added extra benefits such as exercises, outdoor activities, wildlife and dance were mentioned as good outcomes. The experiences recounted suggest that there is a clear divide between the interests of relatively new migrants to the area, such as economic migrants, and those of settled minority ethnic individuals and households. For example, incentives focusing on leisure or social activities appear to be less attractive to individuals whose prime motive for being in Wales is work. This type of incentive is more attractive to those who have time and financial stability as opposed to concerns about accessing basic services or exploitation in the workplace, which are high on the agenda of new migrants.

A number of positives were identified from involvement in consultations, ranging from the tangible and specific outcomes as a result of input – although it was acknowledged that progress through consultation was slow and that dramatic policy change was only very occasionally effected – to more general benefits, such as increased confidence and knowledge about local services and how to access them. Most pertinent were a number of responses that reflected a greater sense of inclusion and empowerment: of feeling involved; of being part of the community; and of effective consultation creating a "positive energy" that promoted community cohesion as different people and groups came together.

Overall, the study demonstrated that people's motivation for involvement reflected many of the known prompts and constraints on committing voluntary effort but it was also clear that some were constrained by fear of discrimination and racism towards their perceived outsiderness. At the same time, the minority participants welcomed the opportunities that consultation provided, particularly so when it resulted in clear outcomes.

## Action research with service providers

Over a period of 18 months, a number of service providers in the area were selected for developmental work on consultation, with varying levels of intervention from the project worker. They were surveyed to identify the major constraints on consultation in practice. A workshop was held to discuss messages from the literature and to introduce the range and variety of consultation mechanisms available to them. Of the original 18 participants, three partners were selected for in-depth work and 11 partners for second-tier working, principally the dissemination of research messages as an ongoing part of the process. Seven of these continued to input into the progress and tracking cycle post-seminar and the researchers were able to evaluate methodologies with five partners. Looking at the experience of the provider partners as a whole, a number of overarching themes and key messages emerged from this study:

- *Enthusiasm and commitment by front-line workers regarding engagement with minority ethnic individuals and households.* There were initially very high levels of commitment, involvement and expectation among the partners, which demonstrates considerable commitment to inclusive engagement with minority ethnic residents, but this was often undermined by organisational or institutional constraints.

- *A lack of leadership from the top in terms of commitment to initiatives and the allocation of appropriate resources.* Good leadership at the strategic and policy level sends out important messages, not only to personnel within an organisation, but also by cascading through to service users and the wider community. This is particularly significant with regards to work with minority or marginalised groups. Without a proactive stance and drive from above, project staff often felt isolated and demoralised. Lack of funding and time were cited as recurring constraints for the majority of partners. Many felt that there were overwhelming obstacles such that there exists a danger that passive resistance or a tokenistic approach of 'jumping through the hoops' becomes the only solution. Capacity issues cannot be allowed to undermine the implementation of an authority's statutory duty to consult inclusively, and the responsibility for tackling this should not rest on individual staff at the front line or on single departments alone. Without leadership from the top to ensure that realistic budgets are allocated, staff tasked with engagement and consultation inevitably decide that their only option is to move on and try to find individuals who are willing to voluntarily contribute on their terms. This can present substantial limitations, particularly in terms of securing democratic representation and participation. It also leaves untapped the knowledge base of people who have quite often contributed voluntarily for years and have simply become disillusioned with the process.

- *A need for more creative, innovative techniques in reaching out.* The barriers of rurality and the sparsity of BME individuals and households are challenges that require lateral solutions. Networking, identifying key players and building relationships and trust are all vital tools for effective engagement. Techniques such as snowballing from staff and other known contacts can be deployed to identify individuals beyond 'the usual suspects'. Piggybacking on other events was a popular technique and can be an effective practice, but one that needs to be utilised with caution. Piggybacking should not be regarded as a quick, simple option, particularly if the event is a BME-focused consultation with a specific agenda. There remains a danger that the number of potential consulters can become hugely disproportionate to the number of consultees and participating individuals find themselves targeted on issues beyond the agreed programme. More constructive piggybacking taps into non-consultation events at community, local or regional level. Less formalised events such as village and county shows, or food, culture or sporting festivals, all offer opportunities for engagement. For example, one partner created a highly visual stand at a popular regional food festival outlining the strategy under consultation. Stickers were used to encourage and enable people to identify their key priorities and additional input could be given 'graffiti wall'-style on post-it notes. Some community events required specific invitation through gatekeepers. These 'closed' events were seen as particularly important as they allowed access to individuals that may be impossible to engage with in any other way. It was clear from the dialogue with agencies that organisations need to move beyond models where they set the prescriptive agenda of date, time, venue and process. Exploring alternative and innovative participatory models, such as informal meetings revolving around food, participatory diagramming, multi-media techniques, activity-based incentives and so on, while working cooperatively on the individual and community levels, can generate more sustainable and meaningful dialogue.

- *Greater use of mixed methodologies needed.* Utilising a single mainstream methodology excludes and marginalises many minority ethnic individuals. A flexible approach that employs a variety of techniques will increase the likelihood of engagement, while synergistic working or partnerships with third sector organisations or other statutory agencies can also broaden the potential audience by ensuring that a variety of channels are being deployed.

- *Cross-authority working and the development of partnerships in equality practice is a positive step.* Partnership working has much to recommend it. The sharing of expertise and ideas, as well as resources, can result in more ambitious and innovative solutions. Collaborative working that crosses departmental, organisational or sector boundaries also capitalises on the limited availability of the target audience and lessens the likelihood of 'consultation fatigue'. For partnerships that aim to function as a sustainable entity, it is essential that structures and protocols are formalised. One of the project partners recounted that setting up strong frameworks helped to delineate responsibilities and encouraged stakeholders to take ownership of the work. For example, the research project group participants were organising meetings internally across departments within their own local authority to disseminate progress on the project and gain feedback on current and ongoing issues within their county boundary.

- *Community key players and third sector organisations are vital in supporting effective consultation and engagement.* Working with key community players or third sector organisations can allow access to individuals and networks that are impossible to engage with in any other way, but partnerships of this type raise some particular issues. There is an inherent imbalance of power here that can result, albeit inadvertently, in unequal outcomes. Partnerships must benefit all parties; otherwise, there is no incentive for cooperation. A reliance on key players, whether for access to closed events, as facilitators or as major participants, necessitates careful handling. Any contribution and input from individuals or groups must be negotiated clearly, sensitively and equitably. There may be multiple issues of capacity – time, financial and knowledge – which need to be taken into consideration, and assumptions and expectations on both sides need to be carefully managed. Funding can also be a key issue here. Project staff may "appreciate the difficulties" of capacity for individuals and community organisations but without the authority to access funds (for remuneration, additional resources or incentives), the result is simply frustration on both sides.

- *Institutional cycles and staff turnover impact on institutional memory through the loss of expertise, capital and established networks.* Effective engagement with minority groups and individuals requires specific expertise and is heavily dependent on good networking. These attributes are often lost with infrastructural changes and staff turnover, resulting in poor 'institutional memory'. Leadership and strategic protocols are needed to capture and disseminate expertise and good practice, capitalising on the successes made by front-line staff.

- *Innovation is relative to organisational experience.* Innovation and perceived creativity is a continuum, and organisational change can only be measured from each organisation's unique starting point. In areas where there is little apparent history of BME engagement, organisations often do not have a repository of tacit or explicit knowledge to draw on. Expectations and evaluations of process and outcomes need to be assessed within this context. Given this deficit of experiential learning and tacit knowledge with regards to effective and inclusive engagement with minority individuals and groups, it could be argued that much of the success and progress lies not in big ideas but in attention to detail. Examples from this project include:
  - including a member of the target audience on a steering or advisory group at planning stage;
  - presenting a range of options so that individuals can choose their mode of participation;
  - providing translated material in appropriate key languages;
  - extending personal invitations through a short visit, phone call or by personalising print and email invitations;
  - offering honorariums or other incentives to demonstrate that people's contribution is valuable;
  - ensuring that evaluation and the opportunity for anonymous input is integral to the timetable rather than a final pre-departure tag-on;
  - acknowledging people's time and effort by providing feedback on consultation; and
  - demonstrating that input is meaningful by disseminating resultant actions or explaining why action is not possible.

Much of the preceding may seem commonsensical. However, such points are too frequently sidelined and perceived as tangential rather than pivotal to success.

There remain concerns about the production of a genuine and open dialogue in the consultation process in which outcomes are followed through and appropriate feedback is given to participants. However, this study showed that there exists a good amount of enthusiasm and commitment by front-line workers towards engagement with minority ethnic individuals and households, but participants lacked learning from available resources or from tacit knowledge within the organisation. Many public organisations are daunted by the challenges of engagement in rural areas and considerable support is needed. Institutional memory is poor and organisational cycles produce their own constraints on the development of good practices, with staff turnover leading to a loss of expertise, capital and established networks. Cross-authority working and the development of partnerships in equality practice is a positive step and there was evidence of this emerging in the study area, but the role of third sector organisations needs to be sustainably utilised and efforts still need to be made to increase the representation of minority ethnic individuals on decision-making bodies and forums. Critically, there is a lack of leadership from the top in terms of commitment to initiatives, the allocation of appropriate resources and capitalising on gains made by front-line workers.

There is no quick solution, nor a single idea or model that will meet the needs of a diverse community. Meeting and talking to people on their terms empowers individuals and builds confidence and trust. Capacity-building, particularly in under-represented areas such as on decision-making bodies, is vital. This is time- and resource-intensive but will ultimately pay dividends in terms of building meaningful and sustained channels for inclusive engagement.

## Conclusion

The concern to build strong and responsive communities that have a voice in the design and delivery of public services is a core policy mandate. This extends to building the capacity of the most marginal voices in order that they can be heard in the policy process. Local authorities and other public bodies are increasingly acknowledging the issues involved in effective engagement with minority individuals and households in their area. This study illustrated the struggles to ensure robust and representative engagement in making and shaping policy that directly affects the well-being of BME populations. These struggles lie at the heart of transformative practice.

While the population of minority ethnic communities in rural and remote areas is relatively small compared to their presence in the UK population as a whole, there is no local authority area without a minority presence, including those considered the most remote. These communities have been subject to considerable transformation in recent years, with both the settled minority ethnic population of rural areas growing and the substantial growth of migrant worker populations in rural areas. Diversity is now the norm.

At the same time, minority ethnic individuals and groups within rural areas have struggled to be visible in terms of public policy and service delivery. Their lack of concentration and the fragmented and diverse nature of this population mean that they lack political clout, effective representation and a collective voice, such that they continue to be overlooked and marginalised. It is well established that the impact of racism and discrimination in these communities is no less substantive than in areas where they are more populous; indeed, these issues form a complex interplay with service delivery that continues to ensure the denial of access to key services for many. The low numbers of minority groups living in rural areas typically means that networks, minority organisations and other forms of social support that may be available in areas of more dense populations have not developed in the locality. Accordingly, many of the assumptions of partnership working, community engagement and community consultation at the heart of contemporary policy have to be rethought.

This study is unique in that it sought to explore two sides of the engagement conundrum – the perspective and activities of public service providers and the perspective and activities of minority ethnic people in the local community – acknowledging the difficulties and challenges faced by both partners. From the perspective of providers, there are clearly a number of expressed challenges that arise in seeking to develop effective engagement with minority ethnic groups in the area. In this study, major constraints were identified as a result of the diversity, dispersal and low aggregate numbers of minority ethnic individuals and households, and the paucity and vulnerability of minority ethnic organisations and networks in the area. From the perspective of individuals in the community, their willingness to participate is conditioned by fears of being overburdened with consultation processes that are ill-planned and have few demonstrable results.

Public sector organisations in rural areas often lack the infrastructure, skills, commitment, leadership and resources required to respond appropriately to diverse communities. This study found the goodwill and commitment on the part of front-line workers falling into attrition in the face of inadequate support from the top. Organisational constraints such as lack of appropriate funding, time and resources deployed to consultation activities and failure to give scope for innovation and creativity at the front line hamper progress. The effect of competing priorities easily shifts attention away from the equalities agenda and accordingly inhibits the accumulation of expertise and sustainable practices. This lack of leadership and support must be addressed.

At the same time, the study identified glimmers of positive practice, most notably, the emergence of partnership working across authorities, drawing sensitively on expertise and guidance from local voluntary organisations, and building positive relationships with individuals and households in the community. Considerable information exists on techniques, methodologies and good practice guidelines for engagement with minority groups but what is clearly needed is support to build capacity and to promote sensitive experimentation and innovation. Without this, consultation will only ever be tokenistic and exploitative.

The gains accrued to good consultation and genuine engagement are many and should form the bedrock of transformative practice. Not only does it enhance and legitimate policy decisions through incorporating the valuable insights and experiences of marginal groups, but it also fosters investment, inclusion and good integration for people from traditionally excluded sections of the community. Minority ethnic and migrant households are making a vital contribution (economic, social and civic) to rural communities. Their contribution needs to be recognised, valued and appropriately engaged in the development of policy and practice.

## References

Agyeman, J. and Spooner, R. (1997) 'Ethnicity and the rural environment', in P. Cloke and J. Little (eds) *Contested countryside cultures*, London: Routledge.

Ahmad, N. and Pinnock, K. (2007) 'Civic participation: potential differences between ethnic groups', Policy Research Institute.

BEN (Black Environment Network) (2006) 'Health and care consultation with the Chinese Women's Society Report', Gwynedd County Council.

BEST (Black and Ethnic Minority Support Team) Partnership (2004) 'North Wales BME communities mapping', prepared by North Wales Race Equality Network.

Boag-Munroe, G. and Evangelou, M. (2012) 'From hard to reach to how to reach: a systematic review of the literature on hard-to-reach families', *Research Papers in Education*, 27(2): 209–39.

Brackertz, N. (2007) 'Who is hard to reach and why?', ISR Working Paper. Available at: http://www.sisr.net/publications/0701brackertz.pdf

Brackertz, N. and Meredyth, D.(2007) 'Community consultation and the "hard to reach"', Nillumbik Shire Council case study report, council plan and strategic resource plan, 2005–06.

Browne, C., Codling, C., Musyoki, L., Page, R. and Russell, C. (2005) 'Community cohesion: seven steps, a practitioner's toolkit', Home Office.

Cabinet Office (2008) 'Better together: improving consultation with the third sector'. Available at: www.cabinetoffice.gov.uk?media/99612/better%20 together.pdf

Campbell, C. and McLean, C. (2002) 'Ethnic identity, social capital and health inequalities: factors shaping African–Caribbean participation in local community networks', *Social Science and Medicine*, 55(4): 643–57.

Caust, M., Berzins, K., Fleming, T., Kandola, M., Khan, A., Landry, C. and Wood, P. (2006) 'Planning and engaging with intercultural communities: building the knowledge and skills base', Comedia and The Academy for Sustainable Communities.

Community Action Hampshire (2006) 'Engaging with your local black and ethnic minority communities: making it happen, good practice guide guidance', web link no longer available.

COSLA (Convention of Scottish Local Authorities) (2008) 'National standards for community engagement', Scottish Executive.

Craig, G. and Lachman, R. (2008) 'Black and minority ethnic voluntary and community sector organisations in rural areas and DEFRA', a think piece from the North Yorkshire Black and Minority Ethnic Strategy Board (NYBSB) in response to the DEFRA consultation document.

CRE (Commission for Racial Equality) (2007) 'Annual report'. Available at: https://www.gov.uk/government/publications/commission-for-racial-equality-annual-report-and-accounts-2006-to-2007

Crew, T., Holmes, M. and Morgan, J. (2007) 'Isolated households. BME participation in the rural labour market in North Wales: developing an evidence base for effective interventions', North Wales Race Equality Network.

Cynwys Project (2007) 'Enabling minority groups to access advice and information', Legal Services Commission, The Community Fund, National Assembly of Wales. Available at: www.legalservices.gov.uk

DCLG (Department for Communities and Local Government) (2006) '2005 citizenship survey – active communities topic report', London.

Dean, J., Wollin, J., Stewart, D., Debattista, J. and Mitchell, M. (2012) 'Hidden yet visible: methodological challenges researching sexual health in Sudanese refugee communities', *Culture, Health & Sexuality: An International Journal for Research, Intervention and Care*, DOI:10.1080/13691058.2012.709639.

De Lima, P. (2004) 'John O' Groats to Land's End: racial equality in rural Britain?', in N. Chakraborti and J. Garland (eds) *Rural racism*, Devon: Willan Publishing.

Derbyshire, H. (1994) 'Not in Norfolk. Tackling the invisibility of racism', Norwich and Norfolk Race Equality Council.

Devon Race Equality Council (2003) 'Multi-ethnic Devon – a rural handbook'.

Dhalech, M. (1999) *Challenging the rural idyll: the final report of the Rural Racial Equality Project*, London: National Association of Citizens Advice Bureaux.

Dunlop, J. (2004) 'Community engagement toolkit. Involving the community. A portfolio of techniques', Dundee City Council.

Garland, J., Spalek, B. and Chakraborti, N. (2006) 'Hearing lost voices – issues in researching 'hidden' minority ethnic communities', *British Journal of Criminology*, 46: 423–37.

Groundwork East London (2005) 'Models for community consultation'.

Hashagen, S. (2002) 'Models of community engagement', Scottish Community Development Centre.

HSE (Health and Safety Executive) (2004) 'Successful interventions with hard to reach groups', Social Inclusion Policy Unit, Health and Safety Executive. Available at: http://www.hse.gov.uk/research/misc/hardtoreach.pdf

Hold, M., Korszon, S., Kotchetkova, E. and Grzesiak, F. (2007) 'Migrant workers in Flintshire', North Wales Race Equality Network.

Holder, D. and Lanao, C. (2002) 'Mid-Ulster: other voices. A listening session with a rural minority ethnic community in 2002', Multi Cultural Resource Centre, Northern Ireland.

Jay, E. (1992) *Keep them in Birmingham: challenging racism in South West England*, London: Commission for Racial Equality.

Kenny, N. (1997) 'It doesn't happen here? A report on racial harassment in Taunton Dean', Somerset Racial Equality Network.

LifeSwap (2007) 'Projects matching groups of young people with councillors and senior officers in their local authority, using mobile phone technology to create better understanding', web link no longer available.

MEWN Cymru (Minority Ethnic Women's Network Wales) (2006) 'Voices from within'. Available at: http://www.mewn-cymru.org.uk/

Neal, S. (2002) 'Rural Landscapes, representations and racism, examining multicultural citizenship and policy making in the English countryside', *Ethnic and Racial Studies*, 25(3): 442–61.

Northern Ireland Forum (2008) 'Promoting the voice of young people. I'm a councillor, get me out of here!'. Available at: www.bigvote.org.uk

NWREN (North Wales Race Equality Network) (2003) 'Criminal justice & the consultation process', North Wales Criminal Justice.

NWREN (2005) 'Workers From outside the UK in the Conwy Local Authority Area', Conwy Community Safety Partnership.

NWREN (2006) 'Race equality consultation scheme report', Welsh Development Agency.

NWREP (North Wales RSL Equality Partnership) (2004) 'The housing and related experience of black, minority ethnic communities in North Wales'.

Participation Cymru (2011) 'National principles for public engagement'. Available at: http://www.participationcymru.org.uk/national-principles

Pugh, R. (2004) 'Difference and discrimination in rural areas', *Rural Social Work*, 9: 255–64.

Ray, L. and Reed, K. (2005) 'Community, mobility and racism in a semi-rural area: comparing minority experience in East Kent', *Ethnic and Racial Studies*, 28(2): 212–34.

Robinson, V. and Gardner, R. (2004) 'Unravelling a stereotype: the lived experience of black and minority ethnic people in rural Wales', in N. Chakraborti and J. Garland (eds) *Rural racism*, Devon: Willan Publishing.

Russell, P., Morrison, A. and Davidson, P. (2001) 'Effective engagement: a guide to principles and practice', Effective Interventions Unit and The Scottish Drugs Forum.

Saltus, R. and Folkes, L. (2012) *In their own words: voices of African-Caribbean and black Welsh men and women*, Pontypridd: University of Glamorgan.

Scottish Executive (2002) 'Good practice guidance – consultation with equalities groups', Prepared by Reid-Howie Associates Ltd on behalf of the Scottish Executive.

Scottish Executive Involving People Team (2002) 'Building strong foundations – involving people in the NHS', Scottish Executive Health Department.

Stonewall Cymru (2007) 'The Inside Out Project report', Stonewall Cymru, University of Central Lancashire and Government Department for Communities and Local Government.

Taylor, D. (2005) 'Film-making in Elton', Community Development Worker Programme: Case Study Summaries, Commission for Rural Communities.

Twitchen, C. and Adams, D. (2011) 'Increasing levels of public participation in planning using Web 2.0 technology', School of Property, Construction and Planning, Birmingham City University, Working Paper Series, no 5.

UK Community Participation Network (1999) 'Participation works! 21 techniques of community participation for the 21st century', New Economics Foundation.

WAG (Welsh Assembly Government) (2004) 'Making connections: delivering better services for Wales'. Available at: http://www.cewales.org.uk/cew/wp-content/uploads/making_the_connections.pdf

WAG (2009) 'Getting on together – a community cohesion strategy for Wales'. Available at: http://www.gavowales.org.uk/file/CoCo_WG_Getting_on_Together_Action_Plan.pdf

Wellcome Trust (2011) 'Community engagement – under the microscope'. Available at: http://www.wellcome.ac.uk/stellent/groups/corporatesite/@msh_grants/documents/web_document/wtvm054326.pdf

Williams, C. (2006) 'Revisiting the rural/race debates: a view from the Welsh countryside', *Ethnic and Racial Studies*, 30(5): 741–65.

# NINE

# Multidisciplinary contexts: insights from mental health

*Frank Keating and Stefan Brown*

## Introduction

This chapter will start from the premise that multidisciplinary teams are microcosms of broader society, and in a racialised society, will reflect these dynamics. Lowe (2013) argues that racial hierarchies that exist in society are reproduced in organisational contexts. He further suggests that what occurs in work-group situations is informed or influenced not so much by the task, but by the more subtle dynamics of discrimination and domination. This chapter will discuss policy developments in relation to race equality in mental health in the UK. We will draw on insights gained from a consultation with mental health social workers to explore their experiences, perspectives and challenges of working across cultures in a community-based setting. Community-based settings were selected because we assumed that these practitioners are more likely to be in direct contact with service users in situ and that there is greater scope to understand individuals in their social and cultural context. A critical discourse framework will be applied to identify the discourse(s) about cultural diversity from the consultation exercise. We will specifically highlight the prevailing or dominant discourses on diversity and point to the need for counter- or critical discourses. We will also highlight some of the inherent tensions in practice. Suggestions for how these challenges and tensions can be addressed will be explored. Informed by insights from critical race theory (CRT), whiteness studies and intersectionality, social determinants of health, and social justice, we offer suggestions for transformative practice.

## Situating racial disparities in the UK

Racial disparities in mental health in the UK have been a long-standing issue of concern and there is documented evidence of the failure by mental health services to appropriately deal with racial inequalities (Department of Health, 2003; Morgan and Hutchinson, 2009). To understand or analyse these disparities, it is important to consider and appreciate the contexts and position of black and minority ethnic (BME) communities[1] in the UK. These groups are disadvantaged across all indicators of social, health and emotional well-being (Williams and

Johnson, 2010). They experience higher rates of exclusion from schools and higher levels of unemployment, are more likely to live in poorer housing conditions, and are disproportionately represented in the prison populations – the litany of racial disadvantage is endless. Evidence shows that high levels of systematic discrimination can have significant mental (ill-)health effects (Karlsen and Nazroo, 2002). The failure to meet the needs of BME groups is most stark in mental health and there is a large literature that captures the challenges in relation to mental health and cultural diversity (see, eg, Bhui, 2002; Fernando, 2003; Bhui et al, 2007; Fernando and Keating, 2009; Sewell, 2009; Karlsen et al, 2012; Keating, 2012). There is well-documented evidence which shows that BME groups come into contact with mental health services through more adversarial pathways, which often include the police and the criminal justice system (Morgan and Hutchinson, 2009). BME groups are also more likely to be subject to compulsory hospital admissions under the Mental Health Act 2007 (Department of Health, 2007). They are over-represented in hospital admissions and are meted out the harsher end of treatments, such as control and restraint, and are less likely to be referred for more socially oriented approaches, such as talking therapies (Davies, 2014). Prior to considering working with cultural diversity in multidisciplinary contexts, it is important to review the policy contexts in which mental health services operate.

## Policy contexts

Against the backdrop presented earlier, there have been numerous initiatives to address cultural diversity more generally (Gunaratnam and Lewis, 2001; Bhavnani et al, 2005), and more specifically in mental health services (Keating et al, 2003). The Modernisation Agenda in Health and Social Care introduced by the Labour Government in 1997 promised scope for change. National Service Frameworks (NSFs) were introduced to set standards for service delivery. The *National Service Framework for mental health* (Department of Health, 1999), for example, set a standard that required services to combat stigma and discrimination towards people with mental illness. It also required mental health services to be responsive to individual need regardless of 'race', culture, sex, disability and so on. A review of this policy five years on (Department of Health, 2004) revealed that there was a raft of new mental health services, as well as a new cadre of mental health practitioners. However, in relation to issues of discrimination and meeting the mental health needs of BME groups, the report concluded that there remain significant challenges in these areas.

A significant marker for racial inequality in mental health services was the death of Rocky Bennett, an African-Caribbean man who died as a result of being restrained by mental health nurses in a medium-secure ward. After a long and drawn-out struggle by his family to achieve justice, an inquiry report concluded that mental health services are institutionally racist (Blofeld, 2003). The government subsequently published an action plan for *Delivering race equality*

(DRE) (Departmental of Health, 2005). This was an ambitious initiative to have better information, improved services and more engagement with communities. The programme was concluded in 2010 and final evaluation reports indicated that there is now better information, staff have been trained in cultural competence and there are pockets of good practice in terms of community engagement. For example, Fountain and Hicks (2010), in their evaluation of the DRE programme, found that the profile of community organisations was raised and that there were stronger links between these organisations and primary care trusts. However, the overall finding was that racial disparities have remained, that the situation is complex and that there were no clear-cut explanations for these 'differences'. Craig and Walker (2012) posited that DRE has failed to achieve a sustainable shift in developing culturally sensitive and more accessible services. Interestingly (or should we note, sadly) The Chief Medical Officer's report in 2014 (Davies, 2014) confirmed that there are still significant challenges in relation to race equality in mental health services.

DRE introduced a shift to a more inclusive discourse focusing on social issues, such as greater engagement, building cultural competence and assessing how ethnic diversity is represented across hospital and community-based services (Craig and Walker, 2012). However, a fundamental flaw in this policy initiative was the assumption that the medicalised approach(es) to mental health care is the most effective way of responding to mental distress. Evidence shows that a narrow medicalised approach overlooks the complex and structural dynamics of social causes that influence access to mental health care (Daley and MacDonnell, 2011). Keating (2007) has argued that the disparities in mental health are social, cultural, economic and political, and that a narrow medicalised approach to redress these is inadequate.

Given that issues of race equality have been pushed to the fore of the policy agenda, it is interesting to note that subsequent policies in relation to mental health have a much-reduced focus on race equality. This invisibilising of 'race' and ethnicity is fuelled by a neoliberal agenda that promotes managerialism, monitoring and individualism, and thwarts the quest for racial equality (Bhui, 2006; Bhatti-Sinclair, 2011; Harrison and Turner, 2011; Singh, 2014). A new mental health strategy was introduced in 2009 to create a shared vision for mental health. The strategy specifically aimed to promote equal access to services and to reduce stigma and discrimination towards people with mental health problems (HM Government, 2009). In 2011, a new government came into office, which meant that the 2009 policy was superseded with the introduction of *No health without mental health* (HM Government, 2011). Reducing stigma and discrimination on the basis of mental illness continued to be a prominent theme and the strategy also included a specific focus on developing culturally appropriate services in order to increase access to services. It should not go unnoticed that there was, at the same time, another policy/legislative initiative to bring all 'single strand discrimination' legislation under one umbrella, with certain characteristics defined as 'protected' (which includes ethnicity), that is, the Equality Act 2010.

The Act calls for all health and social care policies to be subjected to an equalities impact assessment prior to implementation. This development, arguably, may (to a certain extent) explain this reduced focus on race equality (Singh, 2014). Race equality therefore seems to have been subsumed under the broader notion of equality. Activists and advocates for racial equality fear that the new Act will 'water down' or weaken the focus on race equality (Pears, 2013).

A common thread that runs through these policy developments is that although there is a focus on reducing stigma and discrimination, this has not been extended to racism, except for the DRE programme, which particularly aimed to address racial inequalities. While there has been a focus on addressing culture, this is being promoted under the rubric of meeting individual need, which seems to make it easier for practitioners to ignore the individual's social and cultural context. Responding to culture or providing culturally appropriate services have often been limited to dietary needs and the need for separate meeting spaces, such as prayer rooms. The more complex issues of identity, spirituality, embodiment, social exclusion, racialisation and racism are overlooked; this is the challenge for transformative social work practice.

## Working with diversity in multidisciplinary contexts

Multidisciplinary teams (MDTs) have now become to the most accepted and established way of providing effective mental health services (Department of Health, 1999). Good communication, consistency of purpose and autonomy of service users are promoted as key factors for success (Colombo et al, 2003). However, evidence shows that shared decision-making is poor, and power and status are at the heart of the interactions between practitioners and service users (Colombo et al, 2003; Abenstern et al, 2012). There is role conflict due to differing professional perspectives and on the best way to respond to mental health problems (Carpenter et al, 2003). A significant feature of MDTs is the predominance of the medical model in policy and practice (Carpenter and Barnes, 2001; Beresford et al, 2010; Walker, 2013). It has been argued elsewhere (Robinson et al, 2011; Viruell-Fuentes et al, 2012) that a medicalised approach to mental health means that containment, control and compliance become essential features of mental health practices. This has particular resonance for BME groups, who lack trust in the ability of mental health services to respond appropriately to their needs (Keating et al, 2002; Davies, 2014).

To inform our ideas for this chapter, we arranged a consultation with social workers working in a multidisciplinary community setting known as a community mental health resource centre. We approached team leaders of community mental health teams in the London area to ask whether they would be interested in engaging in discussions about mental health and working with cultural diversity. We chose London because this is the most culturally diverse region in the UK and also the area where we expected that social work practitioners would be in a strong position to make useful observations about mental health and cultural diversity.

A community mental health team in one of the London Boroughs agreed to meet with us for a two-hour consultation in January 2015. Nine social workers participated in the consultation, ranging from a student and newly qualified social workers to a manager with significant experience. The group was ethnically diverse and included a gender mix. The broad discussion topics included: perspectives on culture and diversity in mental health, and practice issues and challenges for working with and across cultural diversity in the organisational context. To ease the flow of the discussion, we started with general discussions about their personal backgrounds and their professional journeys into mental health social work. The discussion was co-facilitated by the authors and both took notes during the discussion. We compiled our notes and identified the themes that emerged from the discussion independently, followed by a joint exploration of our findings and analyses in order to compile a final set of themes. We acknowledge that the insights gained from the consultation cannot be generalised broadly, but given our own experience and research in this field, we believe that the findings from this consultation resonate with what is known about cultural diversity and mental health. A further limitation is that we are offering the perspectives of professionals and appreciate that service users and carers will have different and differing narratives about their experiences of mental health and cultural diversity.

Drawing on a model proposed by Daley and MacDonnell (2011), we identified that there are different discourses in MDTs in relation to diversity and race (in) equality, that is, dominant discourses and counter-discourses. The former refers to discourses that maintain and reinforce the status quo and the latter refers to discourses that offer a different analysis of the situation. These discourses are sometimes referred to as downstream and upstream.

In our consultation with mental health social workers[2] on the challenges of working in a multi-ethnic milieu, we identified discourses that operate at three levels: individual practitioner level, team level and organisational level. At an individual practitioner level, there was a clear commitment to anti-oppressive practice, whereas at the team level, the discourse was more closely aligned to working with cultural diversity. However, we noted that these discourses did not translate into broader organisational practices. Bhavnani et al (2005), in a review of race equality initiatives, found that an overemphasis on outcomes creates barriers to organisational change. Organisational discourses can be classified as managerialism and individualism, which include a focus on resources, targets, measurement, monitoring and individual rights. Bhatti-Sinclair (2011), for example, argued that organisational practices and the modernisation agenda in the UK limited access to services and exacerbated the difficulties for BME communities. Discourses at the broader organisational level dominated and influenced decisions and practice at the individual and team levels.

When social workers were asked how ethnic and cultural diversity is addressed in practice, they stated that it is "part of what we do". In other words, working with cultural diversity was perceived to be at the core of their everyday practice. However, when this statement was unpacked, it became evident that there are more dominant discourses that neutralise this commitment to working with diversity. A more individualistic focus on meeting need seems to influence decisions about resource allocation. Practitioners reported that they are expected to assess need according to a set of thresholds for need and rank need according to level of severity, rather than taking into account contextual factors, such as dissemination and marginalisation. Moreover, they have to meet targets and work to time limits, which reduces opportunities to gain a fuller understanding of the individual's context. This supports Harrison and Turner's (2011) finding that organisational structures and priorities undermine the ability of practitioners to provide culturally appropriate service responses. Social workers reported that in order to obtain resources for service users, they have to assimilate to the organisational culture. As one eloquently stated: "attainment of resources requires assimilation of a view [different to yours]". What this worker implied was that he is committed to addressing inequality and promoting diversity, but if he wants to obtain resources to meet the needs of the service users with whom he works, he has to fit his requests or assessments to organisational requirements. It seems that at the front-line level, there is a commitment to embrace diversity, but at the top layers of the organisation, this commitment seems to be phrased differently, that is, under the mantra of resources, cost-effectiveness, thresholds for meeting individual need and meeting organisational targets. This supports views which suggest that organisational culture plays an important role in how issues of 'race' and racism are silenced (Harrison and Turner, 2011; Lowe, 2013).

Social workers have been integrated into health services to work alongside health professionals. Unfortunately, this meant the adoption of a more individualistic and medicalised approach to practice. For example, some of the terminology used to describe a focus on social issues still reflected the medical model, such as the introduction of what was termed a 'Social Care Clinic'. Moreover, practitioners are required to use a shared central computerised system to document and record client/service user information. Even though this system is geared towards use in a multidisciplinary context, social workers reported that it is distinctly oriented towards capturing information of a more medicalised nature, for example, diagnoses, medication, symptom control and compliance with medication. As outlined earlier, the dominance of the medial model has devastating implications for BME communities. Despite suggestions that sociocultural issues should be central to general discussions about mental health (Keenan et al, 2004), practitioners reported that they do not have sufficient time to take social histories. Therefore, they rely on what is already documented, de facto meaning that they may inadvertently act on discourses or narratives that may no longer apply to the individual's current context. This situation also seems to reflect the decline of the role and standing of social work in MDT contexts (McLaughlin, 2005; Singh and Cowden 2009) and, by implication, a lesser focus on sociocultural factors.

Another example of silencing or invisibilising 'race' and racism in organisations is the fact that BME communities are often narrowly construed as service users only and it is seldom acknowledged that they are also represented in service provision as administrators, clinicians/practitioners and service providers (Bhatti-Sinclair, 2011). Williams (2014) reviewed the strategies for anti-racism and the employment of black workers in health and social care and argued that they were catalysts for change and promoting race equality, but, at the same time, they operate from positions of relative powerlessness as they are not represented in the upper echelons of organisational structures (Lewis, 2000). Practitioners experience a range of processes of social exclusion, which includes isolation, marginalisation of their concerns and interpersonal racism (Mirza, 2006). We should therefore acknowledge that racial inequality structures the experience of both service users and practitioners in and out of the workplace. Practitioners reported that there was a distinct lack of formal spaces to discuss and talk safely about issues of diversity. This is a clear example of how the cultural and racialised context for staff is overlooked or silenced (Bhui, 2006; Harrison and Turner, 2011). Conversations of this important nature seem to have been relegated to other social spaces, such as the pub or drinks in the bar. Of course, this means that individuals who do not frequent such spaces are inadvertently excluded from participation in these exchanges. Invisibilising 'race' in the workforce can lead to a fear of talking about issues of 'race' and to racism becoming enforced and entrenched in practice (Keating et al, 2002).

The previous sections explored the context for BME communities in general and highlighted the disparities in mental health. Policy developments were traced and theoretical stances towards cultural diversity were reviewed. Insights from mental health social workers were presented to illustrate the discourses that operate within practice and the organisational context. We conclude from this that the current contexts for BME groups, both as service users and practitioners, require a different approach; thus, the final section of the chapter will explore ideas and suggestions for transformative practice in mental health social work.

## A framework for transformative practice

From our consultations, we found that at the practitioner and team level, there is an expressed commitment to working with cultural diversity and promoting race equality in mental health. However, at the organisational level, it was clear that managerialism drives the way in which services are delivered. Drawing on the insights gained from the literature and our discussions with mental health social workers, we propose that there is a need for counter-discourses that should enable practitioners to address the needs of service users, but also give them greater scope for service user involvement. We have learnt from our consultation with practitioners that 'race' and racism is invisibilised, that medicalised approaches to mental health care still prevail, and that the construction of need is individualised. We propose that a range of interlocking discourses offer a way to build and develop transformative practice: CRT, whiteness studies and intersectionality, social determinants of health, and social justice.

## Critical race theory, whiteness studies and intersectionality

There is clearly a need for a different discourse around achieving race equality. This would require a shift from the invisibilising of 'race' and the narrow cultural competence framework. As highlighted earlier, cultural competence can challenge Eurocentric assumptions and the deficit view of communities (Gunaratnam and Lewis, 2001; Williams and Johnson, 2010), but it does not equip practitioners to deal with the harsher and deleterious effects of racism at systemic and institutional levels. It also focuses on marginalised groups as distinct from white groups and therefore problematises the experiences of those subjected to 'race' and racism (Jeyasingham, 2012). Moreover, it ignores the fact that white groups are also racialised and that they are not an undifferentiated category (Frankenberg, 1997; Hunter, 2010).

A starting point will be to adopt a CRT stance, which holds promise for overcoming these limitations (Abrams and Moio, 2009). CRT was introduced in the US as a counter-argument to the positivistic and liberal discourse on civil rights (Crenshaw, 1991; Delgado and Stefancic, 2001). In essence, it argues that racism is endemic, that it is real (lived experience), that black people embody multiple identities (ethnicity is only one dimension of BME identities) and that power and privilege are maintained and sustained by law and policy. The primary interest of CRT is to analyse and transform the interactions and connections between 'race', racism and power (Delgado and Stefancic, 2001). Limbert and Bullock (2005) suggest that CRT is 'anchored' in the lived experiences of both the oppressed and the oppressor and therefore enables a focus on privilege, advantage and power. On a more applied basis, CRT can assist to locate social policy in the broader context of power relations and provides tools to explore the ways in which restrictive policies (such as those found in mental health services) maintain and sustain racial inequality (Limbert and Bullock, 2005).

As pointed out earlier, the writings on anti-racism provide an analysis that only focuses on the oppressed, which means that whiteness or issues of white identity are invisible, despite the fact that there have been much earlier debates about whiteness (Jeyasingham, 2012). In order to progress and advance our understanding of 'race' and racism, it has been suggested that the analysis should include how white identities operate within racial hierarchies (Warren, 2001; Garner, 2007; Jeyasingham, 2012). According to Jeyasingham (2012: 672–3), including whiteness in our analysis of racism can facilitate a study of the nuances of everyday living and how hegemonic power operates within this. He further suggests that we can 'problematize the normative practices that sustain white centrality' (ie where whiteness is the standard for comparisons between groups) and the experiences of different white groups. This will help us to understand that white groups are not homogeneous: they are also diverse and will be affected differentially by racialisation (Garner, 2007). A focus on whiteness can also inform and make visible our understanding of privilege and locate it in the broader institutional and historical processes that maintain and reinforce white privilege (Grossman and Charmaraman, 2009).

Intersectionality (Crenshaw, 1991; Larson, 2008) is a counter-discourse that highlights the interconnectedness of all forms of oppression and the struggle for equality. These ideas can help us understand and take account of how people construct their reality and acknowledge that such constructions may include racism and discrimination.

## Social determinants of health

A discourse on the social determinants of health acknowledges that there are social factors that have a significant impact on health (and mental health) and can also lead to racial inequality. We have highlighted earlier that BME groups fare worse across all indicators of well-being, so there is a need to analyse the structural features of mental health care (Jackson et al, 2004). A focus on the structures of power and how this informs the experience of care by BME groups becomes vital. Engaging with the social determinants of health inevitably requires a shift away from an individualistic pathology or 'blaming the victim' approach to mental ill-health. Forde and Raine (2008) suggest that a focus on the social determinants of health should include an acknowledgement that individuals have agency and that the role of their own actions in relation to mental health should be integrated with a social determinants of health approach. Moreover, a focus on the social determinants of health can enable practitioners to engage with narratives from the perspective of BME groups by acknowledging that racism is one of the determinants of well-being. Tew (2011) posits that in mental health practice, a focus on the social dimensions of distress gives agency to service users who have been excluded and marginalised by emphasising issues of stigma and power, and by situating an analysis of oppression at the heart of practice.

## A social justice approach

Racial inequality is unjust and unethical, and efforts or attempts to eradicate it from mental health care should be informed by a social justice stance. Social and political factors, especially power in and outside the workplace (Williams, 2014), impact significantly on how BME groups experience mental health care – this should underpin our analysis. Social justice is also at the heart of social work practice (O'Brien, 2011; Graham, 2009) and has been embraced in the definition of social work adopted by the International Federation of Social Workers (IFSW, 2014). Social justice involves the total acceptance of difference and diversity as positive features of both organisations and communities. Such an approach should be underpinned by value of fairness and equality, fully recognising the dignity and worth of the individual. Essentially, it entails meeting basic human needs and maximising life chances (Craig, 2002).

Adopting a social justice approach in practice suggests that we should be valuing human worth, building mutually respectful relationships, addressing the broader psychosocial impacts of inequality and providing support to maximise the life chances and opportunities of minority groups who experience mental health problems.

Following the lead of Ortiz and Jani (2010: 184), we suggest that drawing on the aforementioned discourses will enable mental health practitioners to critique: a) the theoretical presuppositions of services; b) how they fit with the people they are designed for; c) to what extent services reflect what service users understand or construct as needs; and d) those questions that are not being asked or those conversations that are silenced.

Combining insights from the discourses described earlier will enable mental health social workers in multidisciplinary contexts to engage more fully with issues of identity, spirituality, embodiment, social exclusion, racism and racialisation. It will place them in an ideal position to reflect on their own racialised positions, validate individuals' narratives of distress and racialisation, and be more equipped to conduct an organisational and structural analysis that includes a focus on issues of power and privilege. It should equip them to work towards what Closson (2010: 278) terms 'a personal ethic of social justice'.

## Conclusion

We suggest that to fully embrace cultural diversity, mental health social workers should aim to reduce the over-inclusion of unhelpful interventions and increase the inclusion of helpful interventions (those defined by BME communities) – this should be at the heart of transformative practice. We should also embrace the fact that BME communities are unequally represented in those who use services and similarly in those who provide services, particularly at the higher echelons of the organisational hierarchy. Given the long-standing nature of racial disparities in mental health, we acknowledge that addressing this will not be an easy task. It is imperative that there is organisational commitment, support and leadership to achieve racial equality – a suggestion that has been promoted numerously, but still requires reiterating. We need a workforce that is adequately equipped and supported to work with issues of emotional and mental distress in racialised contexts. We need a workforce that fully understands and appreciates the dynamics of racialisation, including that of power and privilege. Attempts to achieve change should be done collectively, that is, combining the knowledge and resources within both organisations and communities. Transformative practice in mental health social work should be inclusive, accessible, sensitive, equitable and socially just.

## Notes

[1] The terms 'BME' or 'minority groups' will be used as shorthand for racialised groups in the UK, but this does not mean that we ignore the heterogeneity within and across these groups.

[2] We acknowledge that this offers a social work perspective and that practitioners from other disciplines may have different perspectives on these discourses. We also wish to acknowledge the practitioners who gave up valuable time to participate in the consultation.

## References

Abendstern, M., Harrington, V., Brand, C., Tucker, S., Wilberforce, M. and Challis, D. (2012) 'Variations in structures, processes and outcomes of community mental health teams for older people: a systematic review of the literature', *Aging & Mental Health*, 16(7): 861–73.

Abrams, L.S. and Moio, J.A. (2009) 'Critical race theory and the cultural competence dilemma in social work education', *Journal of Social Work Education*, 45(2): 245–61.

Beresford, P., Nettle, M. and Perring, R. (2010) *Towards a social model of madness or distress? Exploring what services users say*, York: Joseph Rowntree Foundation.

Bhatti-Sinclair, K. (2011) *Anti-racist practice in social work*, Basingstoke: Palgrave MacMillan.

Bhavnani, R., Mirza, H.S. and Meetoo, V. (2005) *Tackling the roots of racism: lessons for success*, Bristol: The Policy Press.

Bhui, H.S. (2006) 'Anti-racist practice in NOMs: reconciling managerialist and professional realities', *The Howard Journal*, 45(2): 171–90.

Bhui, K. (2002) *Racism and mental health: prejudice and suffering*, London: Jessica Kingsley Publishers.

Bhui, K., Warfa, N., Edonya, P., McKenzie, K. and Bhugra, D. (2007) 'Cultural competence in mental health care: a review of model evaluations', *BMC Health Services Research*, 7(15), DOI: 10.1186/1472-6963-7-15.

Blofeld, J. (2003) *Independent inquiry into the death of David Bennett*, Cambridge: Norfolk, Suffolk and Cambridgeshire Strategic Health Authority.

Carpenter, J. and Barnes, M. (2001) 'Integrating health and social services', in G. Thornicroft and G. Szmuckler (eds) *Community psychiatry*, Oxford: Oxford University Press.

Carpenter, J., Schneider, J., Brandon, T. and Woolff, D. (2003) 'Working in multi- disciplinary community mental health teams: the impact of social workers and health professionals of integrated mental health care', *British Journal of Social Work*, 33(8): 1081–103.

Closson, R.B. (2010) 'Critical race theory and adult education', *Adult Education Quarterly*, 60(3): 261–83.

Colombo, A., Bendelowa, G., Fulford, B. and Williams, S. (2003) 'Evaluating the influence of implicit models of mental disorder on processes of shared decision making within community-based multi-disciplinary teams', *Social Science & Medicine*, 56: 1557–70.

Craig, G. (2002) 'Poverty, social work and social justice', *British Journal of Social Work*, 32(2): 669–82.

Craig, G. and Walker, R. (2012) '"Race" on the welfare margins: the UK government's Delivering Race Equality Mental Health programme', *Community Development Journal*, 47(4): 491–505.

Crenshaw, K. (1991) 'Mapping the margins: intersectionality, identity politics and violence against women of color', *Stanford Law Review*, 43: 1241–99.

Daley, A.E. and MacDonnell, J.A. (2011) 'Gender, sexuality and the discursive representation of equity in health services literature: implications for LGBT communities', *International Journal for Equity in Health*, 10(40), doi:10.1186/1475-9276-10-40.

Davies, S. (2014) *Annual report of the Chief Medical Officer 2013: public mental health*, London: Department of Health.

Delgado, R. and Stefancic, J. (2001) *Critical race theory: an introduction*, New York, NY: New York University Press.

Department of Health (1999) *National Service Framework for mental health: modern standards and service models*, London: The Stationery Office.

Department of Health (2003) *Inside outside: improving mental health services for black and minority ethnic communities*, London: The Stationery Office.

Department of Health (2004) *National Service Framework for mental health – five years on*, London: The Stationery Office.

Department of Health (2005) *Delivering race equality: an action plan for reform inside and outside services*, London: The Stationery Office.

Department of Health (2007) *The Mental Health Act (Amended) 2007*, London: The Stationery Office.

Fernando, S. (2003) *Cultural diversity, mental health n psychiatry: the struggle against racism*, Hove: Brunner Routledge.

Fernando, S. and Keating, F. (2009) *Mental health in a multi-ethnic society*, London: Routledge.

Forde, I. and Raine, R. (2008) 'Placing the individual within a social determinants approach to health inequity', *Lancet*, 372: 1694–6.

Fountain, J. and Hicks, J. (2010) *Delivering race equality in mental health care: report on the findings and outcomes of the community engagement programme 2005–2008*, Preston: University of Lancashire.

Frankenberg, R. (1997) *Displacing whiteness: essays in social and cultural criticism*, Durham, NC: Duke University Press.

Garner, S. (2007) *Whiteness: an introduction*, London: Routledge.

Graham, M. (2009) 'Reframing black perspectives in social work: new directions?', *Social Work Education: The International Journal*, 28(3): 268–80.

Grossman, J.M. and Charmaraman, L. (2009) 'Race, context, and privilege: white adolescents' explanations of racial-ethnic centrality', *Journal of Youth and Adolescence*, 38(2): 139–52.

Gunaratnam, Y. and Lewis, G. (2001) 'Racializing emotional labour and emotionalising racialized labour: anger, fear and shame in social welfare', *Journal of Social Work Practice: Psychotherapeutic Approaches in Health, Welfare and the Community*, 15(2): 131–48.

Harrison, G. and Turner, R. (2011) 'Being a "culturally competent" social worker: making sense of a murky concept in practice', *British Journal of Social Work*, 41(2): 333–50.

HM Government (2009) *New horizons: a shared vision for mental health*, London: The Stationery Office.

HM Government (2011) *No health without mental health*, London: Department of Health.

Hunter, S. (2010) 'What a white shame: race, gender, and white shame in the relational economy of primary health care organizations in England', *Social Politics*, 17(4): 450–76.

IFSW (International Federation of Social Workers) (2014) 'Global definition of social work'. Available at: http://ifsw.org/policies/definition-of-social-work/ (accessed 24 April 2015).

Jackson, B.E., Pederson, A., Armstrong, P., Boscoe, M., Clow, B., Grant, K.R., Guberman, W. and Wilson, K. (2004) '"Quality care is like a carton of eggs": a gender- based diversity analysis to assess quality of health care', *Canadian Woman Studies*, 24(1): 15–22.

Jeyasingham, D. (2012) 'White noise: a critical evaluation of social education's engagement with whiteness studies', *British Journal of Social Work*, 42: 669–86.

Karlsen, S. and Nazroo, J. (2002) 'Relation between racial discrimination, social class, and health among ethnic minority groups', *American Journal of Public Health*, 92: 624–31.

Karlsen, S., Becares, L. and Roth, M. (2012) 'Minorities' experience of health services', in G. Craig, K. Atkin, S. Chattoo and R. Flynn (eds) *Understanding 'race' and ethnicity*, Bristol: The Policy Press.

Keating, F. (2007) *African and Caribbean men and mental health: a briefing paper*, London: Race Equality Foundation.

Keating, F. (2012) 'Understanding "race", ethnicity and mental health', in G. Craig, K. Atkin, S. Chattoo and R. Flynn (eds) *Understanding 'race' and ethnicity*, Bristol: The Policy Press.

Keating, F., Robertson, D., Francis, E. and McCulloch, A. (2002) *Breaking circles of fear: a review of the relationship between mental health services and the African and Caribbean communities*, London: Sainsbury Centre for Mental Health.

Keating, F., Robertson, D. and Kotecha, N. (2003) *Ethnic diversity and mental health in London: Recent developments*, London: King's Fund.

Keenan, E.K., Tsang, A.K.T., Bogo, M. and George, U. (2004) 'Do social workers integrate sociocultural issues in mental health session dialogue?', *Social Work in Mental Health*, 2(4): 37–62.

Larson, G. (2008) 'Anti-oppressive practice in mental health', *Journal of Progressive Human Services*, 19(1): 39–54.

Lewis, G. (2000) *Race, gender and social welfare: encounters in a post-colonial society*, Cambridge: Polity Press.

Limbert, W.M. and Bullock, H.E. (2005) '"Playing the fool": U.S. welfare policy from a critical race perspective', *Feminism and Psychology*, 15: 253–74.

Lowe, F. (2013) 'Keeping leadership white: invisible blocks to black leadership and its denial in white organisations', *Journal of Social Work Practice: Psychotherapeutic Approaches in Health, Welfare and the Community*, 27(2): 149–62.

McLaughlin, K. (2005) 'From ridicule to institutionalisation: anti-oppression, the state and social work', *Critical Social Policy*, 25(3): 283–305.

Mirza, H.S. (2006) 'Transcendence of diversity: Black women in the academy', *Policy Futures in Education*, 4(2): 101–13.

Morgan, C. and Hutchinson, G. (2009) 'The social determinants of psychosis in migrant and ethnic minority populations: a public health tragedy', *Psychological Medicine*, 40: 705–9.

O'Brien, M. (2011) 'Equality and fairness: linking social justice and social work practice', *Journal of Social Work*, 11(2): 143–58.

Ortiz, L. and Jani, J. (2010) 'Critical race theory: a transformational model for teaching diversity', *Journal of Social Work Education*, 46 (2): 175–93.

Pears, E. (2013) 'Is race equality being taken off the political agenda?', *The Voice*, 13 April. Available at: http://www.voice-online.co.uk/article/race-equality-being-taken-political-agenda

Robinson, M., Keating, F. and Robertson, S. (2011) 'Ethnicity, gender and mental health', *Diversity in Health and Care*, 8: 81–92.

Sewell, H. (2009) *Working with ethnicity, race and culture in mental health: a handbook for practitioners*, London: Jessica Kingsley Publishers.

Singh, G. (2014) 'Rethinking anti-racist social work in a neoliberal age', in M. Lavalette and L. Penketh (eds) *Race, racism and social work*, Bristol: Policy Press, pp 17–32.

Singh, G. and Cowden, S. (2009) 'The social worker as intellectual', *European Journal of Social Work*, 12(4): 479–93.

Tew, J. (2011) *Social approaches to mental distress*, Basingstoke: Palgrave MacMillan.

Viruell-Fuentes, E., Miranda, P.Y. and Abdulrahim, S. (2012) 'More than culture: structural racism, intersectionality theory, and immigrant health', *Social Science & Medicine*, 75: 2099–106.

Walker, S. (ed) (2013) *Modern mental health critical perspectives on psychiatric practice*, St Albans: Critical Publishing.

Warren, J.T. (2001) 'Doing whiteness: on the performative dimensions of race in the classroom', *Communication Education*, 50(2): 91–108.

Williams, C. (2014) 'The catalysers: "black" professionals and the anti-racist movement', in M. Lavalette and L. Penketh (eds) *Race, racism and social work*, Bristol: The Policy Press, pp 53–70.

Williams, C. and Johnson, M. (2010) *Race and ethnicity in a welfare society*, Maidenhead: Open University Press.

# TEN

# Outreach: care experiences among Gypsy, Traveller and Roma families

*Sarah Cemlyn and Dan Allen*

## Introduction

'Outreach' is a term that we use in this chapter to capture a number of key elements, but that also needs some definition and differentiation in relation to its different uses. Pierson and Thomas (2002: 324) define it simply as 'any attempt to take a service to people who need it and who would otherwise probably not use the service', while Andersson (2013: 184) draws up a much more rounded definition based on research among outreach workers:

> Outreach work is a contact-making and resource-mediating social activity, performed in surroundings and situations that the outreach worker does not control or organise, and targeted at individuals and groups who otherwise are hard to reach and who need easy accessible linkage to support.

Some elements of this definition hold relevance for the approach we describe in this chapter, particularly in relation to reaching out to make contact and the reference to outreach work relinquishing control of the contact environment since 'outreach workers do not build their relations to people in settings where professional power is mediated through spatial structures' (Andersson, 2013: 179). However, the pervasive notion of 'hard to reach' is one that we critique, implying as it does a pathologisation of the groups being worked with rather than an analysis of the troubled or complex mutual relationship between such groups and social work services, and the political context in which such interactions occur. Therefore, within most analyses, outreach work, while being more open and flexible than much office-based social work, nonetheless focuses largely on work with individuals who are affected by similar social circumstances, though this may also include negative previous experiences of services, as often also holds for Gypsies, Travellers and Roma.

We link outreach to a community social work model and to engagement with a discriminated minority ethnic group, so it involves an emphasis on anti-racism, as well as community engagement, empowerment and partnership, and to an understanding of previous failures to provide culturally appropriate services to Gypsies, Travellers and Roma (Cemlyn, 2000a; Cemlyn et al, 2009; Greenfields et al, 2015). Hartknoll et al (quoted in EMCDDA, 1999: 14) refer to outreach as 'A community-oriented activity undertaken in order to contact individuals or groups from particular target populations, who are not effectively contacted or reached by existing services or through traditional health education channels'. However, this continues the emphasis on a one-way engagement between services and those who are perceived as not capable of being reached in traditional ways. In the approach we discuss in this chapter, within the framework of transformatory practice (see Chapter One), there is instead a strong element of working collaboratively and co-productively with minority communities, of mutual learning, engagement and responsiveness, and of listening to and reflecting critically on the voices and experiences of Gypsy, Traveller and Roma children to enable them to act as a powerful advocate for their rights. One such voice provides our starting point:

> In my soul there is a hole that nothing can quite fill.
>> I've searched across the miles, for me time has stood still.
>> I'm still that convoy member, Travellers across the land.
>> We have morals and we're Christian, our loyal moral band.
>> We believe in freedom, in love and light and hope.
>> Even though I keep searching, I cannot sit and mope.
>> I have these precious memories and future happy dreams.
>> So, one day I hope to find my kin, and then my life begins!

(Poem by a Traveller who lived in a trans-racial placement)

These words are taken from a poem quoted in Allen's (2012a) research study, which examined the experiences of Gypsies and Travellers who lived in care as children. The poem was provided by a woman who lived in care as a child. At the age of 11, she discovered a bundle of papers in her father's writing desk stating that her biological family were Travellers. When she turned 16, she left her home and took to the road in search of her family. However, as she had been raised in care away from her community and culture, she had not been taught the key skills needed to live in a world that she perceived as being determined to assimilate and control her. Over time, she experienced aggressive and violent eviction, exploitation, and the removal of her own children into care. Despite these extreme challenges, she remains driven by a commitment to find her sense of identity. However, each time she attempts to integrate with the Traveller community, she is rejected as a masquerading imposter. As an adult, she struggles to come to terms with the fact that she is not able to be part of the Travelling community for the simple fact that she was raised away from her Traveller community as a child.

In order to examine how trans-racial placements can impact on the lives of Gypsy, Traveller and Roma people, we draw on Allen's (2012a) study in order to bring the voices of those with this experience directly into view. Centralising this critical discussion around the themes of power relationships between Gypsy, Traveller and Roma communities and the wider society, of notions of cultural difference, and of institutionalised discrimination, injustice and insensitivity towards marginalised groups, we set out the approaches needed to counter these difficulties, including political contextualisation, community and cultural engagement, outreach, dialogic practice, and human rights-based practice.

To frame the discussion, and acknowledging the misinformation or lack of realistic information surrounding these groups, we first sketch the political and social context for Gypsies, Travellers and Roma, and summarise previous research findings about social work responses to and provision for these communities, including historical and international experiences of children's 'welfare' services, where fundamental distortions of social work values have led to their characterisation as '(dys)welfare' (Cemlyn and Briskman, 2002).

The groups we refer to as 'Gypsies', 'Travellers' or 'Roma' in this chapter actually constitute a rich and diverse group of communities who each go under different names, and often distinguish themselves carefully from one another. Although a fuller exploration of these differences might be useful, any additional detail is beyond the scope of this discussion. For readers new to this topic, the book *Social work with Gypsy, Roma and Traveller children* (Allen and Adams, 2013) provides an accessible foundation from which to better understand the unique challenges experienced by Romani Gypsies, Roma, Irish Travellers, Scottish Gypsies and Travellers, Welsh Gypsies, New Travellers, Showmen, Circus People and Boat People within a British context.

While this chapter focuses on the position of Gypsy and Traveller children, we do, at different points in this discussion, also refer to Roma communities. When possible, the key messages that we describe are transferred to include Roma children in recognition of the historical, experiential and increasingly political links that exist between Roma, Gypsy and Traveller groups. Alongside the urgent and neglected experiences of Gypsy and Traveller children in care, which are the predominant focus of this chapter, there is evidence of similarly urgent issues affecting Roma children and their experiences with child welfare authorities. We hope to address this task more fully in the near future, but in the meantime, the context for Gypsies and Travellers will be considered with reference to the challenges being faced by Roma children wherever possible.

## Context

The presence of English Romani Gypsies in the UK, some of whom had travelled from India through Europe, has been noted since the early 16th century. However, Acton (1979) argues that it was the intense moral panics and legislation against 'vagrants' in the late 16th and early 17th centuries that shaped the ethnicity of diverse nomadic groups, who had to band together in the face of persecution.

Travellers, who are indigenous to Ireland, have migrated to the UK and throughout the world. They share significant experiences, especially of racism and harassment, and some cultural norms with English Romani Gypsies. The latter also share some cultural and historical features with 'Roma' (itself an umbrella term), who have migrated to the UK mainly since the late 1990s, first as asylum seekers fleeing persecution and discrimination in different countries in Central and Eastern Europe, and subsequently as migrants from the 'A8' European Union (EU) accession countries, namely, Czech Republic, Estonia, Hungary, Latvia, Lithuania, Poland, Slovakia, Slovenia, and then the 'A2' countries of Romania and Bulgaria (Fremlova and Ureche, 2009).

There are considerable difficulties in calculating the numbers of people who identify as Gypsies, Travellers or Roma; however, we may assume that there are between 125,000 and 250,000 Gypsies and Travellers (Ryder et al, 2014), broadly similar to the British Bangladeshi population, and probably round 200,000 Roma people living in the UK.[1]

As previously indicated, there is significant diversity across all of the groups of communities referred to as 'Gypsies', 'Travellers' and 'Roma', but they all experience similar aspects of exclusion, discrimination and poor outcomes across multiple domains, in accommodation, education, health, criminal justice and employment (Ryder et al, 2014). Lack of adequate, secure and culturally appropriate accommodation, which for nomadic or semi-nomadic Gypsies and Travellers, is a legal site for their caravan, underpins unequal access to education, health, employment and other services (Cemlyn et al, 2009; Richardson and Ryder, 2012). This combines with racism, institutionalised discrimination, problematic professional attitudes and the strengthening neoliberal context of privatisation and reduced budgets to create entrenched exclusion. Gypsies and Travellers in housing, especially if the choice is a forced one for lack of an alternative, can experience different pressures, including psychological problems due to cultural aversion to bricks and mortar, isolation, and racism from neighbours (Smith and Greenfields, 2013). For Roma, who until 2014 had restrictions on employment and now face further benefit curbs, accommodation is predominantly in poor and exploitative conditions in the private rented sector. The situation of all the groups is frequently exacerbated by stereotypical treatment in the media and prejudiced and sometimes inflammatory political and public discourse (NFGLG, 2014).

The discrimination experienced by Gypsies, Travellers and Roma has parallels with that experienced by other minority groups, for example, in criminal justice. However, the specific history of their relationships with majority sedentary society requires a broadened frame of reference within which policymakers and practitioners can find space to reflect on the ideological dominance of sedentarism (McVeigh, 1997) and the myths and distortions that pervade perceptions. In parallel with the importance of mindfulness of slavery and colonisation in relation to other black and minority ethnic groups, it is essential to remember the centuries of harassment of Roma, Gypsies and Travellers across Europe, including genocidal policies in the 16th and 20th centuries (Kenrick and Puxon, 1995; Acton, 1997).

However, a crucial part of the political context is also the achievement of political alliances and solidarity between Gypsy, Traveller and Roma communities in pursuit of equality and human rights and their promotion of more informed and fruitful engagement between their communities and the majority society, as represented by organisations such as the former Gypsy and Traveller Law Reform Coalition, the National Federation of Gypsy Liaison Groups and the All Party Parliamentary Group on Gypsies, Travellers and Roma. These coalitions draw from common experiences of discrimination and from the strengths of community experience, drive and commitment to achieve change (Ryder et al, 2014). In specific relation to child protection, social change also requires social work agencies to acknowledge oppression and to take proactive steps to meaningfully engage Gypsy, Traveller and Roma communities, both collectively and individually.

## Social work services

Previous research about social work provision for Gypsy, Traveller and Roma communities has highlighted how the broader social and political context affects interaction between social workers and the communities, and despite some examples of positive practice and committed individual initiatives (O'Higgins, 1993; Pemberton, 1999; Allen and Adams, 2013), a wider failure on the part of social work to engage with and respond sensitively to meeting children's needs, as summarised in Cemlyn et al (2009). The current structures of children and family social work, which have moved far from any community social work orientation, have not helped social work practitioners in the task of sensitive engagement. Moreover, in the corporate local authority context, in which control of unauthorised camping is still often a primary mode of engagement with local Gypsies and Travellers, social work may become caught up in assessments of need that remain framed by sedentarist assumptions and prejudice (Cemlyn, 2000b, 2008; Harrington, 2014).

A prevalent theme in the research highlights the implication of mutual avoidance and fear because of misapprehension and a lack of cultural understanding, and sometimes overt discrimination on the part of social workers (Greenfields, 2002; Garrett, 2004, 2005; Harrington, 2014), and fear of authority generally on the part of Gypsies and Travellers because of eviction or harassment, and threats to children in particular (Cemlyn, 2000b; Allen and Adams, 2013). This is compounded by historical community experiences of the removal of children in the UK and across Europe, sometimes systematically and as part of a strategy for 'educating' them away from their culture as a form of cultural genocide (Cemlyn and Briskman, 2002; Vanderbeck, 2005). These destructive practices have recently been seen in relation to Roma families in the UK, with numerous Roma children being wrongly removed from their families as part of police anti-trafficking operations (Foster and Norton, 2012), and in high-profile cases of fair-skinned Roma children being removed from their families in Greece and the Republic of Ireland based upon suspicions of child abduction.

## The position of Gypsy, Traveller and Roma children in care

The impact of the sedentarist prejudice described by McVeigh (1997) has been seen to lead to a pathologising approach to Gypsy, Traveller and Roma families, including the removal of children into care. Until 2009, however, it was not possible to comment with any accuracy on how many of these children had been taken into care because that data did not exist. To some extent, it is still not easy to comment with great accuracy on this situation because, with the exception of data from England and Northern Ireland, there are no 'official' government sanctioned data sets on the proportion of Gypsy, Traveller or Roma children living in care throughout Europe.

The reason cited for this lack of information reflects various constitutional privileges throughout Europe that prohibit data collection that might be used to reduce a person to a socially constructed ethnic label, such as 'Gypsy', 'Roma' and 'Traveller'. While the avoidance of ethnic compartmentalisation might serve to reduce discrimination, it also presents a significant barrier for social work practice and its responsibility to develop meaningful communication between those people who access services and those people who provide them. For Gypsy, Traveller and Roma children, their specific exclusion means that they are homogenised within Eurocentric data sets, which then conceal the concern that children from these communities are over-represented in various care systems across Europe.

Within the English context, Table 10.1 shows the number of children identified as 'Travellers of Irish Heritage' and 'Gypsy/Roma' in care since 2009, the first year that these ethnic groups were recorded. While small, these numbers represent significant increases: the number of Travellers of Irish Heritage in care is up by 250% on 2009 figures and the number of Gypsy/Roma children is up by 425%.

Before moving on to discuss these statistics in further detail, it is important to note that the decision of the Department for Education (DfE) to group the terms 'Gypsy' and 'Roma' is inappropriate because it suggests homogeneity. The fact that both groups maintain their own sense of identity and separateness from one another is not represented here. The joining of these two terms highlight not

**Table 10.1: Numbers of Gypsies and Travellers living in care in England 2010–14**

| Ethnicity | Year | | | | | | |
|---|---|---|---|---|---|---|---|
| | 2009 | 2010 | 2011 | 2012 | 2013 | 2014 | 2015 |
| Traveller of Irish heritage | 20 | 40 | 50 | 50 | 70 | 70 | 90 |
| Gypsy/Roma* | 40 | 70 | 90 | 120 | 190 | 210 | 250 |

Source: Taken from DfE (2015).

Note: * It is important to point out that from 2016 the ethnicity of Gypsy/Roma will be split to respect the fact that Gypsies and Roma are two distinct groups. Whilst this policy change is welcomed, it is equally important to point out that any census information published before 2016 will remain limited to those categories shown above.

only the inability of the DfE to recognise the importance of ethnicity, but also, consistent with broader concerns across Europe, the failure to value the importance of individual representation or individual circumstance. In response to the rise of Far Right anti-Roma discourse in the UK in particular, it could be argued, for instance, that the 425% increase is less likely to be impacting on Gypsy children and more likely to be directly related to Roma. With no differentiation between 'Gypsy' and 'Roma', this hypothesis cannot be easily substantiated. However, Allen and Adams (2013) summarise communications from organisations working with Roma and refer to the miscommunication, misunderstandings and resultant poor practice that can arise when professionals, with no knowledge of a community's language and working through an interpreter who may only know the national language rather than the specific Romani dialect, attempt to discuss within limited imposed timescales complex concerns and support packages for which the client has no framework of understanding. Where meaningful attempts are not made to verify responses through more direct and deliberate forms of inquiry, false assumptions can be made that heighten any awareness of risk.

The methodological weaknesses in the approach to reporting such figures notwithstanding, it is important to note that they do give credence to a long-held suspicion that Gypsy, Traveller and Roma children are being taken into care at a disproportionate rate. Similar statistical data in Northern Ireland show that 'Traveller' children make up the largest minority ethnic group of children living in care in that country (Department of Health, Social Services and Public Safety, 2015), and further data sets reveal that this pattern is echoed across other EU member states (see Table 10.2).

Based on a series of research studies published by the European Roma Rights Centre (2011), Table 10.2 uses the information collected from government representatives and child protection authorities in Bulgaria, the Czech Republic, Hungary, Italy, Romania and Slovakia to show that the proportion of Roma children living in institutional care is significantly disproportionate to the overall population of Roma people. Taken together with data published in England and Northern Ireland, these figures show that Gypsy, Traveller and Roma children *are* being taken away from their families and communities at a disproportionate rate.

Table 10.2: Representation of Romani children in institutional care in EU member states

|  | Bulgaria | Czech Republic | Hungary | Italy | Romania | Slovakia |
|---|---|---|---|---|---|---|
| Percentage of Roma children in children's homes visited | 63.0% | 40.6% | 65.9% | 10.4% | 28.0% | 2.5% |
| Share of Roma in the total population | 10% | 3% | 7% | 0.23% | 9% | 9% |

## Social work and a continuity of care

Arguably, one of the most important aspects of social work practice relates to the support of children and young people who live in foster care. In addition to the complex roles and responsibilities that accompany this task more generally, there is a requirement that where a child is unable to live with a birth parent, then consideration must be given in the first instance to them living with a family member or friend. Although the legal frameworks are different in each country in the UK, they all allow for children to be placed directly into public care from home, and require local authorities to provide appropriate support according to the circumstances of the case so that cultural and biological links to families can be maintained. The same holds true for countries throughout Europe. However, for all the good intentions of these directives, it is reported that this duty rarely extends to include Gypsy, Traveller and Roma communities in the UK (Allen and Adams, 2013) and, again with the exception of the Republic of Ireland, other European member states (European Roma Rights Centre, 2011).

Understanding why these communities may not be included in friends and family placement planning is complicated. One of the main challenges facing social work practice with Gypsy, Traveller and Roma families is located within a stereotypical perspective that has emerged from a general ignorance, or projected racism, within the population at large (Richardson, 2006; Cemlyn et al, 2009). Frequently characterised as being 'socially deviant' within the media and domestic populism (Stewart, 2012), it is argued that negative representation has become manifest in social care practice, with social work practitioners often (unwittingly) viewing Gypsy, Traveller and Roma communities and cultures as objects of concern (European Roma Rights Centre, 2011; Allen, 2012b). With the exception of the research and transformative approach to social work practice in the Republic of Ireland that enabled the Shared Rearing service to be developed (see, eg, O'Higgins, 1993; Pemberton, 1999), previous research into social work services has identified a general lack of development of fostering services among Gypsy, Traveller and Roma communities to provide culturally appropriate and supportive services to children who can no longer live with their families (Cemlyn, 2000a).

At the time of writing, it is not possible to say how many of the 280 Gypsy and Traveller children living in care in England (National Statistics, 2014a) or the 186 Traveller children living in care in Northern Ireland (National Statistics, 2014b) might be living in kinship care arrangements, as there is no known data available to inform that discussion. Within Europe, however, a research team working for the European Roma Rights Centre interviewed 1,109 people, including Roma children themselves, living in Bulgaria, the Czech Republic, Hungary, Italy, Romania and Slovakia, and showed that the nature of populist hatred towards Roma meant that potential Roma carers are being excluded as suitable carers. What is more, potential foster-carers and adoptive parents who are not Roma were seen to refuse to care for Roma children, sentencing them to a life in institutional care (European Roma Rights Centre, 2011). As Roma children grew up in institutionalised environments away from their families and communities, the study also found that very little support was being provided to them to help maintain and develop a proud sense of identity. The limitation of this study within the current context is that until 2012, it was not possible to extrapolate these findings to generate transferability in the UK. Alongside the work of Pemberton (1999) and O'Higgins (1993), the research by Allen (2012a) was one of the first to fully identify the impact on Gypsy and Traveller children thus wrenched from their cultural milieu.

## The research

The following sections derive from a larger study with six women and four men that utilised interpretive phenomenological analysis (IPA) (Smith et al, 2009) to uncover the lived experiences of Gypsies and Travellers who lived in care as children. For the purposes of this chapter, only the views and experiences of the women who took part in the wider study will be described. Of these six women, one was a Romani Gypsy, four were Irish Travellers and one was from the Showmen community. Each had some experience of living in trans-racial fostering or residential arrangements in either England or the Republic of Ireland between the 1980s and 2000s. To uncover the detail of lived experience, each person was invited to describe their life in care in any way that suited them. Some people chose to talk about their experiences in a one-to-one interview, some chose telephone interviews and one person chose to describe her experiences through poetry. In line with the theoretical framework of IPA, the interpretive analysis presented is a close reading of what each person said.

## Being a Gypsy or Traveller

The impact of being taken into care was emphasised for each person as they explained how their early childhood experiences of being a 'Gypsy' or a 'Traveller' had reinforced their internalisation of a cultural identity, and created an indelible imprint that cemented an understanding of how their customs and mores were unique. Before going into care, each remembered how they were taught to be separate from, and suspicious of, wider Gorgio, non-Gypsy/Traveller, influences: "Growing up we soon learnt that Gorgio people hated us. They hated us and they hated our culture."

Reflecting on these social constructions, each person remembered that when they were removed from their families and placed in trans-racial placements with carers who were not Gypsies or Travellers, their sense of vulnerability became acute. Instead of feeling safe, as consistent with their hopes, dreams and aspirations, each person described the perceived need to conceal their Gypsy or Traveller identity so that any cultural difference did not make them targets of anti-Traveller racism:

"The kids at my new school picked on me because of my [Irish Traveller] accent. I told my foster family but they didn't care, so I thought 'Oh well, I won't speak with an accent anymore that way no one will know I am a Traveller'. I wanted to make the Traveller me invisible."

The sense of cultural isolation brought about through cultural dislocation led each person to question those principles that composed the identity while engendering a great deal of social and emotional confusion. As a result of these complex dilemmas, each person reported the cultural and social uncertainty that they encountered as they attempted to search for an object of cultural familiarity that could inspire an investment in permanence. For each, however, this object of familiarity did not exist.

While the experience of cultural separation and loss may be typical across the care system more generally, it is important to point out that the object that the Gypsies and Travellers who took part in this study were searching for was not. While some children living in care are able to recognise, with some level of familiarity, their own mores (even if this is the more general act of living in a house), Gypsy and Traveller children, particularly those used to living on sites, remain in a place and space of confusion as they attempt to make sense of complete cultural displacement. For those who took part in Allen's (2012a) study, trans-racial placements compounded the need for cultural assimilation as a strategy to experience some feeling of acceptance within the new social context. Over time, each person described how they began to feel guilty for abandoning their culture. In order to overcome these feelings of guilt, each person described an obligation to maintain their Gypsy or Traveller identity:

"I got back [from school] to the foster house and watched telly. I remember having chewing gum in my hair from the girls at lunchtime, I saw Kylie Minogue on the telly, and I decided that I was going to be like her. I suppose I just wanted to feel normal and I went upstairs [and] cut my hair…. [Laughing] fuckin idiot aren't I. Anyways, it didn't work and [the girls at school] called me all the more. I had made a right job of my hair all sticking up all over the place but from that day, I decided that I am who I am and that's the way it is. A Traveller through and through [laughing] I found out that I fight good as well. Me Da would have been proud."

Each person described how their ideological commitment to a Gypsy or Traveller identity reduced their preparedness to accept cultural change, and increased their resilience to undermine the conventions associated with their new in-care experience. For three women, the determination to remain a Gypsy or Traveller became manifest in what they described as aggressive behaviour:

"I didn't do anything that the carers wanted me to do. I feel bad about it now because I used to give them real trouble. I think that I must have been restrained every day. But I thought that if I did what they said, I would become like them."

For three others, self-harm and emotional and social isolation became the common coping mechanism:

"When it all got too much and I started to cut myself and I refused to speak, no one helped me…. They didn't know the pain I felt in my heart from not knowing who I was, from being, from being [sobbing], from being treated like animals, worse than animals. No one cared about me as a Traveller."

In each instance, each person's attempts to maintain a Gypsy or Traveller identity were labelled with broader anti-Traveller stereotypes. Instead of responding to this behaviour with empathy, each recalled how their carers attempted to achieve control and enforced cultural assimilation in more extreme and abusive ways. In spite of the challenges presented, people explained that the ability to survive in care while experiencing cultural severance and displacement was only the beginning of a personal fight to maintain a secure Gypsy and Traveller identity.

## The impact of rejection

Despite individual attempts to demonstrate a certain resilience against the threat of cultural assimilation, the six women who took part in the study explained that when they were old enough to leave care and reintegrate into their Gypsy or Traveller community, they were often marginalised as a direct result of living with non-Gypsy and Traveller carers. As they had grown up in care away from their culture and community, they were seen to be contaminated by non-Gypsy/ Traveller influences. For this reason, some explained that they were unable to marry, and were instead positioned as subservient to the rest of the community:

"When I left care, I tried to get back in with my family. My Uncle and Aunty took me on and let me live in their Trailer for a while. When we went to fairs and that, all the boys would all look down at me and call me dirty. They knew that I had been in care and they all thought that I was like a Gorgio girl. That I had been having sex, that I had been to nightclubs and that I had taken drugs. You see, the Gorgio people look at us and see what they think are Gypsies. The same way the Gypsy boys looked at me and saw a Gorgio girl. Because what they have seen on the television, and that, they think that I am dirty, and because of this, no man in his right mind would marry me. If someone did, they would be outcast."

While some women explained that they were able to conceal the fact that they lived in care as children so as to experience some sense of community inclusion, they reported that the need to hide the truth about their childhood has been a significant factor in their ability to enjoy and experience positive emotional well-being. Despite surviving a journey through care that was enabled by a firm commitment to an internal ideology of what a Gypsy or Traveller woman should be, as adults, they remain alienated and shamed by their own communities because of stereotypical assumptions about the type of people Gorgio are, in interaction with cultural expectations about Gypsy and Traveller women's behaviour. Due to cultural gender expectations, each woman explained that they have never been fully supported to overcome the feelings of complete cultural abandonment and isolation, or the childhood sense of loss and confusion that continues to haunt them to this day.

## The importance of this understanding

Comparable with the report entitled *A life sentence* (European Roma Rights Centre, 2011), which explored the experiences of Roma children living in care in Europe, Allen's (2012a) research has shown that the journey through care for Gypsy and Traveller children living in the UK can present a number of challenges that can force feelings of insecurity. As social stigma is encountered and perceived from the new 'in-care' social networks, the testimonies provided enabled a preliminary understanding of how various different acculturation and resistance strategies were used by Gypsies and Travellers as they attempted to make sense of the traumatic and culturally assimilative experience of cultural dislocation.

By centralising the voices of Gypsy and Traveller women who lived in care as children in this way, it has also been possible to expose some of the possible ramifications of decisions when no careful consideration is given to the ethnicity of the child, or the centralisation of specific mores that might be important to them. When the time came for each person to leave care, they were disadvantaged in multiple ways. Allen (2012a) has shown how and why Gypsy and Traveller women can feel ill-prepared to reintegrate into their own communities as adults. As a direct result of living in care as children, growing up in institutional care or trans-racial placements, they each explained how the experience of being in care created a cycle of oppression from which it is hard, if not impossible, to escape. The clear similarities between the experiences of Gypsy and Traveller children living in care in the UK and those described by Roma children in Bulgaria, the Czech Republic, Hungary, Italy, Romania and Slovakia (European Roma Rights Centre, 2011) once more unites these communities in the most appalling way. Despite constituting a rich and diverse group of communities, it is now clear that the children who live and suffer in care are subject to the same hostility related to the pernicious nature of social injustice, populist discrimination and hatred.

## Responding to the growing crisis

An introduction to the experiences of Gypsies, Travellers and Roma who lived in care as children has enabled this chapter to reveal how the experience of cultural isolation can have long-lasting and harmful implications. Based on the testimonies provided earlier, it could be argued that social care professionals can easily become constrained by prejudice, thus substantiating the concerns of Cemlyn et al (2009). Where this occurs, a lived experience of a life in foster care might be lost within wider racist generalisations. To overcome this challenge, it is clear that if a transition into and out of care is to become safe and effective, cultural continuity must become a centralised feature of any care-planning process. In other words, it is essential that Gypsy, Traveller and Roma children experience continued cultural inclusion. While effective placement planning for Gypsy and Traveller children might only be achieved through friends and family foster-care, where this is not possible, there remains an urgent need for professionals to spend time with the child and to listen and talk to them, as any reasonable parent should. In all cases, this requires a shift in emphasis that sees Gypsies and Travellers less as objects of concern, and more as culturally proud and resilient children who might be losing their identity, their sense of cultural pride, their customs and their distinctive way of life. As shown by research carried out in the Republic of Ireland (Pemberton, 1999), paying more respectful attention to the heritage and lived experience of Gypsy and Traveller children is the only way to promote resilience, protect transitions and reduce the risk of cultural isolation.

A priority is to ensure that Gypsy, Traveller and Roma children are not removed into care because of failures of engagement and assessment informed by political and cultural understanding and culturally competent communication on the part of professionals. Where placement outside the immediate family is essential, the most obvious way to address some of these challenges is to place Gypsy, Traveller and Roma children with appropriate carers in their own communities. However, the reality is that this is unlikely to happen for most children in the foreseeable future, and trans-racial placements are therefore inevitable. For this reason, it is essential that social workers, foster-carers and others involved with Gypsy, Traveller and Roma children are trained in matters of anti-discriminatory practice and cultural competence.

Training programmes that take a reflective approach to cultural awareness-raising and engage with controversial areas, such as oppression, sexism, racism, prejudice, cultural displacement, social marginalisation and forced eviction, are recommended by Allen and Adams (2013) for those working with Gypsy, Traveller and Roma groups. They explain that 'training must support practitioners to recognise that the structural challenges faced by individuals, families, groups and communities are not attributable to lifestyle choices, but rather to their disenfranchised position as distinct ethnic and cultural groups' (Allen and Adams, 2013: 73). Extending to social work education requires training programmes that do not collude with the perpetuation of inequality and disadvantage, and that seek instead the need to establish more challenging approaches that actively support anti-discriminatory and culturally competent practice. While such approaches have formed part of some programmes (Beaumont and Cemlyn, 2004), the continuing evidence about damage to Gypsy, Traveller and Roma children and families shows the need for these to be more widely and firmly embedded. Without this, social work may pathologise families, leading to unnecessarily coercive intervention, or, on the other hand, consider cultural relativism as a reason for non-intervention when services are required.

## Developing community-based outreach

Working to support Gypsy, Traveller and Roma children living in or at risk of entering into care also highlights the need for social work agencies to utilise theories of community outreach engagement and to forge effective links with these communities. Effectively supporting Gypsy, Traveller and Roma families might typically involve putting them in touch with, and working in partnership with, other organisations, including Gypsy, Traveller and Roma community organisations.

The context and issues that we have discussed illustrate the need for a transformative approach to practice that is based upon radical social work theory (Ferguson and Woodward, 2009) and that values diversity and promotes equality and social justice. Moving away from crisis-driven approaches to social work, transformative outreach practice might, among other things, highlight how the local authority is failing to provide appropriate accommodation to children and families, either by providing insufficient or poor-quality sites, by evicting Gypsy and Traveller families, or by forcing them into bricks-and-mortar housing that leaves them feeling depressed and isolated (Parry et al, 2004). Similarly, where appropriate and relevant, it could mean social workers challenging the local authority about failures to offer culturally sensitive services in fostering and adoption, education, health, mental health, domestic violence, and alcohol and substance misuse. Social workers can demonstrate that where these factors are contributing to poor outcomes, the difficulties and risks being experienced by the child are directly linked to failures in accommodation, social care and other service provision.

Working both 'for' and 'with' Gypsy, Traveller and Roma communities requires social workers to challenge the status quo and be proactive in the development of policy and practice that recognise the impact of oppression and discrimination. By proving that local authorities are ready to work with Gypsy, Traveller and Roma families and communities in matters of social justice, as well as family support and protection, practitioners can begin to reverse certain Gypsy/Traveller/Roma–majority community distinctions, and instead promote the core social work traditions of understanding, partnership and meaningful support.

While the recommendations we have advanced here might sound ambitious, it is important to note that Haringey London Borough Council currently implements an award-winning approach to community outreach social work and enables active participatory social work methods to be used in partnership with local Traveller communities. A small Travelling People's Team, with one social worker and one administrative assistant, works with a community social work philosophy of empowerment, reflective practice and anti-racist practice to develop active co-productive partnerships with Gypsy, Traveller and Roma communities in the borough, to promote equality of access to services and culturally competent practice, and to engage families before crises develop. This involves different levels of work at the individual, community, inter-agency and structural levels, for example: co-working child protection cases and challenging discriminatory policies and services that damage families; developing activities that fulfil needs and develop capacity within communities who experience economic and educational disadvantage, for example, welfare rights drop-in sessions and driving theory classes; supporting cultural enrichment and intercultural engagement activities, such as Gypsy, Roma, Traveller History month; working with and supporting community engagement with Gypsy, Traveller and Roma advocacy and support organisations; and contributing more widely to anti-racist policy development. This approach builds trust between social work services and the communities, facilitates more productive relationships and thus more effectively safeguards children; furthermore, by avoiding overreactive or misapplied interventions, it is also financially efficient (Ridge and McCarthy, 2012;Greenfields et al, 2015).

A partnership model is also integral to the work of the Shared Rearing Service in the Republic of Ireland. Specialist work is being supported by Gypsy, Traveller and Roma organisations in the UK and across Europe, sometimes at huge personal cost to individual Gypsy, Traveller and Roma advocates because of the stresses and trauma involved. The need to transform social work practice with these communities can equally cause great pressure for individual practitioners when trying to advocate culturally appropriate, dialogic approaches to practice, particularly when they require management structures to deviate from the norm, and where they are within a local authority and national context where hostility to Gypsies, Travellers and Roma shapes and is shaped by political and media discourses. It is for these reasons that the transformative approaches that we have discussed need to be developed consistently and the over-representation of Gypsy, Traveller and Roma children living in care needs to be addressed.

## Conclusions

This chapter has considered the experiences of Gypsy, Traveller and Roma children living in public care. Although young adults leaving the public care system tend to face significantly more difficulties and are at greater risk of social exclusion when making the transition to adulthood than their contemporaries in the wider population, young Gypsy, Traveller and Roma people are often further disadvantaged due to their particular ethnicity and the endemic and entrenched discrimination that they continue to face as adults.

Given the disenfranchised position of Gypsy, Traveller and Roma communities, we acknowledge the fact that the opportunities for transformative practice may not come easily or quickly. Among the elements of transformative practice discussed in the introduction to this volume, anti-oppressive and critical reflective practice are, in theory, embedded in social work training and practice competence, but the hostile societal context frequently undermines their application in work with Gypsies, Travellers and Roma. Rights-based advocacy, especially in relation to structural aspects of discrimination, and co-production with marginalised communities do not appear to fit well with the current configuration of highly regulated social work. However, the Haringey example shows that a different model is, indeed, possible and that opportunities do exist for good community-based social work practice that facilitates both improved child protection practice and financial efficiency, and that can and should be more widely implemented. This experience can also shore up the approach of committed individual social workers to engage transformatively with Gypsy, Traveller and Roma service users.

More immediately, it is hoped that there will be recognition that the challenges faced by Gypsy, Traveller and Roma children and families are not attributable to a lifestyle choice, but rather reflect their oppressed position in society. Social work can and must rise to the challenges set out in this chapter and ensure that the culture and identity of Gypsy, Traveller and Roma children and families are valued and promoted.

## Note

[1] For an amplified discussion of demographic calculations, see Ryder et al (2014:Appendix 2).

## References

Acton, T. (1979) 'The ethnicity of the British Romani populations', *Roma – Journal of the Indian Institute of Romani Studies*, 11 (formerly 4[4]): 43–53.

Acton, T. (1997) 'Categorising Irish Travellers', in M. McCann, S.O. Siochain and J. Ruane (eds) *Irish Travellers. Culture and ethnicity*, Belfast: Institute of Irish Studies, pp 36–53.

Allen, D. (2012a) *Changing relationships with the self and others: an interpretative phenomenological analysis of a Traveller and Gypsy life in public care*, Leicester: De Montford University.

Allen, D. (2012b) 'Gypsies and Travellers and social policy: marginality and insignificance. A case study of Gypsy and Traveller children in care', in J. Richardson and A. Ryder (eds) *Gypsies and Travellers: accommodation, empowerment and inclusion in British society*, Bristol: The Policy Press, pp 83–99.

Allen, D. and Adams, P. (2013) *Social work with Gypsy, Roma and Traveller children, good practice guide*, London: BAAF.

Andersson, B. (2013) 'Finding ways to the hard to reach – considerations on the content and concept of outreach work', *European Journal of Social Work*, 16(2): 171–86.

Beaumont, B. and Cemlyn, S. (2004) 'Promoting equality and inclusion', in H. Burgess and I. Taylor (eds) *Effective learning and teaching in social policy and social work*, London: Routledge, Farmer, pp 41–54.

Cemlyn, S. (2000a) 'From neglect to partnership? Challenges for social services in promoting the welfare of Traveller children', *Child Abuse Review*, 9(5): 349–63.

Cemlyn, S. (2000b) 'Assimilation, control, mediation or advocacy? Social work dilemmas in providing anti-oppressive services for Traveller children and families', *Child and Family Social Work*, 5(4): 327–41.

Cemlyn, S. (2008) 'Human rights and Gypsies and Travellers. An exploration of the application of a human rights perspective to social work with a minority community in Britain', *British Journal of Social Work*, 31(1): 153–73.

Cemlyn, S. and Briskman, L. (2002) 'Social (dys)welfare within a hostile state', *Social Work Education*, 21(1): 49–69.

Cemlyn, S., Greenfields, M., Burnett, S., Matthews, Z. and Whitwell, C. (2009) 'Inequalities experienced by Gypsy and Traveller communities: a review', Equality and Human Rights Commission. Available at: http://www.equalityhumanrights.com/uploaded_files/research/12inequalities_experienced_by_gypsy_and_traveller_communities_a_review.pdf (accessed 27 November 2014).

DfE (Department for Education) (2015) 'Children looked after in England (including adoption and care leavers) year ending 31 March 2015', London: Office for National Statistics. Available from: https://www.gov.uk/government/uploads/system/uploads/attachment_data/file/483712/SFR34_2015_National_Tables.xlsx (accessed 13 January 2016).

Department of Health, Social services and Public Safety (2015) 'Children in care in Northern Ireland 2013/14', Belfast: Office for National Statistics, https://www.dhsspsni.gov.uk/sites/default/files/publications/dhssps/child-care-ni-13-14.pdf (accessed 13 January 2016).

EMCDDA (European Monitoring Centre for Drugs and Drug Addiction (1999) 'Outreach work among drug users in Europe: concepts, practice and terminology'. Available at: http://www.emcdda.europa.eu/html.cfm/index34000EN.html

European Roma Rights Centre (2011) *A life sentence: Romani children in institutional care*, Budapest: European Roma Rights Centre.

Ferguson, I. and Woodward, R. (2009) *Radical social work in practice: making a difference*, Bristol: The Policy Press.

Foster, B. and Norton, P. (2012) 'Educational equality for Gypsy, Roma and Traveller young people in the UK', Equal Rights Trust. Available at: http://www.equalrightstrust.org/ertdocumentbank/ERR8_Brian_Foster_and_Peter_Norton.pdf (accessed 20 November 2014).

Fremlova, L. and Ureche, H. (2009) *Patterns of settlement and current situation of new Roma communities in England: a report prepared for DCSF*, London: European Dialogue.

Garrett, P.M. (2004) *Social work and Irish people in Britain*, Bristol: Policy Press.

Garrett, P.M. (2005) 'Irish social workers in Britain and the politics of (mis) recognition', *British Journal of Social Work*, 35(8): 1357–76.

Greenfields, M. (2002) 'The impact of Section 8 Children Act applications on Travelling families', unpublished PhD dissertation, University of Bath, UK.

Greenfields, M., Cemlyn, S. and Berlin, J. (2015) 'Bridging the gap between academics and policy makers: Gypsy, Traveller and Roma health and social work engagement'. Available at: http://bucks.ac.uk/content/documents/Research/ INSTAL/Bridging_the_Gap_Health_and_Social_Care_Report.pdf

Harrington, K. (2014) *Serious case review: Family A*, London: NSPCC. Available at: http://www.westsussexscb.org.uk/wp-content/uploads/2014Southampton FamilyAOverview.pdf (accessed 27 November 2014).

Kenrick, D. and Puxon, G. (1995) *Gypsies under the Swastika*, Hatfield: University of Hertfordshire Press.

McVeigh, R. (1997) 'Theorising sedentarism: the roots of anti-nomadism', in T. Acton (ed) *Gypsy politics and Traveller identity*, Hatfield: University of Hertfordshire Press, pp 7–25.

NFGLG (National Federation of Gypsy Liaison Groups) (2014) 'Civil society monitoring on the implementation of the National Roma Integration Strategy in the United Kingdom', Andrew Ryder and Sarah Cemlyn, Decade for Roma Inclusion/Open Society Foundations.

O'Higgins, K. (1993) 'Surviving separation: Traveller children in substitute care', in H. Ferguson, R. Gilligan and R. Torode (ed) *Surviving childhood adversity: issues for policy and practice*, Dublin: Social Studies Press, pp 146–56.

Parry, G., Van Cleemput, P., Peters, J., Moore, J., Walters, S., Thomas, K. and Cooper, C. (2004) *The health status of Gypsies and Travellers in England*, Sheffield: University of Sheffield Press.

Pemberton, D. (1999) 'Fostering in a minority community: Travellers in Ireland', in R. Greeff (ed) *Fostering kinship: an international perspective on kinship foster care*, Aldershot: Ashgate, pp 167–80.

Pierson, J. and Thomas, M. (eds) (2002) *Collins dictionary of social work*, Glasgow: HarperCollins.

Richardson, J. (2006) 'Talking about Gypsies: the notion of discourse as control', *Housing Studies*, 21(1): 77–96.

Richardson, J. and Ryder, A. (eds) (2012) *Gypsies and Travellers: accommodation, empowerment and inclusion in British society*, Bristol: The Policy Press.

Ridge, M. and McCarthy, B. (2012) 'Community partnership social work with Gypsy, Roma, Traveller communities', presentation to BASW Student Social Worker and NQSW Conference, 30 June, London.

Ryder, A., Cemlyn, S. and Acton, T. (eds) (2014) *Hearing the voices of Gypsy, Roma and Traveller communities: inclusive community development*, Bristol: The Policy Press.

Smith, J.A., Flowers, B. and Larkin, M. (2009) *Doing interpretative phenomenological analysis*, London: Sage.

Smith, D. and Greenfields, M. (2013) *Gypsies and Travellers in housing. The decline of nomadism*, Bristol: The Policy Press.

Stewart, M. (2012) *The Gypsy 'menace': populism and the new anti-Gypsy politics*, New York, NY: Columbia University Press.

Vanderbeck, R. (2005) 'Anti-nomadism, institutions and the geographies of childhood: environment and planning', *Society and Space*, 23: 71–94.

. . . . . . . . . . . . . . . . . . . . . . . . . . . . . . . . . . . . . . . . . .

. . . . . . . . . . . . . . . . . . . . . . . . . . . . . . . . . . . . . . . . . .

. . . . . . . . . . . . . . . . . . . . . . . . . . . . . . . . . . . . . . . . . .
. . . . . . . . . . . . . . . . . . . . . . . . . . . . . . . . . . . . . . . . . .

. . . . . . . . . . . . . . . . . . . . . . . . . . . . . . . . . . . . . . . . . .

. . . . . . . . . . . . . . . . . . . . . . . . . . . . . . . . . . . . . . . . . .
. . . . . . . . . . . . . . . . . . . . . . . . . . . . . . . . . . . . . . . . . .

# ELEVEN

# Active involvement and co-production with people with intellectual disabilities from minority ethnic communities

*Raghu Raghavan*

## Introduction

There is considerable evidence that inequality and exclusion are characteristics of the experiences of black and minority ethnic (BME) communities in the UK. The UK population is becoming more diverse and complex in terms of ethnicity, culture and religion. This chapter will focus on people with intellectual disabilities (ID) from BME communities as they face inequalities, discrimination and marginalisation. The key issues and themes in the health and social care of people with ID and their families from minority ethnic communities will be explored in the context of transformative practice for making a difference for minority ethnic communities. This chapter will cover:

- ID in minority ethnic communities;
- The minority experience;
- Transformative care;
- Co-production;
- The liaison worker model; and
- Improving the transition experience.

In England, the *Valuing people* White Paper (Department of Health, 2001) outlined the government's strategy for improving the lives of people with an ID (learning disability) and their families. This policy is based on the recognition of their rights as citizens exercising their choice in their daily lives and enabling opportunities to achieve independence. *Valuing people* highlighted that many people from minority ethnic communities are even more excluded than white people with ID and stated that 'the needs of people from minority ethnic communities are often overlooked' (Department of Health, 2001: 2), demanding an improvement of services to meet the needs of all people and valuing them as citizens.

It is well recognised that people with ID from BME groups are under-represented in services compared to their white counterparts (Emerson, 2012). They experience even further isolation as many of these people face greater inequalities in relation to race, disability, and gender, and exclusion in health, employment and education (Mir et al, 2001). Along with other minority ethnic groups in the UK, British Asians face substantial inequalities, discrimination and disadvantage. They are more likely to live in substandard housing in inner-city areas, be employed in semi-skilled or unskilled jobs, be unemployed, and experience discrimination in education, health and social services (Karlsen, 2007). The nature of experiences of discrimination and social exclusion of people from BME communities creates a negative impact on their health, well-being and socialisation (Emerson, 2012).

## Intellectual disabilities

ID is characterised by significant limitations both in intellectual functioning (reasoning, learning, problem solving) and in adaptive behaviour, which covers a range of everyday social and practical skills. This disability originates before the age of 18 (Department of Health, 2001). Intellectual and developmental disabilities are associated with increased mortality and morbidity, increased risk of social exclusion, and significant demands on families and health and social care agencies (Karlsen, 2007; Turner and Robinson, 2011).

The World Health Organisation (see: www.who.org) estimates the prevalence of ID to be between 1% and 3%. Reports on the prevalence of ID across many countries range from 2% to 8% depending on the definition and the classification systems used (Roeleveld et al, 1997). A meta-analysis (Maulik et al, 2011) of the prevalence of ID from different studies conducted across different populations estimated the highest rates for low- and middle-income countries, and in children and adolescent populations. The authors stress that the increasing population of children and adolescents in some large low- and middle-income countries (such as Bangladesh, China, India, Nigeria and Pakistan) means that it is of paramount importance that services are developed that facilitate appropriate genetic screening during antenatal periods in such countries.

We are unable to estimate the prevalence of ID in all the ethnic groups in the UK due the lack of prevalence studies in specific communities. Evidence indicates that severe ID is three times more prevalent in South Asian (comprising Indian, Pakistani and Bangladeshi nationalities) children and young adults than in age-matched peers in other ethnic groups. Recent analysis (Emerson, 2012) of the independent effects attributable to household deprivation, neighbourhood characteristics and ethnicity for the identification of ID in a sample of English children aged 7–15 years indicated that:

• lower household socio-economic position was associated with increased rates of identification of intellectual and developmental disabilities, especially less severe forms of ID;

- higher area deprivation was independently associated with increased rates of identification of less severe forms of ID but decreased rates of identification of profound multiple ID and autism spectrum disorder;
- minority ethnic status was, in general, associated with lower rates of identification of intellectual and developmental disabilities; and
- exceptions to this general pattern included higher rates of identification of less severe forms of ID among Gypsy, Romany and Traveller children of Irish heritage, and higher rates of identification of more severe forms of ID among children of Pakistani and Bangladeshi heritage.

## The minority experience

Intellectually disabled people and their families from minority ethnic communities experience a number of barriers in accessing and utilising health and social services. People with ID and their families from all ethnic groups experience discrimination. However, there are life events that are unique to minority ethnic communities that differentiate them from majority white ethnic communities, as outlined in the following.

### Lack of knowledge and awareness of services

A key factor that affects service access and utilisation by minority ethnic communities is the lack of adequate knowledge and awareness of the kind and types of health and social care services in their locality. Lack of knowledge of existing services is a potential obstacle for many South Asian families. Policy guidelines in the UK state that people from different cultural backgrounds may have particular care needs and problems and that minority ethnic communities experience barriers in accessing the full range of services (Learning Disability Task Force, 2004). Ability to communicate using English is a problem for many from the South Asian communities and this is clearly identified as a reason for the lack of knowledge and awareness of services (MENCAP, 2009). Lack of awareness of information about the types of support services available to them puts them at a considerable disadvantage. The Royal Society for Mentally Handicapped Children and Adults (MENCAP, 2009: 7) report *Reaching out* argues that:

> carers from BME communities lack basic knowledge about the services that are available, and they have no understanding of how those services operate and consequently what their rights are. But worst of all, they often have no idea what learning disability (ID) is, how it affects the person they care for and what they can do to help.

Due to the lack of awareness of support services, it is not surprising that unmet needs are reported so highly in some BME communities.

## Language issues

Among South Asian families, many people have difficulty communicating fluently in the English language. Family carers who are unable to speak English face particular problems in communicating their concerns to professionals and also in understanding the meaning of consultations. Access to interpreters or family link-worker schemes remains inadequate, with most families having to rely on their non-disabled children to interpret. Even in families who can speak English, there can be poor communication between them and the professionals, rather than simply language difficulties limiting their understanding of the diagnosis, interventions, service access and utilisation.

Families with children with ID face problems in contacting health or social services to explain the nature of their difficulty and the type of help required for their disabled child. They indicate that there is a lack of a single point of contact about who is aware of the young person's condition and difficulties (Raghavan and Pawson, 2009). Hence, families are reluctant to access some of these services as they find it very traumatic to continuously explain the history of the young person to social care professionals who are unfamiliar with their case.

## Same service for all

Often, services provide a 'colour-blind' universalist approach, where services are offered on the same basis to all regardless of their ethnicity and culture. This type of approach ignores the cultural values and belief systems of minority ethnic communities and fails to acknowledge that services are geared towards the dominant white majority culture. This ignores the needs of BME communities and fails to take account of the barriers they face in accessing services.

## Inappropriate services

The inappropriate nature of services offered to BME communities can have a negative impact in terms of access to health and social care services. The types of services offered may not be appropriate to meet the needs of people with ID and their families. For example, the offer of a support worker who lacks a satisfactory awareness or knowledge of ID creates more stress and work for the family, rather than helping them. Moreover, a lack of awareness of the family's cultural and religious beliefs by a support worker is also likely to cause additional stress for them. This creates a feeling among some BME service users and carers that there is a lack of understanding of the cultural needs of the family and hence their refusal of support services.

## Religious beliefs

Service utilisation may be affected by particular beliefs and perceptions held by families, especially those from South Asian communities. Religious beliefs play a crucial role for most families who may consult religious or traditional healers in the hope that they can make their child 'better' (Raghavan et al, 2005). For many South Asian families, religion is very important in the way they lead their lives. Some members of the South Asian community may make more contact with religious healers than professional services. However, this does not mean that they are less likely to contact health and social care professionals and use existing services. Often, families may access religious or traditional healers abroad because they believe that the professionals and services in the UK are not helping to 'cure' ID. South Asian young people with ID or with mental health problems are often taken to religious or traditional healers in the hope that they will make their child 'better', as one respondent in a study by Raghavan et al (2005) indicates:

> Yeah, we have [used religious/traditional healers] abroad because people said somebody might have done black magic on her ... so we went abroad last year. When she was there, she found it difficult because of the different people and surroundings ... they thought it was to do with black magic ... so they got a religious man to do things ... it didn't work. (A Pakistani family carer, quoted in Raghavan et al, 2005: 72)

The religious beliefs of the family play a major role in accepting the birth of a disabled child, in managing stress and in exploring ways of adapting to life with a disabled child. For example, family carers of young people with ID articulate that the professionals and service providers often overlook the religious and cultural needs of the young person. Religious beliefs may help parents to cope with their own feelings and stigma. Bywaters et al (2003) stress the importance of the religious or spiritual beliefs of the family and the need for health and social care professionals to be sensitive to the family's belief system in service delivery.

In examining the religious beliefs of the South Asian population, it is vital to understand the main religions practised in South Asia. These consist of Hinduism, Islam, Buddhism and Sikhism. It is reported that many Muslims accept disability as 'God's will'. Hindu and Sikh family carers' attitudes towards disability is based on the notion of Karma (Katbamna et al, 2000). Here, disability is seen as God's gift as a result of actions in a past life, reflecting the Hindu belief of reincarnation or rebirth (Gabel, 2004). The belief holds that lessons from a previous life (Karma) must be learned in the present life and that having ID or having a loved one with ID would provide opportunities to learn those lessons. The Hindu belief is that one must suffer through the disability without complaint. In this context, suffering is not a negative connotation, but a learning opportunity, which can provide a chance to learn lessons that can release them from rebirth – being released from the cycle of birth and death is the goal of Hindu life. It is important to note the belief here: suffering is an opportunity to willingly fulfil one's duties in life, and one must do this without complaining. This has major implications in terms of service access and uptake from families following the Hindu religion.

## Stigma

The stigma of having a child with ID is an issue for many South Asian parents in accessing services. Families may be worried about what others say, especially when communities are so close-knit and people do not want sensitive issues to be found out by others. Stigma and family reputations are crucial with regard to ID and mental illness, and most South Asian people want to keep such issues concerning their family members within the family structure, with carers taking extra precautions to hide any conditions associated with mental health (Bashford et al, 2002). Ethnicity alone may not provide the explanation for increased stigma. Information and resources play a crucial role in the support when caring for a disabled child. It is suggested that parents are more likely to move away from looking at disability as being tragic when they have more information that promotes a positive approach and when they are able to manage the circumstances without struggling (Mir and Tovey, 2003).

There are also a number of stereotypical assumptions that have been made about South Asian communities holding different attitudes to the majority white ethnic population. South Asians are often described as being a close-knit community, where the main characteristic of life is that everyone knows each other and close friends are classified as brothers and sisters (Hatton et al, 2002). The stereotypical view of South Asian families is that they stick together and help each other in times of need and hardship. Among single-parent families who have a disabled child, support from outside the immediate family can be limited or even non-existent. Service providers have been slow to acknowledge the experience of single-parent families from BME communities. These stereotypical views have been used to explain why minority ethnic families have a lower uptake of services than white families, which is a way of blaming the victim and minimising the problem of institutional racism. However, evidence shows that South Asian families with a young person with ID receive less support from extended families than white families (Raghavan et al, 2013).

Health and social care professionals may assume that all South Asians are a homogeneous group sharing the same views, culture and religious beliefs. There is, however, a great heterogeneity of views, belief systems, opinions and cultures in this community, as in others, with language differences, religious practices and migration histories playing a role in this diversity. More importantly, within each of these communities, there is great variation in terms of educational and financial status and the degree of acculturation.

## Transformative care

The past three decades have seen a major shift in the service model of ID from a medical model to the social model, which promotes the person with ID as an ordinary citizen with rights of equal access to and use of ordinary community services. The closure of long-stay hospitals has led to the expansion of wide-ranging patterns of services in the voluntary and independent sectors. During this period, the service user and disability rights movements have promoted the idea of people who use services as active participants with resources, rather than passive dependants with needs, resulting in innovative approaches such as service brokerage, direct payments and co-production. The associated move towards 'personalisation' in adult social care services can be seen as a continued response to this need for choice and control (Sims and Gulyurtlu, 2014).

*Valuing people* included recognition of the importance of the social in the lives of people with ID, for example, through its concern with social inclusion. However, its interpretation in practice has been an individualistic one based on the principles of person–centred planning (PCP), an approach encouraged across a range of health, social care and education settings (Small et al, 2013). The aims of PCP are both to personalise the planning experience and to influence strategic planning (Felce, 2004). However, a systematic review of the literature (Claes et al, 2010) concluded that there was little evidence that PCP resulted in increased accessibility for service users and little evidence of its impacting on structural problems of service delivery (Cambridge and Carnaby, 2005). Furthermore, there is no clear evidence of a link between PCP and outcomes for service users (Black et al, 2010). Even though PCP was greeted with much enthusiasm in care planning and delivery during the last decade, we are still struggling to highlight its positive impact for with people with ID from BME communities and their families with examples of good practice.

Despite the formal health policy statements, the landscape of care for the majority of people with ID and their families from BME communities is one of exclusion and disadvantage as a result of racial discrimination and culturally inappropriate forms of care provision. The Social Care Institute for Excellence (SCIE, 2013) report on co-production highlighted that public services need to work with the people who use services and stressed that the failure to listen to the voices of service users and carers has been a key theme in all the high–profile scandals in health and social care in recent years. In England, recent enquires into the abuse and neglect of people who use services have highlighted the need for service providers to develop more equal relationships with people who use services and carers. In this context, co-production provides a concept and the framework to develop these more meaningful relationships for service development, with users and carers playing an equal role with commissioners and professionals.

Commissioners and service providers should be planning culturally sensitive services for people from minority ethnic communities. The services offered should be appropriate to the person with ID and their family from diverse cultures. User and carer narratives from minority ethnic communities stress that they are not seeking a 'specialist service' exclusively created for them (Raghavan et al, 2013). Their wish is for mainstream services to be more accommodative of their views and needs. This can be achieved by involving people with ID and their carers from minority ethnic communities in terms of planning services. 'Hearing the voice' and creating opportunities for the 'visibility' of users and carers from minority ethnic communities is essential in building inclusive services that meet the needs of people in the locality. Users and carers from all sections of the local community should be engaging with their local services. This will require a concerted effort by practitioners and service providers to identify users and carers from minority ethnic communities and enable them to be involved in service planning. For this, users and carers will require additional help and support, such as the availability of an interpreter, flexibility in terms of the timing of the meeting to accommodate their cultural and religious needs, and, more importantly, having the willingness to engage in a dialogue with users and carers from BME communities without any preconceived ideas about the nature of services.

## Co-production

Co-production is a way of working whereby citizens and decision-makers, or people who use services, family carers and service providers, work together to create a decision or service that works for them all (SCIE, 2013). This approach is value-driven and built on the principle that those who use a service are best placed to help design it. A co-production model was undertaken in planning the leisure services for young people with learning disabilities from the South Asian community in a study by Raghavan and Pawson (2009). This involved enabling and coaching a core group of youngsters with ID, representing the heterogeneity in the South Asian community, and providing opportunities for these youngsters and family carers to engage with key service providers in the locality through service planning meetings (Raghavan and Pawson, 2009). This enabled users, cares and service providers to co-produce a clear plan of action for accessing leisure services that was agreed by all parties. The following story highlights that an individualised and personal approach needs to be applied rather than service delivery based on a 'one size fits all'-type of approach.

Kiran is a 19-year-old girl with ID. Kiran comes from a large family and is one of five siblings. Kiran is a very energetic and sociable. She loves to go out on trips, fun activities and shopping. However, Kiran does not access leisure opportunities outside of school and her mother has very little time to take her. The family has no access to their own transport. Planning meetings with the mother enabled the family to have transport arrangements in order for Kiran to be picked up and dropped off to the venue by an approved taxi. Direct payments were explored as an option, utilising funding from the local authority that allows the disabled person to buy the care they need. Kiran's community nurse and social worker helped to apply for direct payments. With the direct payments, Kiran and her family have been able to employ a personal assistant (PA) for seven hours a week and she takes Kiran out on the weekends. Kiran is able to choose what she would like to do and when. She now regularly goes out shopping with her PA or to the cinema, for meals and so on. The PA is female and of South Asian origin and she has her own transport in order to take Kiran out, which is very important. Kiran's mother is very happy and assured by this service as it meets all of Kiran's support needs, is flexible, gives Kiran more control and choice, and is culturally and gender appropriate.

Kiran wanted to have more choice and control over her leisure provision. Her leisure preferences could not be met through mainstream services and her vulnerability as a disabled young woman would not allow her to access the things she wanted to do by herself. Co-production refers to active input by the people who use services, as well as – or instead of – those who have traditionally provided them. Therefore, it contrasts with approaches that treat people as passive recipients of services designed and delivered by someone else (Needham and Carr, 2009). It emphasises that the people who use services have assets that can help to improve those services, rather than simply needs that must be met. These assets are not usually financial, but rather are the skills, expertise and mutual support that service users can contribute to effective public services. Critics of direct payments point to the vulnerabilities of users and carers in exercising choice and to their lack of power to engage in true partnerships. Nevertheless, they do imply more flexible, fine-tuned services, shaped and designed in dialogue with the service user, and therefore suggest a counter to universalist service provision.

## The liaison worker model

The use of a key worker or link worker has been suggested as enabling access to services for young people and family carers from the South Asian community (Emerson and Robertson, 2002). The key emphasis here is for the key worker to be a person from the minority community so that they are able to communicate effectively using the appropriate language. The key worker might also help to link up the family with a range of service providers and professionals, thus helping to access a wider range of services. Such a service model, using the liaison worker, was tested in research with young people with ID and mental health needs from the Pakistani and Bangladeshi community with the aim of improving access to services (Raghavan et al, 2009). The randomised controlled trial undertaken indicates that the liaison worker model was found to be useful by families. Families receiving input from the liaison worker had more frequent contact with more services than did families not receiving this input and, in turn, had more results from such contacts. There was also some indication that family carers receiving support had a better quality of life and the young person with ID had less behavioural problems than those in the control population. This confirms that a liaison worker model may be more effective in supporting and improving access to services for BME communities. The following is a case example of the liaison worker model in working with a minority ethnic family, highlighting the complexity of needs and the brokering of a range of helpful services to make a difference for the family.

Sura is a 22-year-old female of Pakistani origin and has severe learning disabilities, as well as a degenerative brain condition. She was diagnosed as having a disability at the age of five and went to a special needs school. Her parents are her main carers, and she lives at home (a big house) with her two brothers, two sisters-in-law, two sisters, two daughters and nephew. Sura's eldest brother has a mild learning disability and her older sister also has severe learning disabilities.

Sura left school at the age of 16. She got married at 17 and has two daughters. She separated from her husband after five years and lives with her parents along with her children. Sura does not communicate very much and uses non-verbal communication skills. She cries at times and her mother thinks that this is because she is unable to communicate her fears or that she might be in pain. She needs help with all the self-care skills that the carers deal with twice a day but her mother does everything for her the rest of the day and at weekends, as well as looking after Sura's children.

She currently has a support worker that takes her out twice a week for about an hour or so. She tried a day centre but her father disliked the mixed environment of the day centre and hence withdrew her from there. She also has a care services package through social services, whereby carers come to the house to assist her with her self-care. Sura still sees the child and adolescent psychiatrist as and when required and a social worker has been seeing the family for some time. Sura's father goes to a local advice group if he needs help and support.

Sura is very affectionate with her parents. She grabs their hand and will touch their faces. Sura's mother says that Sura tries hard to speak but cannot do it. She is generally happy with others. The family mainly allow relatives into the house so that Sura's contact is with people she knows, and she gets on well with everyone. She is very close to her sister and attaches herself to her when she comes up to visit the family. Sura's mother hopes that she might make a miraculous recovery and find someone to get married to and settle down in life.

How best to help Sura and her family? The intervention of a liaison worker for Sura and her family paved the way for improving her health and social care through the signposting of appropriate services and, more importantly, in supporting the family for culturally appropriate care at home:

- The liaison worker improved the care package for Sura by involving a voluntary agency to advocate on behalf of the family with social services. This helped to make a case to the care managers about the needs of the family in providing better support for Sura and her disabled brother and sister.
- The liaison worker met with a social worker from the local community team to conduct further assessments of Sura's ID. These assessments helped to change her diagnosis from a degenerative brain condition to severe ID and this enabled

access to services from the community team for people with ID. This resulted in a full care assessment by a South Asian social worker from the team.

- The liaison worker was able to signpost the family towards better advice on welfare benefits for Sura, her disabled sister and the family.

- Sura's parents are ageing and they are feeling the stress of their care burden. Her mother is unwell and constantly feels tired. It is becoming very hard for her to manage the family and she is unable to go out for even a short while. Her father is trying to bring his sister over from Pakistan to look after Sura and their other disabled children. If they are successful in getting his sister over from Pakistan, it may help ease the burden, as she will act as a carer for Sura and help her parents to care for the rest of the family. This required supporting letters from professionals and service providers. The liaison worker and the voluntary agency worked with the South Asian social worker and other community team members in developing a case for additional support for the family. A supporting letter for this purpose was agreed by the community team for securing an entry visa.

Often, carers are expected to get on with the demanding task of caring for a young person with ID, as well as seeking help and support from a wide range of practitioners and service agencies. This is a complex and daunting task for many people from minority ethnic communities, and hence services need to reach out to the families that need support, rather than families having to constantly search for help. The complexity and bureaucracy of services can be extremely intimidating for service users and their families. Therefore, services need to make first contact and continue to maintain that contact with people with ID and their families. There are different perceptions among families about what help statutory services can offer them, and clearer information is required from services and professionals about what services are available and how they will help them. People from BME communities rely on the use of voluntary services and this can be very problematic as these organisations are often underfunded and under-resourced, making it difficult for them to cope with the complex demands placed on them.

## Improving transition experience

The transitions involved in leaving school and college can constitute critical times in the lives of young people with ID. Transition from school to a post-school world, and simultaneously for many from children's to adult services, has been of concern to policymakers and professionals for many years. The transition phase is traumatic for the young person with ID and their families from all cultures. Evidence suggests that poor transition between services can lead to poor outcomes, as well as causing confusion and anxiety for people with learning disabilities and family carers (Turner and Robinson, 2011).

Responses to the challenges of managing transition have included interventions such as the Department of Health's 'Getting a Life' project (2008–11). This sought to address shortcomings in established practice by delivering individualised transition support across nine local authority areas (see: http://www.gettingalife. org.uk). Transition planning, and PCP, in choosing to build from the individual out, has advantages in pursuing some of the aims of *Valuing people*. It does recognise the person's rights as a citizen, and it allows the person a voice in what they wish. However, an individualised response has less traction, with aims that are essentially social, that is, the need to support social inclusion and to provide opportunities to achieve independence. More generally, it can be argued that PCP is transposing an individualist ideal onto a group of people whose needs might best be pursued via privileging interdependence.

Lang and Rayner (2012), writing with reference to public health, argue that an ecological approach offers an alternative to the narrow language of individualism and choice that they see as prevalent in health discourse and in service planning. Ecological approaches start from a long-argued position that good health flows from the population level to the individual. Their position is that we must start from, and not be deterred by, complex and multilayered dimensions that shape health. We cannot compartmentalise the biological, material, social and cultural dimensions of a person's world. Lang and Rayner acknowledge that ecological public health is an approach that extends Bronfenbrenner's child development model into public health. According to Bronfenbrenner (1979, 1986), the development of the child is best understood using a framework that focuses on the progressive accommodation between the living organism and the changing environments in which he/she grows. This is embedded within larger social contexts. There are bidirectional influences in which a person's development is influenced by their social setting and where personality shapes how that setting is engaged with. The progressive accommodation between the individual and environment is located in what Bronfenbrenner termed a chronosystem. This recognises that both the individual and their context changes over time.

Bronfenbrenner's model is valuable in considering transition experiences in intellectual disability in a number of ways:

1. It allows a consideration of the influence a person has on his or her social network, as well as the influence that that network has on him or her. This approach allows a sense of active agency to be vested in the individual, which is an important consideration given the frequent marginalisation of the person with ID in discussions about his or her life.
2. If the model is used at different time periods, it can capture how networks change, for example, before and after the young person leaves school.
3. Considering transition ecologically, as a network phenomenon and not simply as something that is the responsibility of the young person in the family or of an interaction between family and school or college, can serve as a useful

context in which to explore the levels of support and assistance that the young person receives, and this can be used to guide service planning.

Research on transition and social networks (Pawson et al, 2005; Raghavan et al, 2013) with school leavers from minority ethnic communities shows that young people with ID have limited social networks, limited involvement in mainstream activities and limited interaction with 'non-disabled' peers. In particular, young people from South Asian communities and severely disabled youngsters in this study were less represented in leisure, although they expressed a desire to participate (Raghavan et al, 2013). Young people with complex disabilities also have less opportunity to be involved in mainstream activities as they are often not tailored to their needs.

In Ragahavan et al's (2013) study, all the young people, irrespective of ethnicity, were similar in terms of their needs. Ethnicity was not found to be the major determinant. In part, this can be explained by invoking Bronfenbrenner's categories in a different way. While there are bidirectional influences, there is a centrality of the micro- and meso-system, specifically the family and the school. Within the family, neither one's subjectivity nor a sense of the objective circumstances of one's own life are presented as being shaped by ethnicity. While identity formation in these young people involved negotiating many of the same domains as any young person – ethnicity, culture, religion, gender and age – it was where one was located in a school–college–post-college continuum that appeared crucial for these young people. Attendance at special schools, and hence a likely geographical separation from the local community, affords the clearest manifestation to a young person of their being 'different', not their ethnicity (see Atkin and Hussain, 2003). It is this characteristic, experienced in the meso-system that resonates with both feelings of belonging and the objective possibilities of engaging with social and leisure activities.

In relation to social networks, Pakistani ethnicity is more generally subsumed in a religious affiliation – the Mosque featured as a significant place in young people's lives in this study. Social networks, and a sense of social inclusion, may be very different for a person from a minority ethnic community living in isolation from their co-ethnic communities. In such a situation, the macro- and the exo-system is less likely to contain features that reflect the lifestyle and ethos of the family. Despite the well-established community, with its impact on all Bronfenbrenner's systems, the young people still had encounters within their neighbourhood (the meso-system), which prompted awareness of their South Asian origin because of hostility from peers, for example, 'they called me [names]'.

Parents of South Asian young people identified cultural sensitivities to be very important when they considered placements and activities for their children. Would appropriate modesty be preserved in new settings? Would customs and practices be understood and respected? These sorts of concerns see ideals and standards that are part of the micro-world interacting with patterns of service provision that are located in the exo-system (and are reflective of belief systems at the macro-level). They may well be transmitted to, and shared by, young people and they may manifest themselves in the networks that young people identify with and in the content of their aspirations. They contextualise the sense of 'fit' between micro-ideals and standards and meso-patterns of service and behaviour.

Ethnicity and religion help shape the idea of the acceptable and therefore influence the range of choices available in terms of living arrangements, work and social life. A feature of Bronfenbrenner's model is that the same words appear in different systems, for example, religious affiliation is a part of the micro- and meso-system. In the exo-system, we also find reference to the religious system, and the macro-system reflects overarching beliefs and values, including religion. Small et al (2013) suggest that religious affiliation is important in providing social support for Pakistani young people through the Mosque. For the families of these young people, the religious system and their beliefs and values define things that have to be in place in the exo-system if services are to be considered acceptable. Thus, we see an example of Bronfenbrenner's conceptualisation of bidirectional influences. Ethnicity needs to be considered in nuanced ways, not as meta-identity, but as facilitator and arbiter of particular support needs. Practitioners need to work within the parameters of the acceptable (otherwise the service will not be accessed) and to recognise that working with community organisations builds on strengths already in place.

## Conclusion

People with ID from minority ethnic communities are likely to face exclusion and discrimination in terms of accessing and using services. As we have seen, a number of factors, such as cultural and religious beliefs, language barriers, lack of adequate knowledge, and awareness of services, act as barriers in accessing and using a range of services and professional help. Services should actively seek to improve cultural appropriateness so that they meet the linguistic and religious needs of people with ID and their families. Services should utilise professional interpreters to assist families in order to enable better communication. The South Asian extended family can be a source of support but also bear the anxieties of responsibility and shame, which can mean that support is not accessed. Being a member of a community that is partly defined by religion might offer extra human capital but may also include the possibility of feeling that you have bought shame to that community. Professionals and service providers should not make assumptions about there being family support beyond the nuclear family without exploring the complex dynamics of family relations. If our aim is promoting independence, then the South Asian understanding of this may be quite different from majority norms. *Interdependence* as a goal of service planning might be more consistent with family wishes and so find more support among these communities. Religion might offer some sense of support in day-to-day life, with deeply held beliefs about consolation and hope.

Building culturally sensitive services has been a slogan for some years in policy directives. However, the impact of these directives on commissioners and service providers in acting to build a culturally sensitive and culturally competent workforce is not very clear. We have limited awareness of the processes and mechanisms used by services in building a culturally competent workforce. This theme warrants closer examination through applied research investigating the initiatives used by services and their impact on service delivery and on user satisfaction. Just paying lip service to cultural competency alone will not have an impact on shaping the future of services. What will help is a culturally competent workforce engaged in reflective practice in order to enrich their capacity and capability to meet the challenges of a diverse society. This will help the workforce to understand the nuanced nature of issues affecting diverse communities and the most helpful ways of positioning service delivery through cultural reciprocity and exchange. We live in an age where users have active involvement in shaping the nature of the services they receive through co-production. In order to make this a reality, it is vital that practitioners are culturally competent and able to respond to their needs and wishes in a responsible manner that respects cultural and belief systems.

## References

Atkin, K. and Hussain, Y. (2003) 'Disability and ethnicity: how young Asian disabled people make sense of their lives', in S.W. Riddell and N. Pearson (eds) *Disability, culture and identity*, Harlow: Prentice Hall, pp 161–79.

Bashford, J., Kaur, J., Winters, M., Williams, R. and Patel, K. (2002) 'What are the mental health needs of Bradford's Pakistani Muslim children and young people and how can they be addressed?', University of Central Lancashire, Preston.

Black, L.A., McConkey, R., Roberts, P. and Ferguson, P. (2010) 'Developing a person-centred support service for families caring for children with severe learning disabilities in rural and urban areas', *Journal of Intellectual Disabilities*, 14(2): 111–31.

Bronfenbrenner, U. (1979) *The ecology of human development: experiments by nature and design*, Cambridge: Harvard University Press.

Bronfenbrenner, U. (1986) 'Ecology of the family as a context for human development: research perspectives', *Developmental Psychology*, 22(6): 723–42.

Bywaters, P., Ali, Z., Fazil, Q., Wallace, L.M. and Singh, G. (2003) 'Attitudes towards disability amongst Pakistani and Bangladeshi parents of disabled children in the UK: considerations for service providers and the disability movement', *Health and Social Care in the Community*, 11(6): 502–9.

Cambridge, P. and Carnaby, S. (eds) (2005) *Person centred planning and care management with people with learning disabilities*, London: Jessica Kingsley.

Claes, C., Hove, G.V., Vendevelde, S., Loon, J. and Schalock, R.L. (2010) 'Person-centred planning: analysis of research and effectiveness', *Intellectual and Developmental Disabilities*, 48(6): 432–53.

Department of Health (2001) *Valuing people: a new strategy for learning disability for the 21st century*, London: The Stationary Office.

Emerson, E. (2012) 'Deprivation, ethnicity and the prevalence of intellectual and developmental disabilities', *Journal of Epidemiology and Community Health*, 66(3): 218–24.

Emerson, E. and Robertson, J. (2002) *Future demand for services with learning disabilities from South Asian and black communities in Birmingham*, Lancaster: Institute for Health Research, Lancaster University.

Felce, D. (2004) Models of strategic planning: what will happen next in Wales? *Journal of Intellectual Disability Research* 48 (6): 493–493.

Gabel, S. (2004) South Asian Indian cultural orientations toward mental retardation. *Mental Retardation*, 42 (1):12-25.

Hatton, C., Akram, Y., Shah, R., Robertson, J. and Emerson, E. (2002) *Supporting South Asian families with a child with disabilities: a report to the Department of Health*, Lancaster: Institute for Health Research, Lancaster University.

Karlsen, S. (2007) *Ethnic inequalities in health: the impact of racism*, London: Race Equality Foundation.

Katbamna, S., Bhakta, P. and Parker, G. (2000) 'Perceptions of disability and care-giving relationships in South Asian communities', in W. Ahmad (ed) *Ethnicity, disability and chronic illness*, Buckingham: Open University Press.

Lang, T. and Rayner, G. (2012) 'Ecological public health: the 21st century's big idea?', *British Medical Journal*, 345(e5466): 1–5.

Learning Disability Task Force (2004) *Rights, independence, choice and inclusion*, London: Learning Disability Task Force.

Maulik, P.K., Mascarenhas, M.N., Mathers, C.D., Dua, T. and Saxena, S (2011) 'Prevalence of intellectual disability: a meta-analysis of population-based studies', *Research in Developmental Disabilities*, 32(2): 419–36.

Mir, G. and Tovey, P. (2003) 'Asian carers' experiences of medical and social care: the case of cerebral palsy', *British Journal of Social Work*, 33(4): 465–79.

Mir, G., Nocon, A., Ahmad, W. and Jones, L. (2001) *Learning difficulties and ethnicity*, London: Department of Health.

MENCAP (The Royal Society for Mentally Handicapped Children and Adults) (2009) *Reaching out: working with black and minority ethnic communities*, London: MENCAP.

Needham, C. and Carr, S. (2009) *Co-production: an emerging evidence base for adult social care transformation*, SCIE Research Briefing 31, London: Social Care Institute for Excellence.

Pawson, N., Raghavan, R., Small, N., Craig, S. and Spencer, M. (2005) 'Social inclusion, social networks and ethnicity: the development of the Social Inclusion Interview Schedule for young people with learning disabilities', *British Journal of Learning Disabilities*, 33(1): 15–22.

Raghavan, R. and Pawson, N. (2009) *Meeting the leisure needs of young people with learning disabilities from South Asian communities*, London: MENCAP.

Raghavan, R., Waseem, F., Small, N. and Newell, R. (2005) 'Supporting young people with learning disabilities and mental health needs from a minority ethnic community', in The Foundation for People with Learning Disabilities, *Making us count: identifying and improving mental health support for young people with learning disabilities*, London: The Foundation for People with Learning Disabilities.

Raghavan, R., Wassem, F., Newell, R. and Small, N. (2009) 'A randomised controlled trial of liaison worker model for young people with learning disabilities and mental health problems', *Journal of Applied Research in Intellectual Disabilities*, 22(3): 256–63.

Raghavan, R., Pawson, N. and Small, N. (2013) 'Family carers' perspectives on post-school transition of young people with intellectual disabilities with special reference to ethnicity', *Journal of Intellectual Disability Research*, 57(10): 936–46.

Roeleveld, H., Zielhuis, G.A. and Gabreels, F. (1997) 'The prevalence of mental retardation: a critical review of recent literature', *Developments in Medical Child Neurology*, 39: 125–32.

SCIE (Social Care Institute of Excellence) (2013) *Co-production in social care: what it is and how to do it*, London: SCIE.

Sims, D. and Gulyurtlu, S.C. (2014) 'A scoping review of personalisation in the UK: approaches to social work and people with learning disabilities', *Health and Social Care in the Community*, 22(1): 13–21.

Small, N., Raghavan, R. and Pawson, N. (2013) 'An ecological approach to seeking and utilising the views of young people with intellectual disabilities in transition planning', *Journal of Intellectual Disabilities*, 17(4): 283–300.

Turner, S. and Robinson, C. (2011) *Health inequalities and people with learning disabilities in the UK: implications and actions for commissioners*, Bath: National Development Team for Inclusion.

# TWELVE

# Boy trouble? Motivational interviewing and communication with black boys and their families

*Roma Thomas*

## Introduction

Public discourses frequently position boys as troubled, or troubling, and young black male identities are even more problematised. While concerns over 'failing' black boys date back generations, arguably, the current austerity climate throws into even sharper relief challenges for social work with young boys and their families. This chapter asks how theories that help to shed light on age, gender and racialised constructions of young male identities can be brought to bear on practice? In doing so, it critiques the dominance of psychological approaches to understanding childhood, and highlights the potential for sociological paradigms to enrich social work practice. The chapter goes on to link these insights to the practical question of how to improve social work communication? Communication, as a key aspect of practice, is surely worthy of our attention as a dimension of transformative practice.

The aim of the chapter is twofold. The first aim of the chapter is to draw on sociological insights to set out a broad context for social work practice with young black boys and their families. Here, the discussion draws on multidisciplinary perspectives, exploring age factors, masculinities and intersectionality. The chapter focuses on boys aged 12–15, a key transition phase in the lives of young people. It argues that sociological theories are an underused resource for a profession that is dominated by psychological frames of knowledge. This section of the chapter begins by contrasting psychological notions of adolescence with sociological conceptualisations of youth before going on to consider racialised masculinities and their implications for practice. A core argument of the chapter is the need for scholarship and practice with black boys to move beyond the narrow confines of race and engage with the complex interplay of factors such as age, race, gender and class (only some of which it is possible to touch on within this chapter). This engagement needs to take account of boys' own constructions of themselves, as well as the ways in which they are constructed by others. Having set the 'theoretical' scene, the second aim of the chapter is to propose a way in which theory can be 'put to work' in the context of communication in social work. Here, Motivational Interviewing (MI) (Miller and Rollnick, 2012) is explored as a potential tool for building transformative practice. While the 'bad behaviour' of black boys is often a focus for social work practice, such practice tends not to be informed by a focus on the performance and intersectionality that theoretical insights can offer. Negotiating this 'implementation gap' calls for nuanced approaches to the behaviours of black boys. Such approaches also need to avoid the trap of essentialist constructions. The central importance of communication for effective practice leads me to suggest that MI is a worthy candidate for consideration in building practice that engages with the identities of black boys. MI, though technique-driven, is not proposed here as a social work 'sleight' of hand intended to bend the will of young clients and their families. Rather, MI is proposed as a way of making practical use (through the medium of worker communication skills) of the knowledge of racialised masculinities in black boys offered by sociological framings.

MI is both an ethos and a set of techniques for helping clients explore and resolve ambivalence. The empathic, directional skills of MI, with its emphasis on respectful, non-authoritarian styles of communication, fit well with the tenets of anti-discriminatory practice and with clients' own agency. Examples from empirical research are included in the chapter. The data referred to here – audio-recordings of simulated practice – are part of a large-scale randomised control trial (RCT) that took place in the UK between 2012 and 2013 in an area-based, urban local authority child protection team (Forrester et al, forthcoming). The study evaluated the impact of training in MI on parental engagement in child protection. Audio-recordings of direct practice, both real and simulated, are used in the main study to explore the practice of over 60 social workers. This chapter draws on my qualitative, secondary analysis of 10 audio-recordings of workers in simulated assessment interviews. The 10 recordings were transcribed and inductive thematic analysis (Braun and Clarke, 2006) was used to examine the practice of the 10 workers. Practice was explored in the context of young people's identities and workers' MI communication skills. The extracts are commented on in the light of the theoretical perspectives and MI skills discussed in this chapter. These glimpses of practice help to bring us closer to a real-world context for the application of theory.

## Social worker-simulated interviews scenario

### Difficult conversations about a boy

The scenario for the simulated interview takes the form of a 30-minute social work assessment meeting. Within the scenario, a distressed single parent of a 15-year-old boy is meeting a social worker. The parent is demanding that the young person is taken into care following an episode of aggressive behaviour where the young boy waved a knife around and stabbed the knife into a bread board in the kitchen. This followed being challenged by his parent for returning home late at night smelling of alcohol. In nine out of 10 of the recordings, the actor parent was a single mother; in one case, the actor parent was a single father. The ethnicity of the boy is not specified within the scenario. However, actors were from diverse ethnic backgrounds, including black. In one case, the actor referred specifically to the black identity of her son. The brief to the actor parent was to 'react' to the social worker, that is, to take their cue from what the social worker said and respond in character. Social workers and actors (who were, in the main, social work students) involved in the study rated the scenario as highly realistic.

My 'borrowings' from multidisciplinary perspectives in this chapter are mainly drawn from the sociology of education literature and childhood and youth studies. The significance of gender, age and racial identities is integral to anti-oppressive practice and person-centred approaches in social work. However, scholarship in the fields of education and youth (alongside criminology) lead the field, ahead of social work, in unpicking the complex interplay between gender, age and racial identity (Connell, 1995; Mac an Ghaill, 1996; Sewell, 1997; Skelton, 2001; Frosh et al, 2002; O'Donnell and Sharpe, 2000; Nayak and Kehily, 2007).

## Sociology for social workers – theories looking for practice

This section of the chapter begins by contrasting psychological notions of adolescence with sociological conceptualisations of youth before going on to consider racialised masculinities and their implications for practice.

### Age and innocence

There is a tendency for young people above the age of 12 to be 'lost' within the homogeneous category of children aged 0–17 in the UK child protection system as greater attention is often focused on the needs of younger children (Rees et al, 2010). The Children's Society report by Rees et al (2010) highlights a lack of research on and policy attention to the maltreatment of adolescents. Evidence also suggests that welfare professionals face greater challenges and complexities when the circumstances for an intervention relate to the behaviours of young people themselves, for example, instances of aggression and conflict between young people and their parents, or risky behaviours by young people (Rees et al, 2010; Holt and Retford, 2013). Insights from my own research[1] correspond with this evidence. During six months of observations and family interviews in a child protection service, I observed a small number of cases where boys from diverse ethnic backgrounds, aged 12–15, were regularly demonstrating aggressive and controlling behaviours. These behaviours were usually directed towards their mothers (often single parents) and sometimes towards siblings. In some cases, the boys had witnessed domestic violence. I observed a sense of struggle and anxiety in the social workers responding to these cases. In their chats with me after a visit, the social worker often commented on the age of the young boy as a key concern. In some workers, there was a sense of pessimism as they felt that it was already too late to intervene. Poor outcomes were often seen as almost inevitable given the boy's age.

It is argued here that there are a number of reasons behind the difficulties that professionals encounter in work with adolescents. Some of these difficulties relate to the dominance of age-related factors in professionals' responses to young people. This privileging of age in social work (and other professions) stems, in part, from the dominance of psychological paradigms and the neglect of other sociological domains of knowledge for practice (Flavell, 1992; Burman, 1994; Hogan, 2005). Coppock (2005) refers to a 'hegemony' where practices and knowledge have converged within the frame of psychology. The contrast between psychological framings of adolescence and sociological conceptualisations of youth exemplify these issues and is briefly discussed in the following.

Broadly speaking, psychoanalytic approaches interpret adolescence as a period of deep vulnerabilities of personality that stem from the onset of puberty. This approach emphasises 'maladaptive behaviour' during this life-stage (Coleman, 2010). Ideas of adolescence as a time of 'storm and stress', based on G. Stanley Hall's (1904) work at the start of the 20th century, remain highly influential in understanding the significance of adolescence for young people. This is despite evidence that the majority of young people negotiate this period of their lives without major trauma (Coleman and Hagell, 2007).

Overall, a psychological framing of childhood emphasises internal processes in the adolescent developmental path. The value of psychological paradigms is not disputed here. It is clear that vulnerabilities can arise during this transition phase in a young person's life. Adolescence is known to be a significant risk period for the onset of mental health problems (Collishaw, 2012). This exposure to risk is understandable given the ways in which the growing sociability of young people also leads to 'key institutions and relationships play[ing] a greater role in shaping the lives of young people' (Hagell, 2012: 6). However, a psychological emphasis on the maladaptive also pathologises adolescence and neglects an understanding of the social worlds of young people (James and Prout, 1990; Hogan, 2005). This is unhelpful for practice and can lead to a pessimism among professionals that stymies engagement and effective interventions with young people. In the case of black boys, whose racial identities are frequently problematised, stigma attached to age is likely to create more barriers to good practice. Conversely, emphasis on the turmoil of adolescence can also lead to the vulnerabilities of young people being overlooked and dismissed as a 'normal part of being a teenager'.

A further issue arising from the dominance of psychological paradigms is the oppositional positioning of childhood versus adulthood. These adult versus child binaries can be significant for young boys, who are sometimes assumed to be operating according to the cultural dynamics of older men (Haywood and Mac an Ghaill, 2003). The transition from childhood is traditionally viewed as a loss of innocence (Moss and Petrie, 2005). This 'crossing over' from childhood innocence to adult responsibility and blame has significant consequences for young people. For example, in cases of abuse and the sexual exploitation of young people, they can be seen as 'imperfect victims' (Rees and Stein, 1999), or as 'consenting' to their exploitation (Pearce, 2013). For black boys and the ways in which racial identity can underscore perceptions of 'trouble-making', age-related factors also play an important part in this positioning. Adolescence is a period of time when we can see young people beginning to be positioned as troubled and troubling. The very term 'youth' in popular discourse is frequently used as a pejorative term, and the term 'black youth' even more so:

> Cultural investments in the idea of childhood as a state of innocence can be contrasted with notions of youth as difficult, 'out of control' and potentially dangerous – a symbol of what is wrong with the neighbourhood or the country more generally. (Nayak and Kehily, 2007: 8)

These ideas are also evoked in Tony Sewell's (1997) 'devils' and 'angels' terminology, used to describe the positioning of African-Caribbean boys in a London secondary school (discussed in the next section).

This discussion is not an attempt to abandon psychological insights in social work. Rather, it is an effort to focus on a contribution from sociology that can be 'crowded out' by the dominance of psychological theories in social work practice. In order to shed light on this further, I will focus on two key contributions that sociological approaches can offer: agency and identity. In narrowing my focus to these two areas, I also recognise the size and diversity of the field encompassed by the sociology of childhood (Qvortrup, 1993; James and Prout, 1997; Mayall, 2002; Jenks, 2005; Kehily, 2013). In-depth appraisal of this arena is well beyond the scope of this chapter. Indeed, this is addressed comprehensively elsewhere (Kehily, 2009; Qvortrup et al, 2009; Mayall, 2013). However, before moving on, I should acknowledge the importance of this scholarship to the theoretical knowledge base of key professions involved in the welfare of children, although sadly much less influential for practice (Graham, 2011). Major themes arising from child social studies include children's agency (Hutchby and Moran-Ellis, 1998; Qvortrup, 2005), closely linked to children's rights agendas (Liebel and Saadi, 2012; Morrow and Pells, 2012). In the last two decades, key themes that have emerged include the impact of digital technologies on the lives of children (Livingstone, 2002; Hutchby and Moran-Ellis, 2013; Holloway and Valentine, 2014), and globalisation and its implications for children (Twum-Danso and Ame, 2012; Spyrou and Christou, 2014). Also, more pertinent to this discussion, there is greater focus on the significance of changes in the political and cultural positioning of children and young people. Jo Moran-Ellis highlights the 'notable shift towards the demonization of teenagers (adolescents) along with rising levels of anxiety concerning children generally' (Moran-Ellis, 2010: 186). It is insights from sociological thought regarding agency and identity to which I now turn.

According to James and Prout (1997, cited in Nayak and Kehily, 2007), key features of the sociological paradigm of childhood and youth include:

- childhood is understood as a social construction;
- childhood is a variable of social analysis;
- children should be seen as social agents; and
- studying childhood involves an engagement with the process of reconstructing childhood in society.

Here, 'youth' is used as a term more frequently adopted in sociological frameworks. This is distinct from the term 'adolescence', which is predominant in psychology. Understanding young people as relational, social agents leads to a view of youth as a socially constructed stage of life, rather than the universal state suggested by adolescence in psychological terms. Usefully, Nayak and Kehily (2007: 8) describe childhood and youth as 'contingent constructions, forever in the making'. An understanding of these 'contingencies' can help to move forward social work practice (and other child welfare professions) from the child versus adult binaries discussed previously.

The sociological approach also brings to the fore questions of the agency of young people and the practice dilemmas that can arise when agency is combined with a social work commitment to empowerment. Before examining this interplay in the practice context of communication, this part of the discussion moves on to focus on black boys' identities, in particular, racialised masculinities.

### Racialised masculinities – boys and trouble

> Yet it has been apparent, at least since the 1930s, that the processes of racialization, gendering and social class differentiation produce specific childhoods for children positioned differently within the social formation. (Phoenix, 2000: 95)

Gender issues relating to young people as clients are underexplored in the social work literature. For instance, child and family social work chiefly addresses the role of fathers in child protection (Scourfield, 2003; Featherstone et al, 2009), gender issues in the social work workforce and women as clients (Dominelli and McLeod, 1989; Dominelli, 1991). There has also been a tendency for this focus to be subsumed within broader categories, such as social work with black families and anti-racist perspectives for practice (Graham, 2007; Okitikpi and Aymer, 2009). While anti-discriminatory practice, as a cornerstone of social work, should provide a foundation for critical thinking about these issues, consideration of the intersections between gender, age and race is also less explored in social work. As a consequence, although there is a general consensus that 'specific childhoods' arise from the social structures and positioning described by Ann Phoenix earlier, there remains a tendency to treat young people as an undifferentiated category.

The dominance of age within the psychological paradigm of social work overlooks important theoretical resources that can be loosely grouped under the sociology banner. For reasons of space, I will confine myself to a brief commentary relating to the identities of black boys and the contribution of masculinities scholarship to this field (Mac an Ghaill, 1994; Connell, 1995; Sewell, 1997; Frosh et al, 2002).

Identity is, of course, not fixed; Stuart Hall's (1990: 222) concept of identity as a 'production', 'which is never complete, always in process, and always constituted within, not outside representation', is useful here, up to a point. However, it still begs the question of how the practitioner is to negotiate her or his way through these unfixed, dissolving concepts? One way forward is to engage more closely with the ways in which black boys negotiate and 'produce' their own identities, as well as understanding the ways in which other key institutions, such as school, family and peer groups, position them.

Sewell's (1997) study of the experience of African-Caribbean boys in an inner-city boys' comprehensive school gives a highly relevant account of the re-production of black masculinities. Sewell finds that black boys are perceived as 'angels and devils' in British and US schools: they are, at the same time, both seen as 'heroes' of youth culture, fashion and street style, and positioned as 'too sexy' for school: 'This experience of being the darling of popular youth sub-culture and the sinner in the classroom has led to the formation of a range of behaviours' (Sewell, 1997: ix). It is these behaviours and responses that Sewell categorises as masculinities: 'They [the responses] are linked to how the boys perceive themselves as males and how others perceive them' (1997: ix).

Connell's (1995, 2005) concept of 'hegemonic masculinities' remains foundational in advancing masculinities scholarship. Although critiqued for being too illusory to apply to men in the real world (Donaldson, 1993), the concept is enormously valuable in understanding how boys measure themselves and can construct 'ideal' dominant types of masculinity. The hyper-masculine 'ideal' of being tough, good at sport and not focused on school work is highlighted across a number of studies of boys (Mac an Ghaill, 1994; Sewell, 1997; Frosh et al, 2002). In the US literature, Majors and Billson's (1993) concept of 'cool pose' addresses similar territory. For social work practice, characteristics of hyper-masculinity should call attention not just to the ways in which black boys are perceived by others (ie the structural formations of society), but also to the ways boys construct themselves. Here, again, regard for the agency of young people is instructive. However, a critique of masculinities scholarship for its own problematising discourses is also highly relevant. Alexander (2000: 17) argues that the 'equation of black male identities solely with "race" has served to focus concerns on violence, criminality and control'. Her clear-eyed ethnographic study of young black men (Alexander, 1996) provides a valuable corrective to deficit portrayals of young black masculinity, hence her use of the term the 'art' of being black to denote the strategies that young men deploy in negotiating the world around them:

> Black British youth identity can best be understood, therefore, as a momentary configuration of images and attitudes, formed in interaction with others and encapsulating a multiplicity of shifting

definitions and interpretations. The interaction between these multiple images is complex and alters with both the context and the individual concerned. (Alexander, 1996: 198)

This is not to minimise the significance of the ways in which racialised and other constructions of identity may impact black boys negatively. For instance, Connolly's (2002) study of racism and gender identities in an inner-city primary school gives a vivid account of racialised processes affecting the lives of small children. He highlights the use by teachers of more explicitly racialised discourses together with other 'signifiers', such as a child being 'easily led' or 'hyperactive', when describing black boys who are five and six years old.

Alongside consideration of the impact of discriminatory processes, this discussion seeks to underline the need to consider the influence of young black boys' own 'take' on their lives in relation to masculinity and other aspects of their identity. O'Donnell and Sharpe (2000) emphasise a multiplicity of views amid the uncertainties of masculinities. Importantly, they acknowledge that there is no absolute relationship between factors such as race, class, age and gender. This, of course, highlights complexities and potential traps for practice. Their study includes findings that the masculinities of white boys are structured decisively by class and the masculinities of African-Caribbean boys are structured decisively by race and by their 'ethnically mediated' response to race (O'Donnell and Sharpe, 2000). This view is supported by many commentators (Willis, 1977; Sewell, 1997; Phoenix, 2000; Frosh et al, 2002).

Sociological perspectives offer the potential for more nuanced approaches in social work assessment and intervention, taking into consideration a wider range of external processes in the lives of young people, as well as their own self-identities. This is a valuable addition to the emphasis on internal factors within psychological frameworks.

## Boy trouble?

A view of 'trouble' and 'troublemaking' is the final brief example in this section of the discussion. Connell et al (1982) suggest that we move away from seeing 'troublemaking' as a pathological syndrome to seeing it as a relationship to school, a type of resistance. Similarly, O'Donnell and Sharpe (2000), in their study of boys in a secondary school, found that troublemaking, including truanting and crime, were regarded as a kind of leisure activity by boys. It was seen as 'fun' and 'just for a laugh'. Greater understanding of 'trouble' as a kind of self-expression and 'resistance' to the regimes of others, such as family and school, is more in tune with the professional identity of youth work than social work. It is also more challenging given the statutory nature of social work compared to the voluntary nature of involvement with youth work. However, demonstrating an understanding of 'trouble' as relational without becoming collusive is also likely to prove more effective in engaging young people and ultimately more effective in direct work. Given the frequent positioning of black boys as 'troubled' and 'troubling', this is highly relevant for practice. It is the question of communication with and engagement of black boys and their families to which I now turn. MI is proposed as a tool that can offer the dialogic engagement that is needed for practice to create lasting change with clients.

## Motivational Interviewing – handling difficult conversations in social work

Despite considerable focus in social work policy and training, problems in communication with service users remain a key concern in contemporary social work. Forrester et al (2008) observe that the use of aggressive and confrontational styles by social workers in their study suggests systemic issues. Clapton et al (2013: 7) describe the rise of 'us and them' attitudes between social workers and service users and 'a coarsening of attitudes towards families in child protection work'. Austerity and proceduralism are brought into sharp focus in the Featherstone et al (2014) critique of the rise of risk-dominated, defensive practice in social work. It is argued here that these issues demonstrate an urgent need to focus on micro-skills for practice in order to operationalise anti-discriminatory practice, and to make use of the theoretical concepts previously discussed. MI has the potential to address the gap between theory and practice by focusing on these micro-skills in ways that take account of the identities and agency of black boys.

MI is a directive, client-centred counselling style, originally developed in therapeutic interventions for alcohol misuse (Miller and Rollnick, 2012). MI has an established, international and growing evidence base for its effectiveness in a variety of settings (Lundahl et al, 2010; Forrester et al, 2012). Central to MI is building empathic, helping relationships and exploring and resolving clients' ambivalence, with the aim of supporting behaviour change. Crucially, changing problem behaviours is set in the context of the client's evaluation of their behaviours, and according to the client's goals and values (Forrester et al, 2008). In relation to child and family social work, a key aspect of MI is that it provides a framework for practice that is capable of addressing client resistance in ways that do not undermine social work values of empowerment and social justice (Forrester et al, 2012). Given the nature of statutory social work and clients' often 'involuntary' involvement, this is highly significant. Forrester et al (2012: 123) point out that 'client resistance is not something that solely exists within the client'; it is 'also a product of the nature and quality of the interaction between client and social worker'. In other words, the communication style of the social worker has a crucial effect on client resistance and levels of engagement (Miller and Rollnick, 2012). At its core, MI seeks to move beyond mere recognition of the client's agency to the active engagement of the client's motivations and ambivalence about change.

An example of MI-consistent practice can be seen in the following, where Social Worker 3 demonstrates an appreciation of the importance of both the boy's and the parents' perspective in a way that is attuned to MI principles:

> Social Worker 3 (SW3): "Well what I would think would be best is if I meet with him and get a feel from his perspective what's happening, because that would be really good if I can manage to do that, to think about that alongside your perspective as well, and then what we need to do is try and decide together what's going to work, because you know him best don't you?"

What follows next is an example of a non-MI, authoritarian interaction in a discussion about boundaries:

> Social Worker 1 (SW1): "so those are the things you're going to have to learn.... I know you've been trying, but it's how, it's the techniques, it's how you've been trying."

Sociological approaches, alongside psychological knowledge, can provide ways of knowing, or, rather, getting to know, clients. Although the theoretical underpinnings of MI owe more to psychology, and are therefore more individualistic than relational, the practical skills of MI provide a way of making use of sociological knowledge. In the case of young black boys, this is a helpful move beyond the analyses of powerlessness that dominate anti-discriminatory frameworks in social work (Dominelli and Campling, 2002; Thompson, 2012). The influence of risk-led, deficit models in social work practice, despite aspirations for strengths-based work, leaves little space for the narratives and understanding of everyday lives that comprise the social worlds of clients. MI at least moves a step further towards an understanding of how boys' lives may be shaped by both their own interpretations and those of their family, school and peers. While it cannot be said that MI theory can fully address the sociological constructions discussed, the practice of MI is inherently empowering and it does offer an important resource. An MI approach to client engagement requires workers to create a dialogue with clients and to provide the conditions for that dialogue to be as equal as possible without losing a focus on central concerns. It is advocated here as a stratagem for engaging more effectively with service users.

In the following extracts, defensiveness and risk, and a corresponding lack of empathy, can be seen in the responses of two of the workers. These were also the two workers who advised calling the police in response to the young person's behaviour. Interestingly, other workers within the same scenario did not advise calling the police. The responses of both workers demonstrate a highly authoritarian (non-MI) tone, telling the parent what to do. There is also at times a 'ratcheting' up of the situation, with a focus on future possible risks:

| | |
|---|---|
| SW1: | "You know, you call the police." |
| Parent: | "But I'm not going to do that on my own son." |
| SW1: | "Well, you wouldn't call the police but you throw him out and put him in care, it's …" |
| Parent: | "You see, that's just a threat, you know, that's a threat, I don't know if I would go through with it." |
| SW1: | "I think that Jordan needs to, and it's about being consistent with boundaries. Threatening you with a knife is not acceptable, it doesn't make a difference that you're his mum, he's your son, that he's 15, that's not acceptable and he needs to hear a clear message…. Or even if you think about it the other way, supposing you didn't call the police and next time round he does something, god forbid, to you, and the police are called because something happens to you, where's he going to end up?" |
| Parent: | "Mm. I don't want him to get a record." |

A second social worker demonstrates similar levels of anxiety and defensiveness against risk:

Social Worker 10 (SW10): "Has he ever actually assaulted you in the past?"

| | |
|---|---|
| Parent: | "No." |
| SW10: | "That at least is one thing, but then again you never know because there might always be a first time…. I realise it's not easy to call the police on your own child, but if you're not capable of disciplining him following that, then it does need to go to someone who will. If he does this to someone in the street or a teacher at school, he's going to be arrested and probably charged." |
| Parent: | Yeah, I know." |
| SW10: | "If you're not able to, as I say, put the boundaries in place at this point, he's going to end up with that happening. What I know at this point, all he's in trouble with the police for is a little bit of anti-social stuff and minor |

shoplifting, but if it's going like this, then he could end
up in prison, which no parent wants."

These interactions demonstrate the coarsening of tone described by Clapton et al (2013). The focus is on fixing the behaviours of the young person and deficit parenting skills. There is a marked lack of empathy and a lack of recognition of either the boy's own agency or that of the parent. The reasons for the young boy's behaviour are very much secondary to the need to manage the risk and, if necessary, pass on the risk to an alternative agency, that is, the police.

By way of contrast, we can see a more MI-consistent approach to the same issue of calling the police:

Parent:          "What if he's still like…. What if he gets back in a rage or something, what am I supposed to do?"

Social Worker 6 (SW6): "Obviously, I don't want you to feel threatened in any way and what I would say would be, if you can't walk away from the situation and you felt threatened, would be to call the police."

Parent:          "That's going to make him worse, isn't it?"

SW6:          "But that's if you can't walk away from the situation. If you know he's going to come in late, rather than getting into any conflict with him …"

Parent:          "Right, just ignore him or what?"

SW6:          "Just try and take yourself away from the situation, take yourself away from Jordan so you can't get embroiled in any argument, not until, I suppose, you feel in the space that you're able to talk about things."

These contrasting examples of simulated practice help to illustrate how the skills of MI can be used to try to create a dialogue with the client, while low-skill, non-MI practice is likely to be a barrier to engagement. MI helps formulate a practical response to the implications for social work arising from the sociological factors discussed.

## Conclusions

In this chapter, I have drawn attention to the primacy of age as a key factor in work with young people. I have also discussed the neglect of other factors such as gender and race and, crucially, the ways in which these factors intersect to construct young people's lives. I have highlighted the positioning of black boys and the implications for social work practice. I have also drawn attention to the need to give greater weight to the way in which young people position themselves. Furthermore, consideration of racialised masculinities calls for greater sophistication rather than simply positioning black boys in terms of their race. This is highly significant for practice with boys because, as Alexander (2000: 12) points out, regarding youth, gender and race, 'the coalescence of all three leads to prophecies of doom'.

I hope that I have made the case for the need for social work to open up more space for sociological theories to influence practice. However, once the space for theory is opened up, the way forward for practice may be less clear-cut. The case for MI skills in social work is not pressed here solely in relation to black boys and their families. The tenets of respect and empathy are clearly good practice for social work communication more generally. However, the intersections between race, gender and age are frequently missing in action in social work with black boys. The case for MI as a technique for building transformative practice is located in this space. MI is advocated here as an approach that helps to build the communication skills needed to attend to individual needs in the context of a complex web of identities within our social world. Given the customary positioning of black boys at the apex of 'trouble', MI is proposed as part of a necessary but insufficient skill set for practice that taps into the resources of service users rather than adopting deficit models of black boys' masculinities. MI does this by offering practitioners a chance to identify and work with (as opposed to 'on') service users' own ambivalence and motivations for change. At its best, that is, in highly skilled hands, this can offer opportunities for co-production with service users.

In closing, I would like to sketch out three pointers for practice arising from this discussion. First, there is a need to recognise the value of greater direct engagement with young people in child and family social work, and the need to move beyond the homogeneous categorisations implicit in psychological paradigms of adolescence. The ideas of agency and identity (or rather identities) discussed bring this issue to the fore.

Second, there is a need for practitioners to examine reasons for 'trouble' more deeply. Biehal (2008: 454) highlights a tendency for social work to focus on 'changing surface actions and behavioural performance', with less attention to 'why' questions. Given what we know about 'troublemaking' as a form of resistance (Connell et al, 1982), sociological conceptual resources can help to bring greater depth for practice.

Finally, the literature suggests that improving social work communication with service users remains a priority. The empirical evidence briefly discussed here further supports this argument. These examples of MI-consistent and non-MI practice draw our attention to the all-important specificities that make up practice encounters. Communication is a key arena and sociological insights can help to improve practice. However, more resources are needed to apply these theoretical insights in transformative ways. MI provides a practice-ready tool for this. MI attempts to honour the difference between authoritarian (sometimes aggressive) risk-dominated practice and strong practice that is theoretically informed. It has the potential to bridge a gap between theory and action by helping workers address the implications of gendered and racialised constructions of black boys. In so doing, MI may be a way for practice to move beyond 'trouble' in work with boys.

## Note

[1.] Fieldwork conducted as part of the study of parental engagement in child protection referred to in this chapter.

## References

Alexander, C.E. (1996) *The art of being black : the creation of black British youth identities*, Clarendon Press.

Alexander, C.E. (2000) *The Asian gang: ethnicity, identity, masculinity*, Berg.

Biehal, N. (2008) 'Preventive services for adolescents: exploring the process of change', *British Journal of Social Work*, 38(3): 444–61.

Braun, V. and Clarke, V. (2006) 'Using thematic analysis in psychology', *Qualitative Research in Psychology*, 3(2): 77–101.

Burman (1994) *Deconstructing developmental psychology*, London: Routledge.

Clapton, G., Cree, V. and Smith, M. (2013) 'Moral panics, claims-making and child protection in the UK', *British Journal of Social Work*, 43(4): 803–12.

Coleman, J.C. (2010) *The nature of adolescence* (4th edn), London: Routledge.

Coleman, J. and Hagell, A. (2007) *Adolescence, risk and resilience: against the odds*, Wiley.

Collishaw, S. (2012) 'Time trends in young people's emotional and behavioural problems', in A. Hagell (ed) *Changing adolescence: social trends and mental health*, Bristol: The Policy Press, pp 9–25.

Connell, R.W. (1995) *Masculinities*, Cambridge: Polity Press.

Connell, R.W. (2005) *Masculinities*, Cambridge: Polity Press.

Connell, R., Ashenden, D., Kessler, S. and Dowsett, G. (1982) *Making the difference: schools, families and social division*, Allen & Unwin Australia.

Connolly, P. (2002) *Racism, gender identities and young children: social relations in a multi-ethnic, inner city primary school*, Taylor & Francis.

Coppock, V. (2005) '"Mad", "bad" or misunderstood?', in H. Hendrick (ed) *Child welfare and social policy* (1st edn), Bristol: The Policy Press, pp 285–301.

Dominelli, L. (1991) '"Race" gender, and social work', in M. Davies (ed) *The sociology of social work*, London: Routledge, pp 182–201.

Dominelli, L. and Campling, J. (2002) *Anti-oppressive social work theory and practice*, New York, NY, and Basingstoke: Palgrave Macmillan.

Dominelli, L. and McLeod, E. (1989) *Feminist social work*, Macmillan Education.

Donaldson, M. (1993) 'What is hegemonic masculinity?', *Theory and Society*, 22: 643–57.

Featherstone, B., Hooper, C.A., Scourfield, J. and Taylor, J. (2009) *Gender and child welfare in society*, Oxford: Wiley-Blackwell.

Featherstone, B., White, S. and Morris, K. (2014) *Re-imagining child protection: towards humane social work with families*, Bristol: The Policy Press.

Flavell, J.H. (1992) 'Cognitive development: past, present and future', *Developmental Psychology*, 28(6): 998–1005.

Forrester, D., McCambridge, J., Waissbein, C. and Rollnick, S. (2008) 'How do child and family social workers talk to parents about child welfare concerns?', *Child Abuse Review*, 17(1): 23–35.

Forrester, D., Westlake, D. and Glynn, G. (2012) 'Parental resistance and social worker skills: towards a theory of motivational social work', *Child & Family Social Work*, 17(2): 118–29.

Forrester, D., Westlake, D., Waits, C., Thomas, R., Antonopoulou, P., Whittaker, C., McCann, M., Killian, M. and Thurnham, A. (forthcoming) 'Engaging parents and protecting children: a randomised controlled trial in motivational interviewing in child protection'.

Frosh, S., Phoenix, A. and Pattman, R. (2002) *Young masculinities: understanding boys in contemporary society*, Basingstoke, Hampshire and New York: Palgrave.

Graham, M. (2007) *Black issues in social work and social care*, Bristol: The Policy Press.

Graham, M. (2011) 'Changing paradigms and conditions of childhood: implications for the social professions and social work', *British Journal of Social Work*, 41(8): 1532–47.

Hagell, A. (ed) (2012) *Changing adolescence: social trends and mental health*, Bristol: The Policy Press.

Hall, G.S. (1904) *Adolescence: its psychology and its relation to physiology, anthropology, sociology, sex, crime, religion, and education*, Englewood Cliffs, NJ: Prentice-Hall.

Hall, S. (1990) 'Cultural identity and the diaspora', in J. Rutherford (ed) *Identity, community, culture, difference*, London: Lawrence and Wishart, pp 222–37.

Haywood, C. and Mac an Ghaill, M. (2003) *Men and masculinities: theory, research and social practice*, Maidenhead: Open University Press.

Hogan, D. (2005) 'Researching "the child" in developmental psychology', in S. Greene and D. Hogan (eds) *Researching children's experiences: approach and methods*, London: Sage.

Holloway, S. and Valentine, G. (2014) *Cyberkids: youth identities and communities in an on-line world*, London and New York: RoutledgeFalmer.

Holt, A. and Retford, S. (2013) 'Practitioner accounts of responding to parent abuse – a case study in ad hoc delivery, perverse outcomes and a policy silence', *Child & Family Social Work*, 18(3): 365–74.

Hutchby, I. and Moran-Ellis, J. (1998) *Children and social competence: arenas of action*, London: Falmer Press.

Hutchby, I. and Moran-Ellis, J. (2013) *Children, technology and culture: the impacts of technologies in children's everyday lives*, Abingdon, Oxon and New York: Taylor and Francis.

James, A. and Prout, A. (1990) *Constructing and reconstructing childhood: contemporary issues in the sociological study of children*, London: Falmer Press.

James, A. and Prout, A. (eds) (1997) *Constructing and reconstructing childhood: contemporary issues in the sociological study of children*, London: Falmer.

Jenks, C. (2005) *Childhood: critical concepts in sociology*, London: Routledge.

Kehily, M.J. (2009) *An introduction to childhood studies* (2nd edn), Maidenhead: Open University Press.

Kehily, M.J. (ed.) (2013) *Understanding childhood: a cross-disciplinary approach*, Bristol: The Policy Press.

Liebel, M. and Saadi, I. (2012) *Children's rights from below: cross-cultural perspectives.* New York, NY, and Basingstoke: Palgrave Macmillan.

Livingstone, S. (2002) *Young people and new media: childhood and the changing media environment*, London: SAGE Publications.

Lundahl, B.W., Kunz, C., Brownell, C., Tollefson, D. and Burke, B.L. (2010) 'A meta-analysis of motivational interviewing: twenty-five years of empirical studies', *Research on Social Work Practice*, 20(2): 137–60.

Mac an Ghaill, M. (1994) *The making of men: masculinities, sexualities and schooling*, Maidenhead: Open University Press.

Mac an Ghaill, M. (1996) *Understanding masculinities: social relations and cultural arenas*, Maidenhead: Open University Press.

Majors, R. and Billson, J.M. (1993) *Cool pose: the dilemmas of black manhood in America*, New York: Simon and Schuster.

Mayall, B. (2002) *Towards a sociology for childhood: thinking from children's lives*, Maidenhead: Open University Press.

Mayall, B. (2013) *A history of the sociology of childhood*, London: Institute of Education Press.

Miller, W.R. and Rollnick, S. (2012) *Motivational interviewing: helping people change*, (3rd ed), New York: Guilford Press.

Moran-Ellis, J. (2010) 'Reflections on the sociology of childhood in the UK', *Current Sociology*, 58(2): 186–205.

Morrow, V. and Pells, K. (2012) 'Integrating children's human rights and child poverty debates: examples from young lives in Ethiopia and India', *Sociology*, 46(5): 906–20.

Moss, P. and Petrie, P. (2005) 'Children – who do we think they are?', in H. Hendrick (ed) *Child welfare and social policy*, Bristol: The Policy Press, pp 85–116.

Nayak, A. and Kehily, M.J. (2007) *Gender, youth and culture: young masculinities and femininities*, New York, NY, and Basingstoke: Palgrave Macmillan.

O'Donnell, M. and Sharpe, S. (2000) *Uncertain masculinities: youth, ethnicity and class in contemporary Britain*, New York and London: Routledge.

Okitikpi, T. and Aymer, C. (2009) *Key concepts in anti-discriminatory social work*, London: SAGE Publications.

Pearce, J. (2013) 'A social model of "abused consent"', in M. Melrose and J. Pearce (eds) *Critical perspectives on child sexual exploitation and related trafficking*, New York, NY, and Basingstoke: Palgrave Macmillan, pp 52–68.

Phoenix, A. (2000) 'Constructing gendered and racialized identities: young men, masculinities and educational policy', in G. Lewis, S. Gewirtz and J. Clarke (eds) *Rethinking social policy*, Maidenhead: Open University, pp 94–110.

Qvortrup, J.E. (1993) *Childhood as a social phenomenon: lessons from an international project*, European Centre.

Qvortrup, J. (2005) *Studies in modern childhood: society, agency, culture*, New York, NY, and Basingstoke: Palgrave Macmillan.

Qvortrup, J., Corsaro, W.A. and Honig, M.-S. (2009) *The Palgrave handbook of childhood studies*, New York, NY, and Basingstoke: Palgrave Macmillan.

Rees, G. and Stein, M. (1999) *The abuse of adolescents in the family*, London: NSPCC.

Rees, G., Gorin, S., Jobe, A., Stein, M., Medforth, R. and Goswami, H. (2010) *Safeguarding young people: responding to young people aged 11–17 who are maltreated*, London: The Children's Society.

Scourfield, J. (2003) *Gender and child protection*, New York, NY, and Basingstoke: Palgrave Macmillan.

Sewell, T. (1997) *Black masculinities and schooling: how black boys survive modern schooling*, Stoke-on-Trent: Trentham Books.

Skelton, C. (2001) *Schooling the boys: masculinities and primary education*, Maidenhead: Open University Press.

Spyrou, S. and Christou, M. (eds) (2014) *Children and borders*, New York, NY, and Basingstoke: Palgrave Macmillan.

Thompson, N. (2012) *Anti-discriminatory practice: equality, diversity and social justice*, New York, NY, and Basingstoke: Palgrave Macmillan.

Twum-Danso, A. and Ame, R.K. (eds) (2012) *Childhoods at the intersection of the local and the global*, New York, NY, and Basingstoke: Palgrave Macmillan.

Willis, P.E. (1977) *Learning to labor: how working class kids get working class jobs*, Columbia University Press.

# THIRTEEN

# Evaluation of serious case reviews and anti-racist practice

*Kish Bhatti-Sinclair and Donna Price*

## Introduction

The aim of this chapter is to consider how findings from recorded serious case reviews (SCRs) that took place during the 1991–2010 period informed or otherwise the development of good practice with black and minority ethnic (BME) children and their families residing in England and Wales. The aims are to consider cultural, linguistic, religious and other service needs within reviews and to examine key principles that may transform professional practice. The primary research question will be as follows: to what extent are issues of culture, language, religion and ethnicity incorporated in the findings of SCRs? The secondary question relates to the lessons learnt on the needs of BME children and families.

Social indicators on income, poverty and housing infer that some BME groups are overwhelmingly disadvantaged in British society. Statistics on looked after children (LACs) suggest that some BME children are not only over-represented, but also likely to remain in care longer than other population groups (Owen and Statham, 2009).

Social workers are increasingly seeking to develop practice methods with BME service users and to have in place review systems that address the impact that they and their organisations have on the lives of individuals and groups. However, challenges brought about by austerity measures and other service demands tend to overwhelm the commitment to targeted improvement in services to some groups. Professionals holding child protection responsibilities are particularly prone to pressures triggered by the detailed scrutiny of practice following a serious incident, the excessive focus on negative messages in review findings and the all-too-frequent public scapegoating of the professionals involved. The argument here is that although social workers offer nuanced responses to individual children, they may not be considering kinship ties, family patterns, linguistic differences and cultural understandings when reviewing and evaluating practice.

## Methodology

The data used to arrive at the findings include a search of the relevant literature, including published and peer-reviewed articles, reports from the UK government, research, and popular media/newspapers. The national online repository of published SCRs, hosted by the National Society for the Prevention of Cruelty to Children (NSPCC), was set up in collaboration with the Association of Independent Local Safeguarding Children's Boards, with the aim of storing all reports in a central location for easy public access.

The NSPCC repository was searched for SCRs lodged during the 1991–2010 period, with a particular focus on BME children. The rationale for the timescale is that the Children Act 1989, enacted in 1991, made special provision for ethnicity, culture and religion. Also, the subsequent 20 years incorporated substantial developments in the recording and reporting of reviews on child deaths and injuries. The inclusion criteria focused on papers from England and Wales with a particular focus on review processes supported by the Every Child Matters agenda and the 'Working together' guidance (HM Government, 2013), supplemented in March 2015 by the guide to inter-agency working (HM Government, 2015), which defined serious harm (as opposed to significant harm) in the context of SCRs.

The focus on one set of documentary evidence held in one archive proved challenging at a number of levels. Mandatory submission of SCRs to the archive did not take place until 2013, and prior to this period, the information held varied in quality and quantity. Applying a set criteria to elicit systemic data on, for example, the ethnicity of the child or young person did not work as this information was not always available in an easy to find place (such as a front page with a basic profile of the child, ie age, sex, religion, etc). Follow-up investigation into selected cases led to anecdotal evidence, found in grey literature and media coverage, and although interesting, this information was inconsistent and laden with bias.

## Serious case reviews

The 'Munro review of child protection' (Munro, 2011) led to the revised 'Working together' guidance (HM Government, 2013), which, in turn, created local safeguarding children's boards (LSCBs) and stipulated terms of reference, timescales and remits for SCRs, which must be undertaken when the abuse or neglect of a child is proven or suspected and where that child has either died or been seriously harmed. The guidance also provides for consideration of the conduct of the local authority or other organisation, particularly if they have not demonstrated working together to safeguard the child or young person. In addition, an SCR should be initiated if a young person dies in custody, while on remand and/or in a secure residential facility, and/or detained under the Mental Capacity Act 2005 and/or has taken her/his own life.

Child death reviews (CDRs) can be conducted whenever a child or young person has died suddenly or in unexpected circumstances. The criteria for initiating SCRs and CDRs are set out in the LSCB Regulations (HM Government, 2013). This is a separate process but should be conducted prior to an SCR. It is the responsibility of the Child Death Overview Panel (CDOP) to alert the Chair of the LSCB that an SCR may be required.

SCRs and CDRs have been conducted for many decades in the UK, founded on the premise that reflection, supervision and learning are at the core of developing good practice. However, reviews on cases such as Victoria Climbié have repeatedly located the responsibility for safeguarding children within organisations and systems set up to protect children. More specifically, the balance between supervising/supporting and public questioning/reprimanding has, on occasion, tipped against transforming and embedding good social work practice. Professional standing and confidence has been undermined rather than boosted as a result of the reviews, leaving social workers with questions about their own experience and understanding and of the value of service interventions.

Contextual pressures on organisations and professionals are increasingly being evidenced in SCRs (Bradford Safeguarding Children Board, 2013; Coventry Safeguarding Children Board, 2013), but, again, the suggestion is that social workers may be using surface-level information, lack capacity to dig deeper and have limited access to time and resources. The issue of beleaguered professionals working with families with significant problems has been considered in detail by Brandon et al (2009) and Jones (2014).

Although SCRs have taken place on BME children in the past, the focus on race, ethnicity, culture, language and religion in SCRs has been more recent. This may be because the overall public funds available to statutory and voluntary sector organisations have shrunk year by year, and although there is more on race, ethnicity, culture, language and religion in SCRs, the needs of BME children remain additional or marginal to mainstream child protection services.

The organisational changes in child protection social work (Jones, 2014) have resulted in greater interference by politicians and senior managers into established and well-rehearsed approaches, such as traditional, person-centred engagement. Greater focus on procedures has meant that social workers have less time on home visits to sit and chat with the family over a cup of tea. Common sense would suggest that understanding the family context and finding common ground prior to the commencement of formal assessment processes is critical to good communication. Cases such as Victoria Climbié and, more recently, Daniel Pelka (Coventry Safeguarding Children Board, 2013) highlight the importance of understanding the caring/family context within decision-making. The statement made by the judge sentencing Daniel Pelka's mother commented on her mitigation (in relation to domestic abuse) that being a victim did not lessen her culpability and that the network of family and friends were significant to the case. Although the SCR included sections on racial, linguistic and religious sensitivity, the conclusions and recommendations did not mention the wider family context (Coventry Safeguarding Children Board, 2013).

The Climbié and Pelka cases highlight the importance of the international dimension to child protection. It is commonly understood that childhood is likely to be conceived differently across the world (Smith, 2010); however, it cannot be assumed that professionals have the same understanding of welfare provision and child protection processes as the immigrant carers and parents of the children involved. It may be that the systems approach addresses this issue in the future but SCRs and related commentary have thus far omitted any comprehensive analysis of the impact of culture and religion on child abuse and neglect. However, Brandon et al (2009: 17, 21), in their in-depth analysis of SCRs, found the following information derived from the child protection database notification reports:

> The ethnicity of the children studied in 2005–2007 closely reflects that of the children in 2003–05. Just under three quarters of the children were classified as white in both time periods. The current study shows a higher proportion of mixed ethnicity and a lower proportion who are black British. Ethnicity was recorded for 173 (92%) of the children in 2005–07 and for 136 (84%) in the earlier study.

Despite the poor evidence of ethnic monitoring in SCRs, it is clear that BME children are in the children protection system and social work managers need to embed the multidimensional nature of race, ethnicity and cultural heritage in service and policy development. The Climbié and Pelka cases suggest that professionals require a complex set of skills, as well as time and energy, when working with children who show physical signs of risk and are living in extraordinary circumstances with adults who misunderstand their responsibilities or use their culture, language and religion to manipulate welfare systems (Featherstone et al, 2014). In contexts such as this, highly competent practitioners are more likely to understand their own capacity, seek relevant information, explore and offer a range of options, and find time to reflect on events. The qualities needed are consistency and effectiveness, along with the capacity to look beyond policies and procedures. Social workers who work beyond obligation and have an enquiring and nurturing approach are more likely to plan a bespoke professional intervention that accounts for the unique demography of the child or young person.

Social work organisations are increasingly looking for personal and professional qualities in their workforce, including the ability to analyse and argue in a manner that is beyond bureaucratic action (Featherstone et al, 2014: 43, 89). Proficiency in the application of social work knowledge and values on, for example, areas such as the 'social context' of child protection work is particularly pertinent. The link between poverty and disadvantaged groups, such as BME families with more than four children (Munro, 2012: 32), is a source of concern, and selected groups who fall into this category are receiving government attention under projects such as family intervention services (Department for Education, 2011).

However, there is a practice/policy gap that relates to the practical consequences of ideas generated by central governments, which have to be implemented by safeguarding services. The main difficulty is that political ideas, often rooted in ideology and personal histories, are whimsical and tend to move and change as often as individual policymakers. This means that there is little time to systematically reflect on and learn from the rising mass of evidence available on important issues such as neglect and abuse. The review approaches developed by child protection organisations, over a number of decades, provide a rare archive of data that can be interrogated for lessons, from a range of angles, to form the evidence for social work practice in the face of public disrespect and policy landmines. The collection is now available on the UK's NSPCC website and includes a repository of approximately 882 reports and executive summaries on enquires that have taken place on every child meeting the criteria for this analysis. This is an invaluable data source for students and professionals, who are increasingly being introduced to findings from SCRs early in their careers in order to develop understanding of the complexities of safeguarding practice (Baverstock et al, 2008).

The quality of the information available, however, is variable. This may be because until 2013, SCRs were mainly produced by and responded to by relevant child protection agencies. Online access will, without doubt, inform the development of child protection as a wider range of people, probably from across the world, interrogate the findings and highlight the gaps. The research on SCRs that took place between 1991 and 2010 on BME children suggests that despite Britain's multi-ethnic population profile, the recording of data on ethnicity, religion and culture is so inconsistent that it is impossible to draw conclusions on this area of practice.

LAC data, however, are collected by the government (Owen and Statham, 2009), but in common with many similar data-collecting exercises, the information is mainly based on country of origin or heritage (Chand, 2008). Poor monitoring of religion and ethnicity is evidenced as a significant shortfall in other areas by organisations such as the Office of National Statistics, which was reported to have omitted the recording of ethnic data on alcohol consumption among young people in 2015. A spokesperson stated that ethnicity was not included because it would add little that was 'new or interesting' (Hill, 2015: 8). Evidence suggests that there needs to be greater understanding of the correlation between ethnicity, faith and/or belief and the identified principal abuse.

## Developments in serious case reviews in the UK

The NSPCC online library was set up in collaboration with the Association of Independent LSCB Chairs, with the aim of storing all reports in a central location for easy public access. The levels of information available on the NSPCC website include summaries, executive summaries, full reports and briefings on key factors. SCRs have been publically available documents from the relevant LSCB websites but neither the NSPCC nor the LSCB websites hold or retain historic (pre-2013) SCRs, which are not offered voluntarily. The NSPCC library in London keeps Web-based and paper copies (not available electronically) that can be accessed in person. There is no doubt that this is a valuable and long-overdue resource, but one that requires continuing development to support user access and systematic analysis of what is, in general, an impressive set of documents . The database is constantly updated, so the information order is inclined to change as more SCRs are added. Earlier material is scarce and sometimes limited to executive summaries alone. Links are provided in some cases to the publishing LSCB's website, where a full report may or may not be available, having been removed after a given period of time. In short, the NSPCC database is extremely useful for scrutiny of individual reports, summaries and commentaries, but for cross-correlating variables and drawing lessons on groups such as BME children, it has limited value in its current form.

In addition to the move towards a central resource base, a significant change relates to the common understanding of the processes, methods of intervention and language used in child protection (Broadhurst et al, 2010). The 'Working together' guidance (HM Government, 2013, 2015) lists a glossary of terms that relate to safeguarding practice, including definitions of children, young people, neglect and different types of abuse.

The Laming report on the death of Victoria Climbié in 2003 (Victoria Climbie Foundation and HCL Social Care, 2014) led to the Every Child Matters agenda and the Children Act 2004. Critics suggest that this significant sequence of events addressed race and ethnicity minimally despite concerns about the relative disadvantages faced by such children in society and, more particularly, the possible under- or over-representation within child welfare services (Chand, 2008). The reforms established important principles but failed to build on Section 22(5c) of Children Act 1989, which provided statutory recognition of the importance of religion, racial origin, culture and language in decision-making processes for children in state care (Kirton, 2000). The 2004 'Working together' document guides professionals to address culture, family patterns and child-rearing practices, and warns against racial discrimination. However, a tick-list such as this provides little on the complex intersections between a child in the care system facing multiple disadvantages rooted in many factors, including poverty and racism. Indeed, the SCR on Hamzah Khan, a dual-heritage child, found that the 'cultural and religious complexity of the family was not enquired into' (Bradford Safeguarding Children Board, 2013) despite the fact that they resided in a geographic area that has an established history of settled BME communities. The SCR included a comment on the lack of recognition and action to support Hamzah's white mother, who suffered from the effects of the 'toxic trio', that is, domestic violence, substance misuse and poor mental health (Bradford Safeguarding Children Board, 2013: 66). Brandon et al found that approximately

75% of children in 2009 lived with domestic violence in their daily lives and that larger families and younger children faced additional problems.

The methods and approaches to investigating child abuse and neglect were further stimulated by the recommendation in the 'Munro review of child protection' (Munro, 2011), which promoted the move away from focusing on the specifics of a particular case to identifying underlying local issues that influence practice more generally, that is, adopting a systems approach. Systems methodology involves the practitioners and first-line managers, as well as senior managers, in building the story of the case, the analysis and the development of recommendations or findings. As a result, it can identify organisational factors that support good practice or that make poor practice more likely, and moves away from the culture of individual blame. Systems methodology also seeks to eliminate hindsight bias (in effect, working backwards from the critical event), which makes it easy for an outside person to criticise practice without taking account of the context (Broadhurst et al, 2010).

The idea is that learning is embedded in teams throughout the process because practitioners are 'done with' and not 'done to', so they change practice even before publication of the review and more readily adopt recommendations. The systems approach also brings the added bonus of role-modelling and encouraging good social work practice with families, who usually respond best to collaboration. The 'Working together' guidance (HM Government, 2013) states that SCR reports should provide a sound analysis of what happened in the case, and why, and what needs to happen in order to reduce the risk of recurrence. Reports should be written in plain, understandable English and be suitable for publication without needing to be amended or redacted. The 2013 and 2015 guidance actively promotes ways of working that are less prescriptive, minimise standard formats (such as the use of genogram/chronology) and allow greater freedom for organisational analysis and critique.

The systems model that was developed (SCIE, 2012) offers a significant way forward, along with the changes in SCR processes, conduct and impact. Professional practice is seen in the broader organisational context, with a continuing focus on understanding what happened and what went wrong but with closer attention to the contributory factors that impact on direct work with families.

The principles followed within all models include greater transparency, immediacy of learning, independence and family/professional involvement in review processes. The overarching aim is to allow reviewers to synthesise, construct emerging themes and foster early learning that can be shared continuously with key organisations. Family history and kinship ties are important to most BME families and while standardisation may not be useful, professionals may learn a great deal from understanding where children sit in relation to immediate parents/siblings and the extended family/community. Holistic social work requires in-depth knowledge of who delivers the care, how care is perceived and what is understood about child-rearing practices by primary carers.

## Serious case reviews and black and minority ethnic children

Documentary evidence on ethnicity, culture and religion in online SCRs is scarce, but during the period 2009–11, government figures suggested that black or black British children in SCRs were 8%, compared with a total child population of 3%. Mixed-race children in SCRs were 6%, compared with the total population of 4% (Department for Education, 2013a). Figures for religion or faith were not available for this period. This research found 576 SCRs, dated between January 1991 and December 2010 (numbered 327–902 at the time) in the repository catalogue, with the oldest cases coming first. The numbers held in the earlier years was considerably fewer, for example, 114 SCRs were held between 1991 and 2006 while 77 were lodged in 2007, 105 in 2008, 158 in 2009 and 122 in 2010. The idiosyncratic nature of the numbering system made it difficult to navigate and draw conclusions, partly because the catalogue numbers changed along with SCRs held at any given time. The quality of information was also variable and some SCRs had an executive summary and a full report, which could both have been counted.

The general content analysis (Flick, 2011) approach led to the emergence of the key themes outlined in Table 13.1.

A finding from more recent SCRs related to the inadequacy of interpretation and translation services. The report on Daniel Pelka stressed the inadequate assessment of his linguistic abilities or, indeed, attention to any real communication with him, with or without the help of Polish interpreters. Child abuse linked to faith and belief appeared to be an area of growing interest. The implication is that witchcraft and spirit possession is more likely to affect large, multi-generation households of newly arrived immigrants but that professionals avoid looking deeper into this complex area. Critics suggest that organisations need to provide detailed guidance on how to recognise, identify, assess and intervene in abuse situations that are unfamiliar or ethically challenging (Simon et al, 2012).

Children and young people of mixed-heritage background is one group that has received even less attention than BME children in general within SCRs. It is difficult to draw conclusions from the data under scrutiny; however, the case of Hamzah Khan (Bradford Safeguarding Children Board, 2013) suggests that his complex ethnic family background was not considered in any great detail. There is also concern that the needs of the growing population of mixed-heritage people are not being given due attention within child protection policy and practice (Chand, 2008).

Finally, an important pointer to the development of good practice relates to the training and development of professional values, knowledge and skills. The capacity to recognise the need for holistic services requires consideration of how social workers perceive and work with difference, and also how they understand how bias and prejudice, ingrained within structures and systems, can be addressed and managed. Supervision approaches can support social workers to recognise and respond to individual needs.

**Table 13.1: Key themes**

| | |
|---|---|
| Organisational responses | The application of law and policy, for example, in the provision of specialist services such as interpretation and translation. The repository is also a unique collection of materials that scrutinise child protection policies and procedures and is, therefore, invaluable for organisational learning and strategic planning. Practice researchers could gather evidence on the voice of BME children and social inequalities. |
| Professional knowledge | Despite the Children Act 1989 and subsequent guidance on religion and culture, we found a glaring absence of systematic data-gathering on the demographic profile of the child and the family/carers within review processes. Although more recent SCRs (eg Daniel Pelka) include some information, there is limited consistent recording of ethnicity, religion, language and cultural aspects. This inconsistency might be because until 2013, SCRs were produced using different publishing styles by local child protection authorities and made available for public use through local systems. |
| Professional judgement | There is an underlying assumption within some SCRs that tidy, clean homes equal happy, healthy children. The focus on cleanliness suggests that those involved in reviewing child abuse and neglect lack in-depth analysis and sensitivity to difference and diversity in its broadest form and may hold biased views on living standards and conditions. This suggests that professionals with limited knowledge of extended families may view practices such as the sharing of sleeping, dressing and bathing areas as abnormal, whereas large families may struggle to retain privacy when living in cramped conditions. Evidence suggests that BME families are more likely to live in groups with four or more children and 65% are more likely to live in poverty (Munro, 2012). |

## Conclusion

The systematic reviewing and reporting of child abuse and neglect is to be recommended to children's services across the world, along with the gathering and storing of SCRs in one place. Both are invaluable for professional development and transforming organisational practice. The public availability of the information is particularly important for students, who are increasingly accessing Web-based materials, and for researchers, who require access to large data sets that can be used to extract, link and extrapolate broad findings on, for example, teenage suicide. SCRs are routinely used in classrooms with social work students and in the development of initiatives such as preventive early help for children and families.

The NSPCC reports, summaries and commentaries are an important resource for social workers seeking guidance on how to assess, analyse and interpret the situations of children and families from diverse ethnic and religious backgrounds, as well as other specialised needs, such as disabilities. However, so much more can be added if indicators such as poverty, the number in households and ethnicity can be made available.

Changes are likely to come about as a result of demands, so professional calls for threshold guidance from neglect to abuse is partly as a result of SCR scrutiny (Brandon et al, 2013). Also, the UK government is expecting inspection reports on children's services from bodies such as the Office of Standards in Education (Ofsted) to include the social work response to ethnicity and sensitivity to culture, religion, language and/or disability (HM Government, 2013).

Although generally positive, SCRs have played a significant part in diminishing the authority and overarching image of social workers in the public eye, who continue to act as lead child protection professionals. This may be a peculiar manifestation of poor professional credibility in British society, which is inclined to look for easy answers to complex problems, as demonstrated by government initiatives such as the 'Troubled families' agenda, which seeks to monitor families on low incomes and in poor housing. BME groups often fall into categories such as 'disadvantaged' and are seen to require resources that are over and above those provided and needed by families in the most economically deprived brackets. The protection of children from neglect and abuse is a universal right and information should be routinely collected and used to improve the life chances and well-being across the class and income spectrum. So, what should social workers and other professionals involved look for in assessment and review processes? Evidence suggests that children reflect the general population and are more likely to be from diverse backgrounds. If they have a history of immigration and move regularly across countries, they may demonstrate signs of instability or face identity and attachment issues. Unless they have well-developed family and community support (and as the Victoria Climbié case demonstrated, this cannot be assumed), they may be isolated or have carers/parents who may be shy, secretive and perhaps wary of being judged by external bodies. Families can display a universal range of characteristics, including manipulation or coping strategies, which may be construed as quiet and undemanding. It may be that professionals are out of their sphere of influence or understanding, but behaviour such as this can make some groups invisible to external scrutiny from statutory authorities.

Individuals who have faced trauma and change through seeking asylum and refugee status, with family histories rooted in pre-industrial welfare and family patterns, may be self-sufficiently relying on cultural wisdom on child-rearing practices. Responses such as these may appear secretive and calculating to outsiders but it could be that families are simply managing the available resources in a sensible manner. That said, professionals have the unenviable task of assessing the difference between normal family life and dangerous childcare, and they routinely face the charge that long-term neglect, which may lead to abuse, is not being picked up early enough (Brandon et al, 2013).

A key developmental question for children's services is: what constitutes good intervention, assessment and review? Also, how can information be better gathered to inform decision-making (Broadhurst et al, 2010)? Critics suggest that minority concerns in relation to ethnicity, disability and gender should be mainstreamed (Chand, 2008: 9) as Britain's population becomes increasingly diverse and complex. Embedding good practice should begin with the following question: what are the issues of diversity for this child, young person and family? Also, how can minority concerns be better integrated into assessment and review processes?

However, this does not negate focused attention on the impact of disadvantage, neglect and abuse, and on the provision of specialist services such as well-trained and guided interpretation and translation.

SCRs are commonly used within literature to scrutinise and inform child protection organisations; however, the absence of cultural, religious and ethnic difference is a significant shortfall in knowledge building. A great deal of assumption still remains about the capacity of BME groups to utilise kinship and family to care for both children and vulnerable adults (Bhatti-Sinclair, 2011). There is also ongoing public concern that social workers overlook the needs of the child and privilege parental/carer authority, particularly in unfamiliar contexts that are different in relation to culture, religion and faith.

Professionals are constantly urged to read more widely and receive better, specialist, post-qualifying training on areas that are beyond their immediate concerns, such as international perspectives on child-rearing and notions of childhood (Smith, 2010). Sadly, procedural drivers are still inclined to lead professionals to focus on risk assessment rather than holistic, person-centred approaches.

Finally, despite significant discussion on anti-racist practice in the UK over many decades, social workers still seem unable to fully integrate issues of race and ethnicity into child protection processes. Consideration of how best to profile and monitor children of all backgrounds within SCRs would be a step forward and may lead to a data resource that can be scrutinised for social indicators and variables that can improve understanding of diversity, as well as changes to family patterns and approaches to child-rearing wisdom derived from global sources. British children are multi-ethnic and increasingly cared for by one or more parents and carers from a range of backgrounds. Heritage, therefore, requires a redefinition, a re-conceptualisation and a deeper critical analysis.

## References

Baverstock, A., Bartle, D., Boyd, B. and Finlay, F. (2008) 'Review of child protection training uptake and knowledge of child protection guidelines', *Child Abuse Review*, 17(1): 64–72.

Bhatti-Sinclair, K. (2011) *Anti-racist practice in social work*, Basingstoke: Palgrave Macmillan.

Bradford Safeguarding Children Board (2013) 'A serious case review: Humzah Khan', November.

Brandon, M., Bailey, S., Belderson, P., Gardener, R., Sidebotham, P., Dodsworth, J., Warren, C. and Black, J. (2009) 'Research report DCSF-RR129', June, Department for Children, Schools and Families, University of East Anglia.

Brandon, M., Bailey, S., Belderson, P. and Larsson, B. (2013) 'Neglect and Serious Case Reviews: a report from the University of East Anglia commissioned by the NSPCC', University of East Anglia/NSPCC.

Broadhurst, K., White, S., Fish, S., Munro, E., Fletcher, K. and Lincoln, H. (2010) 'Ten pitfalls and how to avoid them: what research tells us', September, NSPCC.

Chand, A. (2008) 'Every child matters? A critical review of child welfare reforms in the context of minority ethnic children and families', *Child Abuse Review*, 17(1): 6–22.

Coventry Safeguarding Children Board (2013) 'Serious case review: Daniel Pelka', September.

Department for Education (2011) *Monitoring and evaluation of family intervention services and projects between February 2007 and March 2011*, December, London: HM Government.

Department for Education (2013a) 'Equality analysis safeguarding statutory guidance', March.

Featherstone, B., White, S. and Morris, K. (2014) *Re-imagining child protection*, Bristol: The Policy Press.

Flick, U. (2011) *Introducing research methodology: a beginner's guide to doing a research project*, London: Sage.

Hill, A. (2015) 'Young teetotallers cut Britain's alcohol consumption', *The Guardian*, 14 February, p 8.

HM Government (2013) 'Working together to safeguard children – a guide to inter-agency working to safeguard and promote the welfare of children', London: Department for Education. Available at: https://www.gov.uk/government/publications/working-together-to-safeguard-children-equality-analysis

HM Government (2015) 'Working together to safeguard children: a guide to inter-agency working to safeguard and promote the welfare of children', London: Department for Education. Available at: https://www.gov.uk/government/publications/working-together-to-safeguard-children--2

Jones, R. (2014) *The story of Baby P: setting the record straight*, Bristol: The Policy Press.

Kirton, D. (2000) *'Race', ethnicity and adoption*, Buckingham: Open University Press.

Munro, E. (2011) 'The Munro review of child protection: final report, a child centred system', Department of Education, HMSO.

Munro, E. (2012) *Effective child protection* (2nd edn), London: Sage.

Owen, C. and Statham, J. (2009) 'Disproportionality in child welfare', Research Report DCSFRR-124, Thomas Coram Research Unit, June.

SCIE (Social Care Institute for Excellence) (2012) 'Learning together to safeguard children: a systems model for case reviews', January.

Simon, A., Hauari, H., Hollingsworth, K. and Vorhous, J. (2012) *A rapid literature review of evidence on child abuse lined to faith or belief*, October, London: Childhood Wellbeing Research Centre, Institute of Education.

Smith, R. (2010) *A universal child?*, Basingstoke: Palgrave Macmillan.

Victoria Climbie Foundation and HCL Social Care (2014) 'Voices from the front line: supporting our social workers in the delivery of quality services to children', July, Victoria Climbie Foundation.

# CONCLUSION

# Emergent theory for practice

*Charlotte Williams and Mekada J. Graham*

The landscape of practice is rapidly changing as complex modernising agendas and institutional transformations operate to restrict the scope of social work and curtail explicit and focused social justice work. In such a highly regulated environment, it is easy to see how organisations pull practitioners in the opposite direction from critical reflective and ethical practice. Each of the chapters, in turn, has acknowledged the impacts of the neoliberal residualisation and restrictivisation of state services as compounding the disadvantage of black and minority ethnic groups. As these processes roll out, so too do increased expectations of practitioners to exercise skill in holding fast to professional values while navigating what is a fundamentally new terrain.

In the reading and rereading of this collection of essays, we have been heartened by the possibilities of transformative practice with black and minority ethnic communities. This text is full of conversations, of listening, consulting and working together to co-produce outcomes that enhance well-being. The work attests to the strengths embedded within minority communities and how these can be released and brought into service to shape practice. The professional steer is apparent, for example, in terms of accountabilities where there is risk, but these are accounts that eschew the dominance of the professional prerogative in a focus on careful negotiation with service users towards agreed outcomes, as Claudia and Shantel's account well illustrates. The book advances the voice and choice of the service user individual, group and community and attests to the importance of their having opportunity to be heard. Sarah and Dan talk about 'centralising voices' within participatory social work methods; Roma suggests careful listening and reworks the idea of communication in her account of a counter-narrative reading of young black males as 'troubling'; and in Lena and M. Rafik's chapter, conversations with Muslim youth reveal what is salient to them and how their responses are shaped in resistance to wider discourses that discredit them. The point could not be made clearer that a commitment to genuine, sophisticated and engaged listening and the reciprocal nature of communication is fundamental. For Siân, in Chapter Six, this goes well beyond the reductionist approach to an exchange of language and knowledge of specific cultures, towards addressing issues of rights, justice and power.

We suggested the need to build theories from practice as a means to develop an embedded transformatory practice. We use the term 'embedded' in the sense that emergent theory is not ahistorical, but reflects knowledge on the ground of demographies, localities, national cultures and politics past and present. Being attuned to and forming an analysis based on this contextual knowledge is vital. Devolution has produced policy differences across the UK but there are also deeper differences related to cultures of practice, of local knowledges and the particularities of place. In Chaitali and Janet's work in Northern Ireland, the need for work on reconciliation, trust and ethnic collaboration reminds us that intra-ethnic conflict is deeply embedded in social relations in that territory, and that these reverberate across institutional and professional practices. Social work practice is a product of context, and locating action in an understanding of place and the narratives of race and diversity that emerge in particular contexts provides powerful points of leverage for change. What people resident in this area are saying about their experiences and how service providers are responding to them *in context* became a starting point for the work on civic engagement in North Wales undertaken by Tue and Charlotte.

In introducing this text, we signalled our intention to ground this book in practice. There are lots of texts that talk about theory. Indeed, as Lena and M. Rafik suggest in Chapter Five, we have a considerable body of theory but we are still 'failing to respond'. The crafting of theory in practice is very nicely expressed by Roma when she talks about 'theories looking for practice' and asks: how is theory being 'put to work'? In this vein, Chaitali and Janet argue for 'pushing theory' into service and they problematise the notion of cultural competency in pursuit of a *critical* cultural competence informed by an understanding of relations of power. Siân's work also illustrates this crafting in practice when she probes the nuances of practice encounters that involve interpreters. What Siân's contribution demonstrates so well, along with several others in the book, are the ways in which wider, highly stigmatising media discourses infiltrate and warp practices through the 'othering' of minority-language speakers. Developing counter-narratives to these stigmatising accounts should be the bedrock of the social work response, as is argued by Lena and M. Rafik in relation to Muslim youth, by Roma in relation to the framing of black boys' behaviour, by Sarah and Dan in relation to Gypsies, Travellers and Roma peoples, and so on.

As has always been the case, much of the work of advocacy, resistance and reframing, of service provisioning and self-help, goes on beyond the state in relation to black and minority ethnic groups. In this arena, as Michael and Rhetta demonstrate in Chapter Seven, there is scope for innovation, for doing things differently and for using the spaces that open up in civil society to co-produce real and tangible alternatives that have impact. The search for the autonomy and the pull for independence from the state to make this happen have their costs but the benefits for marginalised groups such as refugees and asylum seekers are life-changing. Preventive work of this kind has long-term benefits. Social work must utilise these spaces beyond the state, where broad professional alliances with social care workers and others can be formed, to create innovative responses to diverse needs. Mainstream delivery must change and these wider partnerships, as Sarah and Dan clearly show, are critical to appropriate service delivery.

We proposed a broad framework for articulating the dimensions of work with black and minority ethnic groups built on a strength-based model of high user participation, negotiation and dialogue, and underpinned by value principles well articulated by Beverley and Philomena in Chapter Three. In their chapter and in the chapter prepared by Kish and Donna, the importance of evaluation in steering practice is underlined. Far too much of our work has relied on the moral force of the arguments for change and it is increasingly clear that the need for robust data collection, monitoring and evaluation *in practice* is implied.

What these chapters have illustrated are practices that engage in very innovative ways with the four trajectories we outlined. It was a novel and ambitious methodology for the text. Bringing together busy practitioners and pernickety academics (or vice versa) in dialogue in order to review key practice themes spelled uncertainty and some trepidation on our part about whether this approach would bring about our desired outcomes. Social work is a contested profession that is littered with debates and discussions about its political, moral and social mandates. So, why would we agree about practice approaches and possibilities? We can report that this co-production of knowledge has not come without considerable work and investment of time and no small amount of angst from all parties. Clashes of styles of writing, 'Who are you to talk?' assertions, the pressures of coordinating time commitments and the complexities of balancing and utilising research evidence with practice wisdom all pulled in different directions. There have been some big sighs and associated emoji that clearly demonstrates the complexities of co-production. We largely left it to contributors to determine how they would approach the practice theme of their chapter. Some drew on research or projects in practice, others on case studies and others still on soundings from practice. Ultimately, the contributions revealed some consistent messages:

- The continued marginalisation and vulnerabilities of groups within fields of practice and the overlay of discriminations, stigma, social exclusion and inequalities that persist, fuelled by narrow welfare chauvinism, media hype and political rhetoric was demonstrated.
- The changing nature of ethnic diversity in the UK was outlined, in particular, the complexities of intersections of difference, demonstrating that diversity can no longer be framed through the purview of static homogeneous groups. This assumption and others underlying the old diversity models embedded in much of social work practice, holding onto ethnic compartmentalism and ethnic and linguistic essentialism in assessment, are increasingly redundant. Working with intersectionalities in a super-diverse world of practice calls for a new ways of thinking and doing. Indeed, what was apparent was a more sophisticated questioning of the role of ethnicity as the orchestrating factor in intervention, as in the case of Raghu's analysis of young people with intellectual disabilities in Chapter Eleven. We clearly need deeper analysis of the significance of ethnicity in service delivery and a greater understanding of how diversity is identified and mobilised, both by service users and by practitioners.

- The issues of (the lack of) organisational literacy in responding to minority ethnic groups, as described by Tue and Charlotte, Raghu, and Frank and Stefan, are consistently flagged. Resources, leadership and consistent and sustained commitment from the top and within the culture of organisations is required to ensure that good practices do not go into attrition.
- The need to develop the evidence base and data collection and for evaluation and monitoring to guide practice is clearly important, as Kish and Donna and others point out. It is well known that research and data collection on ethnicity is expensive and complex but the dearth of robust evidence in social work continues to undermine purposive action. There is a wealth of experience in the field and this needs to be systematically captured.
- Social workers are lead practice professionals in critical areas of implementing safeguarding law, and as Claudia and Shantel's, Beverley and Philomena's, Kish and Donna's, and Frank and Stefan's accounts all demonstrate, this balancing act of assessment of risk alongside respect and acknowledgement of the strengths of individuals, groups and communities produces tricky and ethical dilemmas for practice. A skilled practitioner is implied. Time, care and craft are needed, as well as continuing professional development in building knowledge, expertise and critical reflexivity. The 'implementation gap' is in our hands and social work is well positioned to add value.

There are, of course, omissions in this text. Lots of the chapters highlighted the issues for children, youth and their families. We would have liked a focus on caring, on personalisation and advocacy, in adult services but we committed to work with the themes that came forward and we lost some on the way as life interrupted well-laid plans. We are delighted to bring together leading writers in the field of race and ethnicity in this collaboration. We do not know of another text in social work where so many of the contributors come from black and minority ethnic backgrounds themselves and have such considerable experience of working on the front line of practice. This critical mass in UK social work is to be celebrated and together makes a significant collective contribution to advancing practice through their writings.

Finally, it is worth saying that we need to remember to look after ourselves, in particular, in the workplace and within workplace relations. As Frank and Stefan point out, these are microcosms of the broader society with subtle dynamics of discrimination and domination. There is little doubt that black and minority ethnic professionals experience considerable impacts on their well-being as a direct result of the energy and time they commit to transforming social work practice. These professionals are thriving in difficult (often very white) environments, despite the 'race work' they carry out daily on a personal and professional level and the often ambivalent positionings that they have to negotiate. We would argue that the workplace is not depoliticised in this sense, but a highly political terrain in which we recognise that allegiances lie both within and well beyond the bureaucracy in the wider spaces of civil society and seek to work with them. Small and collective acts of resistance from many different quarters across practice domains count in the larger scheme of things and give hope and open up possibilities. As Michael and Rhetta remind us in Chapter Seven, 'solidarity is horizontal', and our collective efforts make a difference to the project that is transformatory practice with black and minority ethnic groups.

# Index

Note: Page numbers followed by the letter n refer to end-of-chapter notes.